Thirty Years Into Yesterday

Thirty Years Into

JEFFERSON REID AND STEPHANIE WHITTLESEY

The University of Arizona Press   Tucson

Yesterday

A History of Archaeology at Grasshopper Pueblo

The University of Arizona Press
© 2005 The Arizona Board of Regents
All rights reserved
♾ This book is printed on acid-free, archival-quality paper.

Manufactured in the United States of America

10 09 08 07 06 05   6 5 4 3 2 1

Library of Congress Cataloging-in-Publication Data
Reid, J. Jefferson.
Thirty years into yesterday : a history of archaeology at Grasshopper Pueblo /
Jefferson Reid and Stephanie Whittlesey.
p. cm.
Includes bibliographical references and index.
ISBN 0-8165-2402-5 (cloth : acid-free paper) —
ISBN 0-8165-2401-7 (pbk. : acid-free paper)
1. Grasshopper Pueblo (Ariz.) 2. Mogollon culture. 3. Excavations (Archaeology)—
Arizona—Fort Apache Indian Reservation—History. 4. Processual archaeology—
Arizona—Fort Apache Indian Reservation. 5. Archaeology—Arizona—Fort Apache
Indian Reservation—Field work. 6. University of Arizona. Archaeological Field
School—History. 7. Fort Apache Indian Reservation (Ariz.)—Antiquities.
I. Whittlesey, Stephanie Michelle. II. Title.
E99.M76R46 2005
979.1'59—dc22
2004015057

Contents

Figures

Maps

Lists of Field School Participants

Preface

In order to qualify as historical, an event must be susceptible to at least two narratives of its occurrence. Unless at least two versions of the same set of events can be imagined, there is no reason for the historian to take upon him [her] self the authority of giving a true account of what really happened.—**Hayden White** (1987:20)

This book is a historical account of a major archaeological project and the intellectual debates it engendered. The University of Arizona Archaeological Field School at Grasshopper—a five-hundred-room Mogollon Pueblo on the Fort Apache Indian Reservation, Arizona, that was occupied during the A.D. 1300s—was more than just a research and training institution that spanned thirty years, although its achievements as such were important enough. The Field School provides an extraordinary window into a changing American archaeology and three different archaeological research programs as they confronted the same sprawling, masonry ruin. Like the enigmatic Mogollon culture it sought to explore, Grasshopper research has spawned decades of controversy and debate among archaeologists of the American Southwest. An intellectual history of Grasshopper research provides a framework for addressing larger issues in the growth and development of southwestern archaeology.

We have several objectives in writing this history. One is to synthesize and complete the progress reports of Thompson and Longacre (1966) and Longacre and Reid (1974) that chronicle each season's work from 1963 through 1973. We summarize their presentations and add our synopsis of the final nineteen years. These sketches provide a sense of pace and personnel that begins to situate the research within the shifting realities of academic archaeology. We avoid the hackneyed histories of archaeology as the thrill of discovery, the challenge of the unknown, and the romance of the exotic. Instead, we seek to paint a realistic picture of academic archaeology's intellectual debates and personal animosities (Snead 2001). In this regard, as well as in format and narrative style, we follow Richard Woodbury's excellent lead in *Sixty Years of Southwestern Archaeology: A History of the Pecos Conference* (1993).

Despite the importance of archaeologists to our story, we record little of their personal histories. Although the research history of Grasshopper is also a social history—the men and women who joined together every summer were crucial research components, and their personalities and foibles defined in many ways our purpose and methods—their stories must be told in another narrative.

A second objective is to chronicle the research questions, methods, theories, and concepts that characterized fieldwork at Grasshopper from 1963 through 1992. We do this to make sense of the intellectual shifts from culture history, to processual archaeology, and then to behavioral archaeology, as each body of questions, concepts, and procedures sought to understand the same archaeological record. We offer our evaluation of these three conceptual schemes' performance in understanding ancient life at Grasshopper.

A third objective is to continue telling the stories of the singular place that is Grasshopper. Grasshopper is a layered landscape that records the lives of prehistoric Mogollon and Anasazi people, the historical Western Apache who came to live in this mountain homeland after the puebloans abandoned it, and the twentieth-century archaeologists who came to reconstruct and explain the past. Grasshopper is defined by those who lived there and by the material residue of their presence, yet its significance will only be realized when the stories of the Mogollon, the Western Apache, and the archaeologists are told.

We have tried to present something of the lives of the ancient Mogollon in the book *Grasshopper Pueblo: A Story of Archaeology and Ancient Life* (Reid and Whittlesey 1999). This book offers a synthesis of everything we know about the people who actually lived at Grasshopper Pueblo and their relations with other communities in the region before the mountains were abandoned forever by Pueblo people around A.D. 1400. It might reasonably be labeled a paleoethnography of a mountain pueblo accentuated at regular intervals by anecdotes about archaeology, archaeologists, and the Cibecue Apache. We wrote it as a summary of thirty years of fieldwork that would be understandable and interesting to the widest possible audience. We especially wanted the Cibecue Apache to know what we had learned about ancient life, and we assigned all royalties from the book to them.

Keith Basso has discussed the lives, landscape, and history of the Western Apache people in numerous publications. Although we do not pretend to add to this scholarly library of the Western Apache, we do consider the importance of the Apache to Grasshopper research. As friends and coworkers, the Apache help us achieve a more intimate knowledge of the land, give us much to think about concerning how people can live effectively in the central Arizona mountain landscape, and teach us the importance of spiritual beliefs to everyday existence.

The current book takes the story to the next level, chronicling the struggles and triumphs of thirty summers of fieldwork at Grasshopper in a shifting, sometimes contentious, always intriguing intellectual climate. In one sense, this book is also the third in a series that we have informally dubbed "The Ancient Life Trilogy." The first was *The Archaeology of Ancient Arizona* (Reid and Whittlesey 1997), in which we interpret the archaeological history and cultural prehistory of Arizona from Clovis to Coronado. It also situates Grasshopper Pueblo and Mogollon culture in time and place. The second was *Grasshopper Pueblo: A Story of Archaeology and Ancient Life*.

Through her study of archaeological histories, Jennifer Croissant (2000) has encouraged us to situate our historical motives, whose roots are deep in our own intellectual history, within a broader intellectual context. Reid documents his interest in personal histories to the spring of 1975, when he spent each Thursday evening recording Emil Haury's autobiographical account of his archaeological career. Sections of this narrative were used to construct the final chapter of *Emil W. Haury's Prehistory of the American Southwest* (Reid and Doyel 1986) and Haury's obituary in *Kiva* (Reid 1993).

During Reid's editorship of *American Antiquity* (1990–1993), he conspired with Douglas Givens, who had published on A. V. Kidder, to expand the traditional associate editor of obituaries to include history of archaeology. The fiftieth anniversary meeting of the Society for American Archaeology in 1985 and subsequent publications on the history of archaeology had signaled a growing interest in historical topics, especially as they were perceived by the pioneer figures. An "Editor's Corner" made the following point (Reid 1991:195):

Of more immediate concern, however, are the men and women who pioneered American archaeology, the people who brought you the past as we know it today. Among the most valuable archaeological resources being lost today are these pioneer archaeologists. . . . Personal loss reminds us, albeit too late, that *people* do archaeology, reconstruct prehistory, present papers, squabble over interpretations, and teach other people to do the same, but, we hope, a little bit better. And these same people have biases, preconceived notions, personal experiences and agendas—dare one call it a subjective element—that must be comprehended at some level if we are to treat the whole past fairly. We must know more of these archaeologists before they depart.

Reid encouraged biographical essays like the ones David Doyel (1994) wrote on Charles Di Peso, and Raymond Thompson (1995) penned on Haury. Reid and Givens also sought autobiographical accounts but were successful only in getting one from George Quimby (1993), although conversations with Jesse Jennings may have encouraged Jennings to write *Accidental Archaeologist* (1994). Reid's standard approach to those senior scholars was that if they did not write about their archaeological careers, then someone else would, and that person may not get it right.

"Getting it right" is vastly more complicated than simply acquiring a first-person account, but personal perspectives are an excellent starting point for initiating discussion. Haury did not shy away from controversy, but he never presented his side of the story. Reid looks back on their oral-history sessions and wishes that he had asked Haury what had ruined his close intellectual relationship with Harold Gladwin or what alienated him from his alma mater, Harvard's Peabody Museum, during the quarter century of the Mogollon debate. He did not, and such questions must go unanswered.

This book is not a social history, except as actions and ideas are attributed to individuals. The authors have squabbled endlessly over this point. Whittlesey has argued compellingly that the history of research cannot be fully comprehended apart from the social network of people, personalities, and the flow of information that makes research possible. Reid's only counter has been to assign most of that social history to another book to avoid diluting this one's perspective. We have tried, nevertheless, to include the most prominent actors and the role each played in Grasshopper fieldwork research.

This brings us to a final objective in writing this history. The data collection–fieldwork phase of Grasshopper research is over, ceasing after the summer of 1992. The Grasshopper Field School truly is history, its buildings carted away to serve other purposes at other places, its cabin and tent platforms swept clean, the bits and pieces, flotsam and jetsam of thirty summers of work smoothed over and left to the cowboys, cattle, and coyotes. The analysis and explanation phase of Grasshopper research, underway for the past decade, is far from complete. We have much to learn still, and we suspect that other stories will require more books to tell them properly.

For the authors, Grasshopper is a highly personal history. Our professional development and life histories are intimately interwoven with the land, the archaeology, the research, and the people. This story therefore is an account of two archaeologists as well as an archaeology growing older, maturing, and looking back with some measure of nostalgia at a youthful time. We endeavor to keep this personal perspective in check, lest it obscure the more general issues and themes that are the focus of this narrative. The reader must be aware that, like all historical reconstructions, this intellectual history of Grasshopper archaeology is our interpretation of facts, patterns, observations of others, and ambiguities of the historical record.

Convention does not provide a standard format for acknowledging the hundreds of people who contributed to Grasshopper research. So that their names will not be forgotten, we have included at the beginning of each year's discussion a list of all of that year's participants grouped under research and teaching staff, support staff, Apache crew, students, and family. These camp rosters also convey considerable information about fieldwork finances and the ebb and flow of the Grasshopper research endeavor. Those persons who began as students and then returned in subsequent years as staff are immortalized through multiple listings and our enduring gratitude for their blood, sweat, and intellect. Erin Reid spent her first fourteen summers at Grasshopper, most of them with just her dad, and contributed in so many wonderful ways to the good memories of those past times.

A number of individuals appearing in the annual Field School rosters also contributed to this intellectual history of research. Charles Riggs prepared several of the Grasshopper Pueblo maps. Susan Luebbermann assisted with the photographs. Joseph Ezzo, Barbara Montgomery, Charles Riggs, and David Tuggle gave us valuable comments on one or more drafts of the manuscript, and Christian Downum reviewed and commented on the Grasshopper–Chavez Pass debate. As we had hoped, Raymond Thompson took the manuscript challenge seriously and proceeded to correct, cut, and annotate profusely, most of which we incorporated into the present narrative. He is, however, absolved of all blame for those instances where we did not follow his sage advice. We also are grateful for his identifications of field-school personnel, his memory still strong after forty years. We especially thank William Longacre for his close inspection and approval of the final review draft. Michael and Claudia Berry, both unconnected to Grasshopper research, deserve special thanks for their comments on an early manuscript from the perspective of analytically critical, innocent bystanders. Two anonymous reviewers need to be thanked personally and profusely for their careful reading of the manuscript and their extremely helpful comments.

When all are acknowledged either here or in the text, we first must apologize for those whom we have overlooked, and then we must reiterate that this story is our personal interpretation of a rather complicated sequence of ideas and events and the people who created this intellectual history.

For all the many reasons discussed above, we offer this record of one of Grasshopper's many pasts—the story of archaeological research—as another in the series of stories that must be told if we are eventually to decipher the palimpsest of time recorded at the place called Grasshopper.

Abbreviations

AAA	American Anthropological Association
APS	Arizona Public Service
ARPA	Archaeological Resources Protection Act
ASM	Arizona State Museum
ASU	Arizona State University
BIA	Bureau of Indian Affairs
CAP	Central Arizona Project
CFM	Chicago Field Museum
CNF	Coconino National Forest
CRM	cultural resource management
CRMD	Cultural Resource Management Division
CUL	construction unit L
LTR	Laboratory of Tree-Ring Research
MNA	Museum of Northern Arizona
NFS	National Forest Service, Southwestern Region
NSF	National Science Foundation
OCRM	Office of Cultural Research Management
SAA	Society for American Archaeology
SARG	Southwestern Anthropological Research Group
SHPO	State Historic Preservation Office

SMU	Southern Methodist University
UA	University of Arizona
UC	University of Chicago
UU	University of Utah

Thirty Years Into Yesterday

1

A camp in an isolated location with some permanent buildings and an assured water supply is an important feature of the University of Arizona program. Archaeological research is often carried out in out-of-the-way places in large measure because so much of the potential evidence is destroyed by urban, industrial, and agricultural expansion near centers of population. Field training therefore should take this fact into account by providing students with both a sample of the kind of living conditions necessary in isolated regions and an opportunity to learn something of the logistic problems they might face themselves as research scientists.—**Emil Haury** (1964:3)

Grasshopper. To those who do not know the place, the word may conjure up odd and uncertain images—insect, plague, perhaps a character in an old martial-arts television show. Grasshopper is, however, none of these things, but rather a place name labeling a remote locale in east-central Arizona, a dot that appears on only the most detailed maps. For those who know it best, Grasshopper is far more than this. It is a place of many pasts that will never live again, a palimpsest recording the traces of diverse peoples who lived and worked there over its six-hundred-year history. People of vastly different cultures came, marked the country to create distinct landscapes, and then left.

The uppermost layer is modern. Grasshopper was the last of the archaeological field schools isolated in the mountain backwoods of central Arizona and the last large, prehistoric pueblo village in the American Southwest to be thoroughly investigated by professional archaeologists working in a field-school situation. In this unique context and stunning natural landscape, dozens of students learned what it takes to become a professional archaeologist, and many of them went on to achieve considerable success in that field.

The next layer bears traces of the Western Apache peoples who lived near Grasshopper for centuries and who own the land today. The lowest layers hide the material record of the more distant past. A rich and unparalleled archaeological record reveals the lives of prehistoric Mogollon and Anasazi peoples who occupied the region long before the Apache and Euroamerican peoples arrived. It is difficult to imagine a richer database for unraveling the complicated threads of past human lives.

Grasshopper is unique in another way. Grasshopper research is a fascinating and revealing historical record of change and development in American archaeology and in the discipline as a whole. The Grasshopper Field School—which, hereafter, we label simply the Field School—reflected in microcosm the paradigm shifts that irrevocably changed the discipline. The Field School began in the era of culture history, rapidly shifted to the emerging processual archaeology, and served as a laboratory and proving ground for behavioral archaeology. In its final years, it absorbed influences that can be attributed broadly to postprocessual archaeology. Perhaps no other archaeological endeavor can claim the longevity necessary to reflect these changes. Moreover, each of Grasshopper's three directors—Raymond Harris Thompson, William Atlas Longacre, and James Jefferson Reid—can claim prominence in the development of the three archaeological programs with which they were associated.

It is remarkable that Grasshopper's unmatched archaeological record could serve the needs of three schools of American archaeology and hold research interests for three decades. We have used this singular situation as an opportunity to chronicle the history of the Field School. This book looks closely at the ways in which three different archaeologies and three directors tackled the same archaeological context, cataloguing their successes and failures.

In addition to this unique window on American archaeology, we tackle this daunting historical task for a number of reasons. In chronicling the bits and pieces of thirty summers of survey and excavation in one of the most remote and beautiful regions of the American Southwest, we sought to catalogue the minor triumphs and seeming disasters that characterize any field endeavor. Emil Haury—longtime director of the University of Arizona (UA) Archaeological Field School, past director of the Arizona State Museum (ASM), head of the Department of Anthropology at the UA, and one of southwestern archaeology's most important scholars—said it well in his history of the Point of Pines field school. He writes (Haury 1989:122), "Technical reports on archaeo-

logical studies seldom, if ever, touch on certain successes and failure, the traumas and pleasure of getting the work done. The feeling that guided me throughout this writing was that the 'other side' of the archaeological effort ought to be told because it, too, is an important part of the human adventure, a part that is not recoverable unless it is reported on in some fashion." Our thirty-year chronicle was worth the writing for this reason alone.

A general view looking north of Grasshopper Pueblo (middle ground) and the Field School camp (in the trees at right).

The Field School is widely viewed as one of the discipline's most eminent training grounds, and we think it is no coincidence that the history of Grasshopper research is so rich and the contributions of the archaeologists who trained there have been so important. The archaeological record of Grasshopper Pueblo and the surrounding region is unmatched in its ability to answer a huge array of research questions. We have sought to explain the role of this record in research and training. Grasshopper drew scholars who were interested in its ability to answer questions about the past and students who were interested in learning from them.

The story of Grasshopper archaeology is, therefore, essentially about archaeologists as people and how they acquire knowledge about the past. One could probably read this narrative without prior exposure to the intellectual subtleties and tortured dialogues that have characterized

American archaeology over the past forty years and come away with a rather clear, if not always flattering, picture of contemporary archaeology and archaeologists. We summarize the major debates—sometimes self-serving, sometimes bitter—and petty squabbles that characterized this history as it was played out at Grasshopper in chapter 8.

Finally, the Grasshopper Field School ended in 1992, and its history demands a record, in part because the field experience that survived for thirty years may not be repeated. Although we often recall our years at Grasshopper with exasperation and regret, such negative thoughts are always tempered with the cold realization that this may never happen again in American archaeology. It may never again be economically feasible to spend three decades working at a single site and region. It certainly will never be politically and socially possible to recover and analyze a suite of seven hundred human burials. Probably never again will we find a virtually undisturbed, five-hundred-room pueblo with intact room floor assemblages, and if we did, it would probably be too costly to recover and analyze. Changing times have affected the field-school experience as well. Today's urban field schools are a different experience than Grasshopper—an eight-week, intensive immersion in research, small-group dynamics, and education that took place in an isolated, primitive environment on an Indian reservation.

In the remainder of this chapter, we introduce the three themes that will dominate our story. First, over its thirty-year history, Grasshopper provides a unique window on archaeological research and changes in American archaeology. Grasshopper research, like the enigmatic Mogollon culture it sought to explore, has created controversy and debate. In chapter 8, we chronicle one of its more important debates as a comparison of two archaeologies.

Second, Grasshopper was both schoolhouse and research laboratory, and a dynamic tension between teaching and research endured throughout its history. We chart the shifting sources of support, struggles with insufficient funds, petty squabbles and scholarly debates, and the shifts in teaching methods that resulted from a maturing discipline and a geometrically increasing material record.

Third, Grasshopper was a unique place, and we attempt to give a sense of its character as an isolated field camp, a remote and stunning landscape, and a bit of the untamed West surviving in a modern world.

Grasshopper's Unique Window on Archaeological Research

For thirty years, Grasshopper research sought to understand the prehistoric Mogollon past and to preserve a record of the early Apache occupation of the region. This perspective is yet another unique feature of the Grasshopper story. No other archaeological project in the Southwest, and few in North America, can claim a similar vantage.

Contemporary intellectual postures and agendas (often hidden) promote a rather simplistic, sometimes distorted view of American archaeology's past. Unsympathetic revisionists may recast our intellectual history in images that fit particular polemical needs, without bringing much evidence to bear upon their interpretations. In response, we take up the challenge to begin a critical reexamination of American archaeology that is well grounded in evidence—verifiable people, places, and practices. We examine the changing Grasshopper research program to bring the historical development of American archaeology into sharper focus, so that significant developments in archaeological theory, method, and practice may be evaluated in a single "laboratory." This evaluation is the subject of chapter 8, "Archaeological Lessons from a Mogollon Pueblo."

Grasshopper research was conceived within the framework of culture history, quickly embraced questions and methods of processual archaeology, and became the spawning ground for behavioral archaeology. Along the way it acquired from Cibecue Apache friends and fellow workers hypotheses and perspectives generally attributed to postprocessual archaeology. We introduce these three archaeologies and summarize their histories at Grasshopper as background.

Culture History

Culture history in the Southwest began in the 1930s and was the dominant paradigm for interpreting the prehistory of the region until sometime in the 1960s. It was concerned with classification and description of prehistoric cultures toward documenting variability in material culture in time and space, and, in this sense, it continues in American archaeology still. Space was divided into branches and time into periods and phases (Reid and Whittlesey 1997:15). Culture history at Grasshopper spanned the years 1963 to 1965, with Raymond Thompson, a second-generation architect of culture history, at the helm. In 1963, Thompson moved the field school from a one-year stint at the Ringo site in southeastern Arizona to Grasshopper, and once again to the mountains of central Arizona, where it had flourished under Byron Cummings and

Haury. Under Thompson's direction, excavation and student training followed in the culture-history tradition as Haury, one of the definers of the approach, had perfected it at Point of Pines. Thompson's credentials as a culture historian would later be broadcast internationally when he was considered as epitomizing the traditional school of archaeological thought. In the introduction to his innovative ethnoarchaeological study of Yucatecan ceramics, Thompson (1958c) wrote that the logic of deductive reasoning was inappropriate to the practice of archaeology, insisting that an inductive approach was more productive. He explained the role of the subjective element in archaeological inference. Thompson (1972) presented a model that admitted the complementarity of induction and deduction, and his chief critic later recognized the usefulness of induction (Binford 1999). Archaeologists have generally failed to acknowledge that Thompson was among the first to grapple with the nature of archaeological inference and to begin the revival of ethnoarchaeology.

Processual Archaeology

Processual archaeology often has been touted as a revolution in American archaeology and was dubbed the "New Archaeology." It began during the 1960s and continues to be the dominant paradigm. Processual archaeology sought to go beyond the simple description of material remains to reconstruct and explain nonmaterial behavior, emphasizing ecological and sociological processes: Archaeology was viewed as anthropology (Binford 1962; Longacre 1970; Reid and Whittlesey 1997: 19). Unlike culture history, whose proponents saw themselves as practicing more art than science, processual archaeology believed the reverse. The deductive nature of inference was paramount, and there was an overt and vital emphasis on testing hypotheses about the past. Processual archaeology at Grasshopper began in 1966 and continued until 1973, under the direction of William Longacre.

In 1966, Longacre assumed the Field School directorship from Thompson and immediately stamped the research program with the imprimatur of processual archaeology as it was practiced in the Hay Hollow Valley. Longacre received his doctorate from the University of Chicago in 1963, where he studied archaeology with Lewis Binford and Paul Sidney Martin. He had been Martin's closest protégé at Vernon, Arizona, locale of the Chicago Field Museum of Natural History Southwest Expedition and always called simply "Vernon." Historians of archaeology count Longacre's (1970) dissertation, *Archaeology as Anthro-*

pology: A Case Study, among the handful of actual field studies that legitimized the initial, seemingly abstract claims of processual archaeology. It was the first test of these claims based on field data.

Behavioral Archaeology

A period of transition, which lasted from 1974 to 1978, followed the processual archaeology years at the Field School. Behavioral archaeology had its halting beginnings at Grasshopper in the summer of 1973. Longacre left Reid, a newly minted UA Ph.D., in charge as acting director of the Field School while he made his first visit to the Kalinga of Northern Luzon, Philippines. Michael Schiffer, who also had just completed his dissertation, joined the Grasshopper staff as assistant director. By 1973, it was apparent that Grasshopper was simply too big and too complicated for processual archaeology. Data-collection techniques and analytical principles were insufficiently developed to provide credible answers to the questions posed by processual archaeology. Furthermore, credible answers to the questions could not be obtained quickly, whereas the false promise of quick answers was one of the alluring qualities of processual archaeology. Behavioral archaeology matured as processual archaeology slowly faded from the conceptualization and practice of Grasshopper research. Longacre (2000:295), who retired as director of the Field School at the end of the 1978 season, has described the creation of behavioral archaeology as a "great refinement and improvement of the New Archaeology."

Behavioral archaeology at Grasshopper, initiated in 1979 and continued until the Field School closed in 1992, developed from real-life attempts to remove obstacles to the resolution of behavioral questions that processual archaeology posed. Behavioral archaeology encompasses principles, concepts, and methods for identifying and separating sources of variability in the archaeological record from the human behaviors that are the object of research scrutiny. It provides a structure for integrating the seemingly disparate investigations of experimental archaeologists, ethnoarchaeologists, and others seeking principles of human behavior to assist in the reconstruction, and ultimately, the explanation of the past. Reid, Schiffer, and William Rathje first published the most general statement of this unifying structure in 1975. Schiffer's (1995a) *Behavioral Archaeology: First Principles* is the essential synthesis of the conceptual framework of the program.

Behavioral archaeology is most widely known through Schiffer's (1987) discussion of formation processes, which exposes as unworkable the central methodological tenet of processual archaeology—that the archaeological record is a direct reflection of past behavior and culture. Although it is often overlooked, formation processes are more than postdepositional processes, and behavioral archaeology is more than the study of formation processes. One facet of behavioral archaeology at Grasshopper was an expansion of the interesting questions that could be asked about human behavior using material culture of the past and present. Another was a rigorous concern with the methods for understanding the formation of the archaeological record in reconstructions and interpretations of past behavior.

In subsequent chapters devoted to each of these different archaeologies, we chronicle the important research directions that drove each summer's investigations, the personnel who directed fieldwork, the methods that were used, and the outcome of fieldwork. We also list some of the major economic, social, and political factors that influenced the research. We leave the summation of these archaeologies and their comparison for chapter 8.

The University of Arizona Legacy

We have said that Grasshopper was a singular place. It also was a unique institution, and we believe that its singularity was mostly a product of an inherited legacy—the deep anthropological tradition of the UA. The field school that was Grasshopper could have emerged from no other context. Aspects of this legacy, which can be traced back to Cummings, influenced research and teaching at Grasshopper for thirty years. From the beginning, the UA was a uniquely southwestern institution, a place where research and teaching focused on the peoples and the places of the American Southwest. Recognizing that Arizona and the Southwest were natural laboratories for the study of desert environments, scientists of international reputation filled the UA's departments and related organizations, such as the Desert Research Laboratory, the ASM, the U.S. Geological Survey, and the Laboratory of Tree-Ring Research. The Department of Anthropology capitalized equally on Arizona's rich natural and cultural landscapes. It did not claim to be a center for Mesoamerican or Near Eastern studies, although anthropologists in these fields would come to teach there. It was part and parcel of the Southwest, and the peoples of the Southwest past and present were its proper frame of study.

An important facet of the UA legacy was the notion that archaeology was anthropology. As we will see in chapter 3, Cummings taught classics in the Department of Archaeology at the UA in a deeply humanist fashion. Not long after, Haury transformed this foundation into a departmental emphasis on anthropology. Ethnography was a vital force in teaching and research, perhaps best exemplified in Haury's Papaguería Project. Moreover, the direct historical approach that Haury used in that and other projects required a strong ethnographic background. A four-field approach—cultural anthropology, linguistics, archaeology, and physical anthropology—would distinguish the UA program for decades and continues there still.

A close relationship between the Western Apache people and UA archaeologists defined the field school from its inception. Beginning with Cummings's field school at Kinishba on the Fort Apache Indian Reservation, UA field schools have been located on Western Apache land. Like Haury's field schools at Forestdale and Point of Pines, Grasshopper benefited from a working relationship with the Apache people in numerous ways. Grasshopper would expand this further, to embrace Western Apache models for living with the unique mountain environment and to consider the importance of spiritual matters to the everyday lives of Native Americans.

The tradition of concentrated fieldwork in the American Southwest as a venue for student training as well as research is perhaps the most obvious element of the UA legacy that also can be traced to Cummings. Haury would transform Cummings's heavily romanticized view of the field into a hard-sciences approach, selecting an area to tackle specific research problems and setting up a long-term program to solve them. As we will see in chapter 8 and elsewhere, arguing theoretical points with the shovel and trowel, rather than with pen and paper, was Haury's modus operandi, and behavioral archaeology would follow his example in the Grasshopper–Chavez Pass debate. Strong empiricism would characterize the UA tradition from its beginning.

Also from its beginning, the UA field school was a joint production of the Department of Anthropology and the ASM. Cummings began his tenure at the UA as dual head of the department and director of the ASM. It was natural that the field school be jointly sponsored by both institutions. One byproduct was to increase the amount of paperwork required by the ASM to catalog artifacts and prepare them for curation. These tasks would consume inordinate amounts of staff time that might otherwise have been invested in analysis.

Last, one of the most enduring aspects of the UA legacy was the field school's commitment to deeply felt although unpopular, even controversial, causes. The best known of these is the controversy over Mogollon distinctiveness and authenticity, which endured for three decades. Haury, who authored the monograph and developed the concept that began the controversy, would devote his field schools at Forestdale and Point of Pines to its resolution. In the 1980s, long after the Mogollon dispute abated, we would return to controversy in the form of the Grasshopper–Chavez Pass debate.

We will elaborate on these themes in chapter 3. Now, we turn to Grasshopper as a schoolhouse, to characterize the teaching program and learning environment of the Field School.

The Grasshopper Schoolhouse

Grasshopper research, both its evaluation and intellectual emphasis, cannot be understood apart from the field-school environment in which it took place. The Field School at Grasshopper continued a long tradition of field training by the UA that we summarize in chapter 3.

Haury's student years with Cummings at the UA taught him that students could not automatically learn proper archaeological field techniques on their own. Simply going through the motions of fieldwork, regardless of how many times the exercises were repeated, would not ensure that the puzzles of prehistory would be resolved. Cummings himself, after countless years of experience and exposure to the archaeological record, typified the sloppy fieldwork of his pioneer generation. Haury also knew that archaeological fieldwork must be taught in an actual field situation, as illustrated by an outstanding recollection of his graduate days at Harvard. A sandbox for teaching excavation techniques stood in the basement of the Peabody Museum. Haury expressed to us great relief at being exempt from the sandbox requirement because of his prior field experience in the Southwest. It would apparently have been an overwhelming humiliation, we sensed from his comments, to have been required to dig in the box (see Haury 1995). Haury knew fieldwork was essential to prehistoric archaeology, knew how to conduct fieldwork, and directed the UA field school to enhance training in fieldwork essentials.

Archaeology is a labor-intensive enterprise. At one time, archaeological field schools may have been a means of obtaining inexpensive labor for a project, and for some low-budget projects, it was the only source of labor. Few could undertake archaeology were it not for the time-honored ability of universities to give credits in lieu of wages. In recent years, the rise of contract archaeology has so inflated archaeological wages that, except for the credit hour, the academic community might be entirely priced out of fieldwork.

There is no evidence that university credit was used to acquire student labor for the UA field schools, although it was always a means of partial compensation. Some students believed that their labor was being bought for credit, others that they were not being taught as much as they expected. This complaint can arise in any class, however. The record is clear that, when skilled manual workers were needed at the UA field schools, as they were almost every summer, they were recruited from local communities and not the student pool. Haury knew that students are poor laborers, as the makeup of his Snaketown crew—primarily locally recruited Pima Indians—attests. Furthermore, we know of few field-school staffs of recent years who thought that students as laborers could do more and do it better than the staff themselves.

Gifford and Morris (1985) recognize that the essential role of the student at the UA field school was to pursue research into prehistory as part of the training and education of future archaeologists. For the undergraduate participant, fieldwork remains as integral to his or her education as the laboratory is to the curricula of the physical and natural sciences. For the graduate student, the field school provides an opportunity to develop and execute a thesis or dissertation research project under the close supervision of experienced faculty.

Advanced Field Training through Research Participation in Archaeology

For eight years, between 1964 and 1971, the Field School participated in the Advanced Science Seminar Program, Division of Scientific Personnel and Education, of the National Science Foundation (NSF). Haury and Thompson designed the initial proposal, which was invited by NSF personnel who had visited Grasshopper with a Summer Institute group. Titled "Advanced Field Training through Research Participation in Archaeology," the proposal set the format and agenda for the teaching program throughout the thirty-year history of the Field School. Therefore, it is instructive to summarize the 1964 program proposal to the NSF (Haury 1964:3–5). The proposal made three major points, as follows:

1. Because much archaeological research takes place in isolated locales, field training should take this into account by exposing students to the kinds of living conditions they are likely to encounter and the logistical problems they might face as research scientists.

2. Equal emphasis is given to excavation, laboratory analysis, and

field interpretation. The latter two phases of the program are thought to be of increased importance because scholars working internationally are often precluded from bringing the collections recovered by excavation back to the United States for study. It is therefore important that students be taught field processing of specimens and the initial field interpretation of data.

3. The routine of participation and instruction includes the following phases:

(1) Each student digs in prehistoric ruins under the supervision of a well-trained field archaeologist and is exposed to the full range of field situations geared to current research problems. "No effort is made to introduce artificial devices in order to expand any student's range of experience. The students participate in a real research situation and learn by sharing not only in the excitement and successes of the investigation but also in the problems, frustration, and failures of specific phases of the research." (Haury 1964:4)

(2) Each student brings the material collected from the completed excavation unit into the laboratory, processes and analyzes it under the supervision of a qualified staff member, prepares a complete record of it, and writes a field report and interpretation based on it. "These analyses, records, and reports are not exercises designed for students, but rather constitute the final scientific record of the research which in time will serve as the underpinnings of the final reports of the Grasshopper research program." (Haury 1964:4)

(3) Field trips will be made to other archaeological sites and areas.

(4) One-hour classroom sessions consisting of lectures, questions and answers, or discussions or activities will be presented each weekday evening to review background material, discuss methodological and interpretive problems, and share individual excavation experiences.

(5) Lectures and field demonstrations by visiting specialists will also be included.

The 1964 budget for student participants included a weekly stipend of seventy-five dollars, a travel allowance of eighty dollars, a dependency allowance, and room and board. Although the stipend was later dropped, student participants were subsidized heavily throughout the eight years of NSF support. Even after the loss of Advanced Science Seminar support, the role of the student remained essentially unchanged, although the vocabulary for expressing it kept pace with the times, as witnessed in the discourse on the teaching and research program by Longacre and Reid (1974:4–12):

> The Field School emphasizes the graduate student's participation and involvement as a research assistant in a long-term program of multidisciplinary research. . . . Students not only participate in testing ongoing hypotheses but are encouraged to contribute to current research through the formulation of new questions, new problems and new hypotheses.
>
> At Grasshopper, teaching and research are inseparable. This critical feedback situation is most vividly portrayed in student projects. . . . They formulate hypotheses, operationalize critical variables and their measure, test the hypotheses, and evaluate the results. These projects are designed to give students research experience in solving specific questions that interest them. In addition, these small scale projects complement the large scale research in which students have been participating all summer. . . . Research interests developed in the process of preparing a summer field project are often pursued through the year and provide the material for term papers, articles, and dissertations.
>
> It is only within the context of professional research that students acquire the theoretical and technical skills necessary to meet the demands of contemporary archaeology. Research is seen as an expanding, dynamic strategy predicated on the proposition that archaeology as anthropology seeks to describe and provide explanations for human behavior through the examination of extinct cultural, behavioral, and environmental systems. These explanations are made more secure when an explicitly scientific method of investigation is pursued. . . . Field school research provides an atmosphere of creative experimentation whereby new methods for the collection of data and recognition of new data sources are devised, employed, and evaluated.

Financial and other factors relevant to the teaching program began to change in the 1970s. It was necessary to place increasing attention on student training for a host of reasons. The Field School had been envisioned primarily as a training program for graduate students. After 1971, when the school ceased being supported by NSF's Advanced Science Seminar Program, we accepted more undergraduates with little prior experience. The expansion of contract archaeology during the 1970s and 1980s further siphoned off experienced students who found it necessary to work during the summer. Increasingly, students had little or no archaeological experience, and they more often came from urban environments where the physical and mechanical activities encountered in archaeological fieldwork were unnecessary and unknown.

As we discovered more about the prehistory of the Grasshopper region, it was necessary to devote more time to lectures about it. The amount of information about the site, the regional environment, the Southwest, excavation and laboratory procedures, and camp life on the Apache reservation required tours and talks during the entire first weekend in camp, followed by evening lectures throughout all but the last week of the session. Resident staff discussing their research projects slowly replaced the visiting lecturers who came often to Grasshopper in its early years. Student projects and exercises devised to teach concepts and procedures replaced previous written requirements that usually had included writing a room report.

To meet such changing teaching and research demands, we recruited experienced staff. It always had been the practice to draw staff members from the pool of former students, and, as at Point of Pines, to encourage them to develop research interests leading to theses and dissertations. With altered teaching requirements, experienced graduate students became essential. Moreover, graduate-student dissertation projects came to dominate research during the final years of Grasshopper. This was small repayment for the time and energy they had expended in student teaching and camp logistics.

Grasshopper and the American Southwest

For centuries, Grasshopper has been a singular place in a unique landscape. In prehistory, it was a special locale that drew diverse peoples who built a five-hundred-room village over the course of several generations. Those who came to Grasshopper in the twentieth century to investigate its past found a place that had remained special despite the passage of centuries. It was a remote camp in an isolated location, set within a uniquely beautiful natural landscape. The rugged terrain, primitive living conditions, and undisputed romantic aura of Native Americans who lived in traditional ways generated a sort of magic-lantern view into the vanished West. In many ways, Grasshopper reflected the essence of the American Southwest—ruggedly beautiful country that could be dangerous, an isolated place where survival called upon technological skills and the importance of family, friends, and culture. Working there demonstrated a not-unimportant lesson to many an urban archaeologist— what life might have been like a century or seven hundred years ago.

Grasshopper was imbued with an indefinable essence, a subtle aura that perhaps had to be experienced to be understood completely.

Throughout our history, we share a sense of its physical beauty, living conditions, and Western heritage. We introduce Grasshopper and attempt to convey a sense of this place in chapter 2.

The Uniqueness of Place

As a dot on the map of Arizona, if indeed it can be found, Grasshopper may not be significantly different from hundreds of other locales in the American Southwest. But Grasshopper is a special place, not only for its unique natural setting. It was important to the people who lived there and who in doing so created a singular material record of their lives. It was special, too, for the archaeologists who deciphered the stories of the past.

Grasshopper research spanned a period of major change in southwestern archaeology. The three directors had respectable pedigrees in three prominent schools of archaeological thought and practice. Because of the Grasshopper research program, we have the unique opportunity to monitor not just the changing rhetoric of archaeology, but also the actions and results of three different archaeologies—culture history, processual archaeology, and behavioral archaeology—as they confronted the same five-hundred-room pueblo ruin tucked away in the mountains of east-central Arizona. This opportunity will not come again, although Grasshopper's magic lingers there still.

2

Grasshopper in the Archaeological Imagination

Archaeology inherits the earth; most places contain the debris and cradle the memory of innumerable past events. —**David Lowenthal** (1985:238)

In this chapter, we catalog the important factors that contributed to archaeology in Arizona and profoundly influenced Field School research. There is much in the conduct of archaeology that is art and much that is subjective, and this is seen perhaps most clearly in fieldwork. Archaeological fieldwork is a unique and compelling mixture of place, personnel, and a special sense of purpose that structures thought and action, and it is unlike data collection in any other science. Archaeology takes place in a landscape of the mind, a landscape of ideas, emotions, and thought as important in structuring action as the character of the physical landscape. Yet it was the landscape that first orchestrated the archaeology of ancient Arizona. Therefore, we must begin by placing Grasshopper in the context of the alluring and wild Southwest, the Southwest of the archaeological imagination—that rich mosaic of places, people, and climate that created a particular breed of archaeologist and a particular kind of archaeology.

We then move on to discuss Grasshopper in its several guises—as part of a unique topographic and cultural region, as a particular place on the landscape, and as a camp. Last, we characterize the rich archaeological record of Grasshopper Pueblo and the Grasshopper region. In doing so, we attempt to demonstrate "that neither a people nor a landscape is truly understandable except in terms of the other" (Hinsley 1996:205). The Southwest, Hinsley goes on to write, "invites and demands a personal commitment beyond military conquest, political sovereignty, or legal ownership. Belonging must be dirt-deep, with the bones of the dead."

The American Southwest: The Allure of Wilderness

Although much denigrated by contemporary archaeologists, the image of the archaeologist-as-explorer so romanticized in Steven Spielberg films was not a fiction. The nineteenth-century Southwest was a challenging and sometimes dangerous place, and only the strongest-willed, most robust and determined archaeologists survived. It was also a glorious land, a place of slick-rock canyons, flint-sharp skies, and towering cloud masses that has inspired writers and artists from Georgia O'Keeffe to Tony Hillerman. Jesse Jennings describes the romantic allure of the Southwest well (Jennings 1994). Arriving in Santa Fe in 1919 as a boy, he went about "gawking and soaking up the aura of romance and learning—never to be forgotten—that indefinable allure of the Southwest, a blend of climate, people, blue sky, architecture, the ever-present piñon and pine clad mountains, the spicy tang of sage and cedar, and the sweet perfume of burning piñon."

Such romantic memories mask the unforgiving side of the land. The rain falls not often enough or, perversely, falls too much. Thunderstorms are accompanied by dangerous lightning that sparks wildfires and destructive hail that hammers crops flat. Flash floods tear up cornfields and destroy homes and barns. Rivers flood, burying the wagons and cars of those who foolishly attempt to cross them in full spate. Yet the destructive power of nature is less evident in the Southwest than in the Midwest's tornadoes or the southern coast's hurricanes. To the easterner used to shades of green, softly blurred skies, and moist air, the Southwest could be frighteningly unfamiliar. The first lesson to be learned was simple—adjust rather than fight, and take the land on its own terms.

The people are an important part of the Southwest's allure, and the American Indian has fascinated nonwesterners since the days of the dime novel and the Wild West show. The easterner arriving in Arizona encountered, often for the first time, living Native Americans who were as exotic as the land. A. V. Kidder (1960:5) wrote of his first trip west on his way to survey the cliff-dwelling country with Sylvanus Morley for the Archaeological Institute of America. His naive wording reflects the year—1907, not the politically correct 1990s—but his admiration is clear: "Yet another feature of this day of new impressions; the Indians. We cut a corner of New Mexico and came through a portion of the Jicarilla Apache reservation. There they were, teepees and all, squaws with red and yellow dresses and leather leggings and long black hair, bucks in sombreros on little switchy-tailed horses. Small brown children waved to us from the open flaps of the teepees. It was all just as it should be."

The reality that these people represented was just as stunning as the make-believe world of John Ford Westerns—they were struggling to make a living and raise their families in a land that could be harsh and often was not their traditional home. To the anthropologist, Indians were the living record of the past, answers to questions made flesh. The descendants of the cliff-dwellers and pueblo-builders served as a reservoir of hypotheses and interpretations about the past.

The rich archaeological record of the Southwest was another factor that made it irresistible to archaeologists. To easterners and midwesterners, in particular, who were accustomed to the fiber-impressed and shell-tempered material that passes for pottery in these regions, the finely decorated, painted, and textured pottery of the Southwest, ubiquitous and abundant, must have seemed as spectacular as the pueblos from which it came. When archaeologists learned through early stratigraphic investigations that pottery was also a rich mine of chronological information, it became a treasure trove indeed.

One of the Southwest's most challenging features was its aridity. Chicago journalist William Curtis wrote in 1883 of Zuni Pueblo, "Everything dries here. The earth dries, the grass dries, the river dries, the wagons dry and fall to pieces" (quoted in Hinsley 1996:196). The arid environment enhances preservation of all materials, however, and hidden in the protected cliff dwellings of plateau and mountains were prizes —preserved textiles, basketry, and wooden artifacts. Entire roofs built with timbers from coniferous trees were preserved in rock shelters. Because roof timbers survived well even in open sites, the smallest and shallowest pueblos in timbered country had a chance of yielding preserved wood. After the advent of tree-ring dating, wood surpassed painted pottery for achieving temporal control.

The intellectual, political, and social forces that underlay the confrontation with the American West have been well catalogued by others. Hinsley (1996) lists some of the most important that combined to produce the turn-of-the-twentieth-century archaeologist: a denial of historical change, an emphasis on temporal stasis, the enticement of fresh discovery in an uninhabited and abandoned land, and an emphasis on natural rhythms and artistic abilities that strongly appealed to easterners caught in the throes of industrial revolution. In addition, there was the desire to build history for a nation without one, put down human roots in a landscape older than time, and create a humanized landscape from the humanless spaces. Underlying all were profoundly influential intellectual myths: the West as physical and spiritual salvation, as pristine wilderness, as a land of unbounded resources—the extraordinary geography of hope that pushed Americans to settle the West all the way to the Pacific Ocean (Whittlesey 2003).

The seductive climate, illimitable expanses of stone and sky, native peoples, and rich archaeological record drew the easterner seeking ruins and archaeological prizes. Constraining the imagination and implementation, however, were the stark realities of this country. Perhaps most important was the wildness, the extraordinary isolation, and the remoteness of the region from centers of civilized activity. Even in the twentieth century, the Southwest was remote. It is difficult to imagine what it must have been like when archaeologists first arrived. The isolation and remoteness of the region, the lack of civilized amenities, and the limited transportation created difficulties that today seem insurmountable. Because little of these archaeologists' struggles comes through in the printed record, we try to give a flavor of what archaeology was like at the turning of the twentieth century.

When Victor and Cosmos Mindeleff, Adolph Bandelier, John Wesley Powell, and others first came to Arizona, the West was scarcely tamed. Bandelier's first explorations in Arizona and New Mexico preceded Geronimo's surrender to General Nelson Miles at Skeleton Canyon in 1886 by a half-dozen years. The native peoples were incompletely inured to reservation life, and although they often served as guides and interpreters to early archaeologists, there were also inevitable clashes, as Neil Judd's account of Byron Cummings recounted in chapter 3 reveals.

Travel was unspeakably difficult. Trains brought the eastern archaeologist into a trackless land. There were no interstate highways; mules, horses, and wagons were the preferred, indeed, usually the only, form of transportation. In his "Reminiscences," Kidder (1960:10–11) describes one of his first days on survey with Morley in the San Juan country near Bluff, Utah. The account gives a certain feel for the circumstances of archaeological survey in 1907:

Wednesday, July 3rd. We got up at four, shook the sand out of our hair and clothes for toilet, saddled up and got away just as daylight began to strengthen. . . . The ride beginning to tell on me, pains beset my poor back and legs, and I could only stand the walk or gallop of my horse, trotting was pure torture. . . . Such a two hours and a half as elapsed before we rode into Holley's ranch on the McElmo I never hope to go through again. I ached in every joint and muscle, my horse was tiring enough to make his gait harder than ever, we had come into country slashed and broken with canyons and barred with endless mesas, and the heat was intense. . . . I don't think I could have gone five miles further. When we reached the ranch I drank deep from the cool water barrel, unsaddled, put my horse in the corral and leaving all the arrangements to Mr. Hewett, lay down in the henyard, which was the nearest shady place and promptly fell asleep.

Excavation was even more difficult, for the archaeologist was charged not only with getting self, food, and water up to the dig, but also excavation equipment, notebooks, and photography equipment. Gustav Nordenskiöld, one of the first to probe the ruins of Mesa Verde, penned the following account of a typical day's work to his parents (quoted in Hinsley 1996:190–91):

[After breakfast] we wash up, whereupon we saddle our horses, the water bottles are filled, and we set off along the narrow path to a place on the mesa above the ruin where we are working. We unsaddle our horses and tie their forelegs together. Then we climb a long, roundabout way down to the ruin. There we dig, sketch, photograph, label finds and so on till the sun is high in the sky. Then we have dinner, a tin of corned beef and a loaf of bread is all we get, for we cannot have much with us; then we resume work again until the sun begins to sink in the west and the shadows on the side of the canyon grow long. Then up in the saddle again and back to camp. Soon the campfire blazes up, the tea can is put on the flame, and supper, with about the same menu as breakfast, is eaten rather faster if possible.

The archaeology and archaeologists who emerged successfully from this challenging environment were tough and unbreakable, well tempered by successive trials. This rugged and fearless breed of archaeologist was also almost entirely male. The archaeologist then was more than an eastern intellectual out for an adventure in the West. He was also required to ride, pack a mule, hobble his horse, dig wagons out of quicksand, shoot a gun, and occasionally skin a rabbit or deer and butcher it for supper. Indiana Jones was real, and archaeologists nourished and enriched his image to pique the interest of wealthy and influential sponsors (Fowler 2000; Hinsley 1996).

Women were therefore few in the early days of southwestern archaeology and most often remained in the background. The women who accompanied their husbands on those early explorations of cliff dwellings and sprawling ruins in Arizona, Utah, and New Mexico possessed even more energy and endurance than most. Mary-Russell Ferrell Colton, wife of Harold Colton and cofounder of the Museum of Northern Arizona, exemplified these traits. During the summer of 1913, the Coltons toured the Southwest. It is exhausting simply to read the account of that trip, horrifying to contemplate actually taking it. Arriving in Glorieta, New Mexico, the Coltons first hiked over the Sangre de Cristo Mountains, with pack burros and a wagon to carry supplies, and toured several pueblos. Then they took the train to Gallup, where they met saddle horses, guides, and a wagon supplied by Lorenzo Hubbell. They rode to Zuni, camping en route, thence back to Gallup and traveled from Hubbell's trading post at Ganado to Canyon de Chelly. From Ganado they rode to Keams Canyon and then on to Polacca and the Hopi villages. A trip (by train) to the Grand Canyon ended the tour.

Mary-Russell's account of that trip reveals the conditions under which southwestern archaeology was conducted, the character and physical stamina needed to endure those conditions, and the exhilaration that this life could create. Mangum and Mangum (1997:30) recount Mary-Russell writing her mother that

> it's an awful chore getting dressed and washed of mornings now, after going for a month with only 3 baths & taking one's clothes off 3 times, life seems terribly complicated.
>
> Riding for a month has caused me to lose flesh, & when I return you will be surprised to find that you have a hipless daughter. . . . But don't think that I am fading away from ill health for I am solid muscle from head to heel and have been enjoying good health all summer. I can be in the saddle from dawn to dark, ride forty-five miles a day, without feeling tired.

Unfortunately, the accomplishments of such women often have been seen in terms of interior decoration and making the field camp a home (e.g., see Hinsley and Wilcox 1996:101).

Grasshopper in the Archaeological Imagination

To describe the landscape and the place that was Grasshopper, we use a number of scales. We open with the mountain transition zone that was home to the Mogollon culture, then focus on the Grasshopper re-

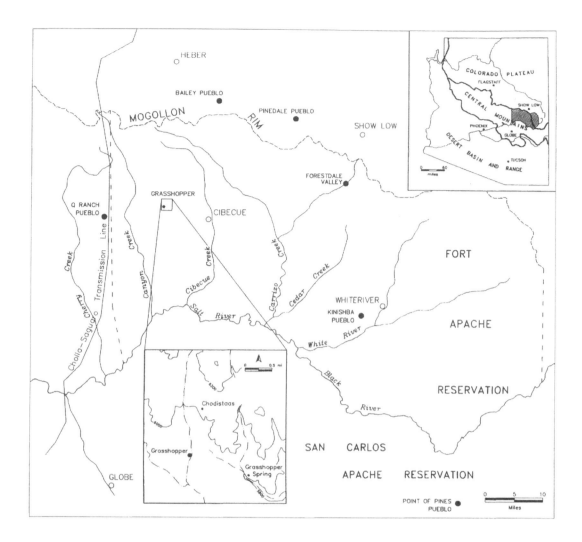

The Grasshopper region in relation to the Fort Apache Indian Reservation and the Cholla Project transmission line.

gion and plateau. We then consider the camp, an oasis of habitation and human companionship in a desert of unsurpassed wildness.

Transition Zone, Region, and Plateau

The Mogollon Rim forms the northern boundary of a mountain zone that runs diagonally from central Arizona to southwestern New Mexico and separates the Basin and Range physiographic province from the Colorado Plateau province. This heavily dissected terrain was produced by faulting and volcanic activity, creating a sharp topography of high peaks, steep canyons, and narrow valleys of unparalleled roughness. Although precipitation in most of the Transition Zone is adequate, about twenty inches each year, it is erratic and unpredictable. The overall high elevation produces a short growing season and cold, snowy winters, both of which make the region only marginal for agriculture using prehistoric techniques. The elevational differences also created vegetation diversity, ranging from western yellow pine above six thousand feet to cactus and desert shrubs below 3,500 feet; the middle elevations are characterized by a mixture of piñon, juniper, oak, and chaparral brush.

This diverse topography and vegetation yield a mosaic of resources that, although often abundant, can vary wildly from year to year. The Mogollon, like the Western Apache who followed, solved these problems of unpredictability and uncertainty with a settlement-and-subsistence strategy emphasizing high mobility, rather haphazard farming during most of their history, and heavy dependence on hunting and wild-plant foods.

The Grasshopper region lies just below the Mogollon Rim, which rises to more than seven thousand feet in elevation. This topographic feature has a marked effect on climate in the adjacent physiographic regions (Whittlesey 2003). The 320-square-mile area region is bounded by the Mogollon Rim on the north, Cibecue Creek on the east, Canyon Creek on the west, and the Salt River on the south. On the south, the land falls sharply down toward Salt River Canyon, and the vegetation shifts rapidly from pine to mixed grassland, juniper, and chaparral before meeting desert vegetation. To the southwest, the Sierra Ancha rises sharply beyond Canyon Creek. Numerous cliff dwellings are tucked away in this high, wide tableland. Cibecue Creek winds through Cibecue Valley to the east, and eventually empties into the Salt River. The White Mountains rise much farther to the east.

The heart of this mountain setting is the Grasshopper Plateau. This uplifted, relatively level province in the center of the Grasshopper region is essentially defined by the Salt River Draw drainage. Grasshopper is located in the northern area of the Grasshopper Plateau.

Much of the transition zone in Arizona, the Grasshopper region, and Grasshopper itself are located on Western Apache land. The Fort Apache Indian Reservation, which is home to the White Mountain Apache tribe, extends from the headwaters of the White River to a point about ten miles west of Grasshopper and from the Mogollon Rim to the Salt River. The reservation abuts National Forest land on three sides, and the San Carlos Apache Reservation joins the Fort Apache Reservation on its southern boundary. Just east of Grasshopper is the tiny community of Cibecue, heart of the traditional territory of the Cibecue Apache (Basso 1970).

Grasshopper the Place

Calvin Stillman (1995:51) observes that "a familiar landscape belongs in a personal sense of the natural." He tells us that "a landscape exists only for its viewer or listener." So it is with Grasshopper. The vision we portray here is highly personal and ours alone. Moreover, Stillman (1995:51) goes on to point out that "details of landscapes have associations. They can arouse memories of persons and events long past. . . . Such a landscape is a continuity." Grasshopper is best remembered as we encountered it first—at the end of a long, often troubled journey from the hot Sonoran Desert of Tucson to the blessed coolness and forest at six thousand feet above sea level.

When we climbed out of the truck to open the barbed-wire gate that kept the cattle out of camp, our first sensation was scent—ponderosa pine bearing just a tinge of vanilla; a bitter undertone of juniper; the dark essence of cow manure; and often the rich perfume of wood smoke from the cowboy camp. Scent was followed by touch—a passing breeze bearing coolness and sometimes a trace of damp. The last sensation was pure emotion—a profound sensation of gratitude and relief that the year of teaching and studying was over and a keen anticipation of what the summer would hold. We were at Grasshopper once again.

To reach Grasshopper required trekking some 150 miles from Tucson to the Cibecue turnoff over good asphalt road, although one was often stuck behind travel trailers and eighteen-wheelers through the steeply winding Salt River Canyon. More than once trucks would break down or flats would slow the journey, making us all the more thankful to reach our destination. From the highway turnoff, we began to leave modern life behind, and by the time we reached the red-rocked hills of Cibecue that gave the place its Apache name, we knew we had reached what was essentially a foreign country—the wilderness of the Fort Apache Indian Reservation. Not a single traffic light graced the streets of Cibecue, and we encountered horses, cows, and children more often than other vehicles.

The pavement stopped at Cibecue, where a dirt-and-gravel road began that wound steeply through grassland, scrub oak, and juniper. Crossing Spring Creek, then climbing the hill, we reached the cattle guard and fence that separated the Cibecue and Grasshopper cattle districts. There we also entered the ponderosa pine forest that marked the eastern extent of the Grasshopper Plateau.

Five miles of flat, straight, dusty road led from the cattle guard to the camp through forest and wooded pastures occupied by cows and their calves. We would rarely encounter other humans, although late in the day we might pass a pickup headed back to Cibecue with a load of firewood. The last leg of the trip signaled the isolation that would characterize camp life at Grasshopper.

With the gate closed securely behind us, it was just a short distance uphill to the camp. The cluster of buildings, which became progressively more decrepit each summer, welcomed us with weathered wood and sagging porches. Stepping out of the trucks and breathing that wonderful air, we knew we had truly arrived. Immediately we began the remarkably time- and energy-consuming process of unloading and preparing the camp to receive another season's worth of students, who would arrive with varying degrees of eagerness to learn about archaeology in what was one of the Southwest's most remote and striking locales.

Although the legends about how Grasshopper got its name are many, we have narrowed them down to two, between which the reader may choose. According to cowboy geographer Will Barnes (1935), who did his field research when there were still people living there, Grasshopper was named for an Apache woman whose limp gave her the name of *Nas chuggi*, meaning "grasshopper." Later researchers and Apache friends recall merely that it was a place of many grasshoppers.

"An archaeological camp," wrote Sylvester Baxter in 1889, "proves to be a very busy place, although it seems a very region of *dolce far niente*, under the serene sky, on the wide and silent sunlit plains basking in the sunlight" (Baxter 1996:162). So it was with the Grasshopper camp, which was a unique mixture of the familiar and the exotic, the old and the new, the busy and the restful. The Field School camp was located on a hill overlooking the ruin to the west and what we called the cowboy camp. During the early years of the twentieth century, a man named Jacques (pronounced locally as "Jockwees") ran a trading post at Grasshopper. Jacques built a log building and another of stone taken from the pueblo. The Grasshopper Store, which closed in the 1940s, today houses Apache cowboys.

The camp served as pasture for white-faced cattle, work horses, range horses, and the occasional mule. The bellows and low rumblings of bulls in the night caused many urban students to wonder if they were going to survive their first (and, for some, only) field experience out West.

It required extraordinary labor to make the camp habitable—removing the leavings of rodents that had wintered in the cabins, setting up the water and plumbing systems, restoring the kitchen to order. It took about eight days to become fully acclimated to the elevation of six thousand feet above sea level, meaning that the trips to the outhouse and

The Apache cowboy camp, once the log cabin and stone house of the historic Grasshopper Trading Post.

down to inspect the ruin during that first week often left us short of breath. The ruin was situated in the center of a flat meadow, clothed in varying degrees of grass and flowers depending on the winter's precipitation and usually dotted with grazing cows and horses. To reach the ruin, we walked downhill through the V-gate—a construction tailored to admit people but not cows—crossed Salt River Draw and negotiated its varying degrees of muddiness, also dependent on the winter's precipitation, and across a refuse area to Room Block 1.

The cowboy camp was off limits to us, but when we knew they were away cowboying, we sometimes sneaked down to the camp at sunset to watch the reflections in the cattle tank of the old buildings and trees, gilded by the last rays of sunlight.

The generator and pump that brought us water were housed at the cowboy camp beneath an ancient windmill alongside a little grove of apple trees. The trees produced tiny, hard, unbearably tart apples that everyone tried and would sample just once. Behind the cowboy camp and stretching all the way to Grasshopper Spring was the meadow, a favorite destination for evening walks, Saturday wine and cheese events, after-hours partying, and romantic encounters. Riding the horses, much less the cattle, was strictly forbidden, but seldom proved problematic. Urban cowboy wanna-bes could seldom catch potential mounts. Moreover, Apache horses are not conditioned by years of selective breeding to produce soft and rideable gaits.

The animal contingent at camp was an amusing, and to students, occasionally frightening mixture of creatures large and small. Black bears often ambled through camp in search of garbage and were known to enter student dormitories in search of hidden snacks. About once each summer, a rattlesnake would be found somewhere in camp. The piercing shriek of a cook's assistant or student often signaled its discovery. Occasionally, skunks would take up residence underneath the camp buildings, and we never found a way to discourage such homesteading. At night, coyotes would sing unseen in the meadows, their lonely calls emblematic of Arizona and the West.

Stories of venomous insects lurking in the outhouses were apocryphal, but some, such as a fuzzy green caterpillar, indeed were dangerous. The innocuous-looking creature could cause a rash or far more serious reaction, depending on the victim's sensitivity. We can recall no incidents of animal-caused injuries, with the exception of the caterpillars. More injuries, real and imagined, were sustained on the volleyball court than either at work on the dig or by Grasshopper's resident critters.

The physical isolation of the camp was intensified by the restriction of access to the outside world. We discouraged students from bringing an automobile to camp, and if they did, we prohibited them from driving. There were good reasons for the prohibition. Not only could the roads become impassable to passenger cars after even the slightest rain, but for most of the season, even had there had been much of anywhere to go, there was no free time. Time off was in such short supply that most students and staff used it to catch up on sleep.

Stillman (1995:51) reminds us that "the home landscape can offer stability, reassurance, prosperity, the familiar, a profound sense of belonging." The Grasshopper camp became our home away from home, a source of familiar comfort in an alien environment. Recreational activities were simple. Those with healthier habits would walk in the meadow or hike to Grasshopper Spring or perhaps farther, to Martinez Ranch, an abandoned Apache wickiup and the site of Longacre and Ayres's (1968) early experiment in ethnoarchaeology. After dinner and before lecture, there was volleyball of astounding creativity and flexible rules. Saturday nights were reserved for a fire at the campfire circle out beyond the volleyball court, a dance in the dining room, or maybe both. On Sundays, a staff member might lead willing participants on a hike to one of the many cliff dwellings or pueblos in the region.

Music and junk food were the two things missed the most, other than the significant others left back home. Without electricity, tunes were supplied by whatever boom box, car-stereo system, or portable CD player that students had brought or could rig. Most of these jerry-built systems consumed inordinate quantities of batteries. Little knots of people would gather nearby whenever music was in the air, whether it was opera, Bach, or Duran Duran. The food was usually wonderful, but despite the home-baked breads, cakes, cookies, and no dearth of nourishing hot meals produced by Grasshopper's many memorable cooks, most of us began to long for a Big Mac, fries, and chocolate shake by the middle of the summer. Mexican food and pizzas were other foods we missed, as neither enchiladas nor pepperoni pizza could be cooked and served easily to twenty or more hungry diners. Staff members would disguise these longings by offering to go on the Show Low run or on errands to Globe or Tucson, where such meals could be obtained. If bribed, they might return with the forbidden fruit for those left behind.

In addition to its fine climate, natural beauty, and exotic wildlife, one of Grasshopper's alluring qualities was its archaeological context. We turn next to the unique archaeological record of pueblo and region.

The Archaeological Context of Grasshopper

Grasshopper archaeology cannot be comprehended fully without understanding the incredible variety and quantity of artifacts in primary, secondary, and de facto refuse contexts. Description alone may be insufficient to convey the enormity of the record. Because most of our colleagues equate the Grasshopper record with the low-yield contexts of their own experience, clearly we have been unsuccessful in all previous efforts.

The reality of a "Pompeii-like" archaeological record has attracted attention in the literature, where it has generally been conceded that few contexts actually fit the definition (Binford 1981a; Schiffer 1985). But Grasshopper and Arizona mountain pueblos, in general, are an exception to the comparatively thin record of other places and other pueblos. They come as close to a Pompeii-like record of domestic behavior as one can find short of a major catastrophe (Ciolek-Torrello 1989). The richness and diversity of this archaeological record lured us and countless others to the Pueblo Southwest. The robust material record of human behavior at Grasshopper held the promise that we actually might use it to reconstruct human behavior and to explain the fascinating events of the past.

Bion Griffin excavating a room floor at Grasshopper Pueblo.

In grant proposals, papers, and presentations, we developed a comparison that begins to convey the immensity of the Grasshopper archaeological record in terms understandable to southwestern archaeologists. We recapitulate that comparison here. At the Hohokam Classic period Escalante Ruin, David Doyel recovered 16,767 sherds in excavations from the compound (Doyel 1974:320) and 3,066 sherds from the adjacent platform mound (Doyel 1974:326). By contrast, a single room at Grasshopper Pueblo yielded a nearly equivalent ceramic sample. Room 164, which was excavated to floor in 1971 by students Stephanie

Whittlesey and Susan Kus, produced 15,563 potsherds—and they only screened the last level above floor. If we were to include the subfloor levels and burials excavated the following summer by students Patricia Gilman and Susan Ciolek-Torrello, Room 164 at Grasshopper Pueblo would be equivalent in excavated ceramic materials to the twenty-two-room, three-plaza Escalante compound (see Doyel 1974:115) and to many entire sites elsewhere in the Southwest.

Comparison with Colorado Plateau pueblo sites is even more instructive. More than 175 excavated rooms at Broken K, Carter Ranch, Hooper Ranch, Joint, Mineral Creek, and Table Rock Pueblos in the Hay Hollow Valley produced around 125,000 potsherds. This number was about twenty thousand more than from the seventeen excavated rooms of Chodistaas Pueblo, a late-thirteenth-century site a mile north of Grasshopper. Moreover, the Chodistaas sherd total (see Montgomery 1992b:260) excludes the nearly three hundred whole or restorable floor vessels, recovered on room floors, that have been the subject of three dissertations (Crown 1981; Montgomery 1992b; Zedeño 1991, 1994). If three hundred whole vessels each produced an estimated seventy potsherds, then the ceramic material recovered from seventeen rooms at Chodistaas would be equal to 175 rooms excavated in and around the Hay Hollow Valley. Other Grasshopper material culture—flaked stone, ground stone, bone, and shell artifacts; faunal remains; even perishable materials—was equally abundant.

The implications for prehistory of the material record of Grasshopper are intriguing. In terms of archaeological research and reporting, the implications are staggering. That a number of southwestern archaeologists see no difference between the archaeological records of Grasshopper and Chavez Pass Pueblos, where no rooms and no undisturbed human remains were excavated, is a dismal comment on the current state of the discipline (see chapter 8). As will be demonstrated in succeeding chapters, each archaeological program approached the record of Grasshopper Pueblo differently and with varying degrees of success. Processual archaeology, for example, assumed that if the lofty scientific goals of processual archaeology were achievable, then Grasshopper would be the proving ground. In time, however, it became apparent that the archaeological record of Grasshopper was simply too big for the theory, methods, finances, and academic schedules of processual archaeology. We take up this thread in chapter 8.

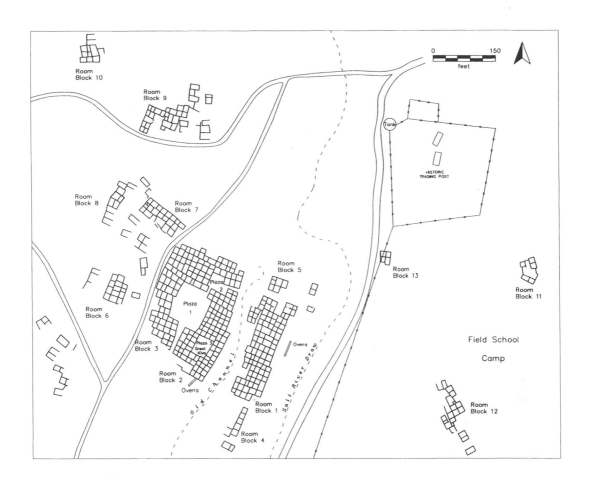

The Record of Grasshopper Ruin

Grasshopper Pueblo, showing the location of the historic trading post and cowboy camp, and the Field School camp.

Grasshopper is a masonry pueblo ruin of roughly five hundred rooms concentrated in three room blocks of the main ruin and further distributed in ten small, outlying room blocks and a number of scattered room groups.

Room Block 1 forms the East Village; Room Blocks 2 and 3, separated from Room Block 1 by the original course of Salt River Draw, represent the West Village. The mean room size of sixteen square meters is twice that of contemporaneous pueblo rooms on the Colorado Plateau. Thus, Grasshopper would be comparable in square footage to an ancestral Hopi pueblo of around one thousand rooms (see Reid 1973, 1978, 1989; Reid and Shimada 1982; Riggs 1999a, 2001; Scarborough and Shimada 1974).

Archaeologists excavated 103 rooms, or about 20 percent of the estimated total, to the last occupation floor, and a large number of these rooms were also excavated to sterile soil or subfloor tested (Riggs 1999a,

2001). Although few of the excavated rooms were selected using random-sampling procedures, statistical tests comparing the size of the excavated rooms against a randomly drawn sample of all rooms show no significant difference (Riggs 1999a, 2001). If the excavated rooms were similar to a random sample of all rooms in size—the only parameter measurable for both groups—then we assume them to be representative of other characteristics as well. Riggs (1999a, 2001) and Hinkes (1983) provide discussions of the representativeness of the Grasshopper record.

Three plazas were defined by the construction of Room Blocks 2 and 3. Plaza 1 was the largest, measuring 750 m²; Plaza 2 measured 152 m²; and Plaza 3, as represented when it was converted into the Great Kiva, was 185 m². Test excavations in Plaza 1 covered approximately 15 percent of the area and in Plaza 2 roughly 50 percent. The Great Kiva–Plaza 3 complex was excavated completely.

The room blocks encompassed approximately ten hectares, a figure that should be taken only as a rough measure of two-dimensional space. Ceramic refuse was most dense around the room blocks and in trash areas, including a large midden to the east of Room Block 1 and several low trash mounds in the flat south of the main ruin. The extramural areas in the alluvium surrounding the main ruin were extensively tested with hand-dug and mechanically excavated trenches. In nonalluviated areas, the underlying bedrock was at or very near the surface.

There was considerable architectural variability at Grasshopper Pueblo. Most obvious was the distinction between the outliers and the main pueblo, where most rooms were single-storied with full-standing masonry walls. The outliers were small room blocks scattered around the main pueblo, some on low hills to the north, west, and east, and they were constructed of masonry or cobble architecture. The low walls suggest a perishable superstructure of poles and brush or jacal. Outlier rooms tended to be larger than rooms in the main pueblo, and activity organization was different (Reid and Whittlesey 1999:150).

Human burials were excavated from 1963 until 1979, when Reid assumed the directorship of the Field School. During that time, 672 burial numbers were assigned, and approximately seven hundred individuals were identified. No burials were removed from Chodistaas, Grasshopper Spring, or any of the small sites excavated after 1979.

All of the human remains were turned over to forensic anthropologist Walter Birkby of the Arizona State Museum for preservation, analysis, and curation. Birkby and students in forensic and biological anthropology performed identification and analysis of human remains

(D. Berry, 1985a, 1985b; Birkby 1973, 1982; Cassels 1972; Ezzo 1991, 1992a, 1992b, 1993, 1994; Fenton 1998; Fulginiti 1993; Hinkes 1983; McClelland 2003; Shipman 1982; Sumner 1984). Lane Beck currently maintains and analyzes the collection at ASM now that Birkby has retired.

Funerary artifacts are curated as a research collection in the ASM (see J. Brown 1969; Clark 1967, 1969; Griffin 1967; Whittlesey 1978, 1984, 1989).

Whole vessels, sherds, and stone tools also are curated in the ASM (see Ciolek-Torrello 1978, 1984, 1985, 1986; Crown 1981; Lorentzen 1993; Mauer 1970; Montgomery 1992b, 1993; Triadan 1989, 1994, 1997; Van Keuren 1994, 1999, 2001; Whittaker 1984, 1987a, 1987b; Zedeño 1991, 1994, 1995).

Faunal remains and bone tools were curated by Stanley Olsen at the Zooarchaeology Laboratory of ASM (Holbrook 1982a, 1982b; Kelley 1974; McKusick 1982; J. Olsen 1980, 1982, 1990; S. J. Olsen 1968, 1982; S. L. Olsen 1979; Olsen and Olsen 1970, 1974). There would be much more small-artifact material had screening been a regular practice before 1974, after which time all dirt from an excavation unit was processed through quarter-inch mesh. Had the entire material collection been recovered, ASM would have run out of curation space far earlier than 2003.

The Record of Grasshopper Region

Site survey in the Grasshopper region was constrained by the heavily dissected, forested, and brushy terrain, the absence of roads, and the lack of maps at a workable scale. It was not until ten years after David Tuggle's 1969 systematic sample survey that 7.5-minute maps were available for the region. Survey in the early years, therefore, required knowledge of the landscape and roads that only could be acquired by personal experience at considerable expense in time and travel funds. The ability to avoid getting lost or helplessly stuck in the midst of nowhere was an additional advantage. Had we enlisted the assistance of the Cibecue Apache from the beginning, rather than late in the research, we could have eliminated many of the obstacles to survey.

Chodistaas and Grasshopper Spring Pueblos. The emphasis on Grasshopper Pueblo in Field School research and publication history has tended to obscure the fact that considerable excavation effort was expended on two earlier, smaller pueblos located near Grasshopper—Chodistaas

Chodistaas Pueblo.

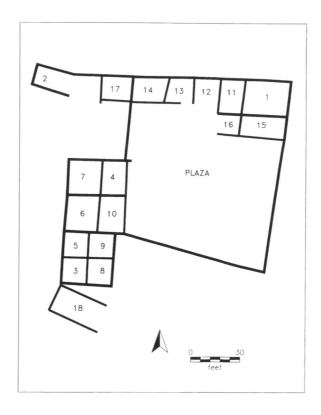

and Grasshopper Spring. Chodistaas is an eighteen-room pueblo about one mile from Grasshopper Pueblo, situated on a bluff overlooking the meadow north of the field camp.

Two room blocks and an enclosed plaza form a compoundlike architectural arrangement. Most of the large rooms were constructed of low masonry walls with arborlike roofs of small beams and brush. Four store rooms built late in the occupation were typical one-story pueblo rooms with full-standing masonry walls. Two inferred ritual rooms each had a distinctive, offset orientation slightly south of east, earthen platforms or benches, and one jacal wall.

Chodistaas was founded in A.D. 1263, occupied on a seasonal basis throughout the A.D. 1270s, and converted to permanent occupation between A.D. 1280 and 1285 at the height of the Great Drought. Sometime in the A.D. 1290s, Chodistaas was destroyed in a rapidly spreading and disastrous fire. The resulting preserved floor assemblages and charred roof beams provided a rich archaeological context with unparalleled chronological control. We recovered almost three hundred whole or reconstructible vessels from the room floors, along with hundreds of stone and bone tools. Although some vessels were smashed when the

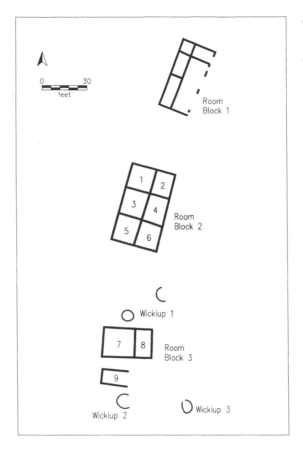

Grasshopper Spring Pueblo and Apache wickiup rings.

burning roofs collapsed, the activity areas on room floors appear to have been otherwise little disturbed. Ceramic and stratigraphic evidence suggests that the fire was intentionally smothered and later buried with dirt and refuse in an act of burial that may have been ritualistic as well as deliberate (Montgomery 1993). The Pompeii-like character of this context is striking.

Grasshopper Spring Pueblo is located a mile east of Grasshopper Pueblo near a lushly vegetated spring. It lies at the edge of the same meadow that Chodistaas Pueblo overlooks and that opens just above where the field camp used to be. No doubt the water, plants, and other resources drew inhabitants to the area, for Grasshopper Spring and its vicinity were occupied from preceramic through early historical times. The site has about fifteen rooms, eight of which appear to have been built and occupied during the late A.D. 1200s, making that component of Grasshopper Spring Pueblo contemporaneous with Chodistaas Pueblo.

Architectural evidence and other information lead us to believe that

Grasshopper Spring was occupied by a group of people related to the Anasazi (also known as the Ancestral Pueblo). Although the architecture was generally similar to Chodistaas, with low-walled masonry rooms and ritual rooms, the village layout was different. Instead of room blocks abutting a plaza, a typically Mogollon kind of settlement organization, Grasshopper Spring Pueblo consists of isolated room blocks separated by open space. There is no plaza or compound. The presence of locally made corrugated pottery that mimics Anasazi gray ware, distinctive hearth styles and inferred cooking technology, and continued reliance on the atlatl and dart when hunters elsewhere had switched to bow and arrow also set Grasshopper Spring apart from Chodistaas (and Grasshopper) and imply a connection to the Colorado Plateau.

Like Chodistaas, Grasshopper Spring Pueblo burned in the late A.D. 1200s, but abandonment processes were as different as other aspects of behavior and material culture. The pueblo collapsed and was filled in by the typical processes of postabandonment disintegration and deposition, not by ritual burial.

Regional Survey. William Longacre was instrumental in organizing the Southwestern Anthropological Research Group (SARG) and focusing it on the pursuit of one question—why sites are located where they are, a standard settlement-pattern question requiring standard survey techniques of data collection. Instead of being at the vanguard of this research effort, Grasshopper was excluded because of our inability to adapt the Colorado Plateau–based recording form to the landscape of the mountains and to submit a minimum number of sites to the data bank. Alan Sullivan would later develop survey interests, but we would continue to experience extreme difficulties in beginning a comprehensive survey due to forest closures when it was too dry, impassable roads when it was too wet, and general logistical problems. Some of this history is presented in other chapters and more completely by Welch (1996).

The majority of the survey effort occurred late in the history of the Field School. Tuggle's (1970) dissertation research during the summer of 1969 was the first systematic survey in the region. Site survey around Grasshopper Pueblo in the mid-1970s provided an inventory of sites within a three-mile radius. The six-year Cholla Project, which we supervised for ASM from 1977 through 1982 (Reid 1982), encompassed three regions along a 135-mile-long transmission-line corridor extending from the Little Colorado River to south of the Salt River (see the map of the Grasshopper region). The Q Ranch region was adjacent to the Grasshopper region, and it was surveyed during the Cholla Project in 1978 (Reid 1982, vol. 3). Three years of extensive survey in the Grasshopper region supervised by Tuggle and partially funded by the Arizona State Historic Preservation Office (SHPO) paralleled the Q Ranch survey. Together, these projects covered 180 square miles within a survey universe of 450 square miles (40 percent coverage).

The Grasshopper survey database includes about 780 sites and seven hundred limited-artifact areas for a total of almost fifteen hundred archaeological localities. Nearly two hundred sites are assigned to the A.D. 1300s. This group includes about ninety pueblos comprising nearly nineteen hundred rooms. These represent sixty-eight surface pueblos ranging in size from two to five hundred rooms and twenty-five cliff dwellings ranging from two to 120 rooms. Archaeological research has concentrated on the largest of the A.D. 1300s sites: ten surface pueblos and one cliff dwelling varying in size from thirty-five to five hundred rooms and totaling about fourteen hundred rooms. Welch (1996) has completed a reevaluation of the settlement data (see Longacre and Reid 1971; Sullivan 1980, 1982; Tuggle and Reid 2001; Tuggle, Reid, and Cole 1984; Welch 1991; Welch and Triadan 1991).

In 1932, as part of his Sierra Ancha expedition for the Gila Pueblo Archaeological Foundation, Emil Haury excavated Canyon Creek Pueblo, the largest cliff dwelling in the Grasshopper region (Haury 1934). It was investigated more recently by Field School archaeologists (Graves 1982a, 1983; Reynolds 1981). In 1970, Haury led a memorable hike back to Canyon Creek Pueblo, his memory strong even after a forty-odd-year hiatus. Thereafter, it became a standard destination for weekend hikes. Red Rock House (Reynolds 1981), located just off the western edge of the Grasshopper Plateau, was another cliff dwelling to which we trekked many times and which served as the venue for student projects. This cliff dwelling was documented and cored for tree-ring samples but was not excavated. Canyon Creek and Red Rock were the subject of Reynolds's (1981) dissertation for Arizona State University. A number of small surface sites identified and recorded during survey were also venues for limited testing during the 1970s and 1980s.

The 155 sites of the Q Ranch region that were recorded and investigated during the Cholla Project form an integral part of the Grasshopper region archaeological record. Intensive surface collections from twenty-five sites produced ceramic collections ranging from two hundred to 12,160 sherds (mean = 1,991) and flaked stone collections ranging from sixty-eight to 2,953 items (mean = 453). In addition, survey, intensive surface collections, and limited excavation in the Chevelon region (Reid

1982, vol. 2) north of Q Ranch and the Tonto-Roosevelt region (Reid 1982, vol. 4) to the south provide additional comparative data. The archaeological record of Grasshopper Pueblo and the mountainous region between the Mogollon Rim on the north, the Salt River on the south, Cibecue Creek on the east, and Cherry Creek on the west is extraordinary.

The landscape of Grasshopper was a complicated composition of form and meaning. The landscape structured our research and at times hampered it. Grasshopper also was a restorative place, renewing and energizing those who lived and worked there when fatigue and failure threatened. As Feltskog (1995:92) wrote of another landscape in another part of the West, the landscape gave us "the wonder and the power and the transcendence which West—reality and dream—had always promised the American imagination of freedom and transformation." Next, we turn to the historical background of Grasshopper archaeology.

3

Prelude to Grasshopper, 1919–1962

All undertaking the course must be able to ride horseback and camp out. The trip will entail some hardship because most of the work done will be on the Navajo Reservation in the midst of "The Great American Desert," where water is scarce and where the only roads are Indian trails. To one who enjoys the Rockies, with their rugged peaks, stretches of lofty mesas and deep-cut box canyons, the country is a delight and the climate full of tone and vigor. To those who enjoy out-of-door life, such a six weeks' experience adds a decade to their allotted three score and ten.—**Byron Cummings** (1919), quoted in Gifford and Morris (1985:399)

The Grasshopper Field School did not emerge *de nouveau* from the red dirt of the Fort Apache Indian Reservation. It was the product of many summers of archaeological research undertaken in a field-school context by the University of Arizona. We trace the history of the Arizona field schools from Byron Cummings's first venture into the cliff dwellings of the Four Corners region to the last field school before Grasshopper. In so doing, we also highlight general patterns in the early history of southwestern archaeology, portray some of the Southwest's best loved and most important personalities, and explore one of its greatest controversies.

Historical Themes in Grasshopper Archaeology: Growth of an Arizona Field-School Tradition

Anthropology at Arizona has first and foremost meant archaeology. *Anthropology* was taught in the *Department of Archaeology*, rather than the reverse, during Cummings's tenure from 1915 until 1937. Although Cummings strove from the beginning to develop a "program in anthropology," the department's title was not changed to "anthropology" until Emil Haury replaced Cummings as head. Until 1980, the three heads of the department—Cummings, Haury, and Raymond Thompson—were archaeologists, and they were also directors of the Arizona State Museum. The dual role of director and head gave these early archaeologists a powerful academic and political base from which to influence the scope and direction of Arizona archaeology, and the leadership of the department remained primarily in the hands of archaeologists after Thompson's retirement from the position. The field school is a major expression of the UA's emphasis on archaeology.

An Arizona field school is more than a summer course with a venerable history. It is also a set of purposes and procedures for conducting archaeological research and teaching, which do not always work smoothly in tandem. Between the two there is often a dynamic tension or a dialectic struggle that can have synergistic effects of increasing productivity and responding to change. Additionally, teaching can add an essential democratizing force to an enterprise that leans naturally toward the autocratic. A field school is a vastly different research context than either the rarified atmosphere of the academic project supported by the National Science Foundation or today's businesslike data-recovery efforts by cultural resource management firms. To comprehend Grasshopper archaeology, one must understand first the field-school context within which it took place.

Arizona is not unique in its attention to archaeological field schools. The American Southwest has a long history of such outings, of which the Arizona tradition is both a part and a product (Joiner 1992; Mills 2005). It is unclear what facets of the regional tradition were incorporated into the Arizona experience, and an investigation in this direction would not be germane to our account, which focuses on how the Arizona field-school tradition influenced Grasshopper archaeology. The reader can find summaries of southwestern field schools in the accounts by Gifford and Morris (1985) and Mills (2005).

Four themes underlie the history of Grasshopper research as it was formulated and carried out within the Arizona field-school tradition: (1) an exploration or, in Walter Taylor's (1954) words, an "expedition" tradition; (2) a strong emphasis on teaching field methods and laboratory techniques; (3) a commitment to scholarly research and publication (regardless of the controversy it might provoke); and (4) a deep respect for Native Americans, especially the Western Apache. To convey a sense

Byron Cummings at Rainbow Bridge in 1935.

of the development of these themes within the Arizona field-school tradition, we summarize its history and chart the dynamic tension between teaching and research.

In the early days of American archaeology, exploration and observation of broad regions were sufficient to begin comprehending the similarities and differences of prehistory's remnant pieces. As understanding increased and questions became more focused, the field of investigation narrowed to more manageable areas and to individual sites that would reveal the sequence of local cultural development. Although we have oversimplified it, this path was taken by Cummings and Haury as they established an Arizona field-school tradition marked by exploration, teaching, research, controversy, and relationships with native peoples.

Exploration, Teaching, and the American Indian: The Legacy of Byron Cummings

The UA field-school tradition began with Cummings (Gifford and Morris 1985). It must have been an extraordinary experience to have been one of Cummings's students, accompanying the dean on his journeys in search of the past at a time when southwestern archaeology was rough and new and the land itself incompletely tamed.

Cummings inaugurated the UA Archaeological Field School in 1919. His contribution to the tradition combined a profound love of the landscape, ruins, and contemporary Native Americans—themes that were then and remain today common denominators of southwestern archaeology. His special gift was a dedication to students that subsequent generations of Arizona archaeologists have not surpassed. Cummings also exemplifies the early years of exploration and defining prehistoric southwestern cultures, a time when most of prehistory remained to be written and archaeologists were relative newcomers to the scene (see Fowler 2000).

Cummings was a man of high intelligence and phenomenal energy and stamina, with a totally selfless dedication to others—his community, his university, his profession as teacher and archaeologist, and, above all, to his students. Clara Lee Tanner (Tanner 1954:19), who knew him well, gives a glimpse of Cummings's essence:

> Dean Cummings rests deep in the hearts of the men and women with whom he came in contact. He gave freely of inspiration, of knowledge, he gave willingly and without reservation. Personal gain was of no concern to him, for whatever he had that another might profit through the sharing, that should be and was shared. With the great and the humble he shared alike. The man in work clothes was as welcome at his professorial door as were the great scientists or the wealthy dowager. Each student with a sincerity of purpose received his attention.

Cummings's selflessness and his devotion to students are best illustrated by an incident that A. E. Douglass, discoverer of tree-ring dating and a longtime colleague of Cummings, relates. In 1918, the year of the great influenza epidemic, Cummings was appointed dean of the College of Liberal Arts at the UA. Although the president closed the university and requested that faculty live off campus, Cummings refused. He believed it to be his responsibility to care for the sick. Douglass (1950: 1–2) writes, "I have always felt that his help day and night in the campus hospital at that time when nurses were scarce and students were dying, saved the lives of many students."

Cummings combined this devotion to students and flair for inspiration with an abiding passion for the outdoors, exploration, and the great ruins of the Southwest—which came together in archaeological field trips to explore the Colorado Plateau country. These were opportunities to undertake a kind of teaching that went far beyond classroom learning, and he accomplished this in unique ways. As Douglass (1950:2) writes, Cummings influenced his students "by his ability on his field trips as a camp manager and even as cook and perhaps especially by his celebrated biscuits and his campfire evenings."

Cummings began exploring southeastern Utah and northeastern Arizona in 1907 while at the University of Utah, where he served as professor of classics and dean of the College of Arts and Sciences. His first half-dozen expeditions were truly trailblazing trips, pioneer undertakings by a pioneer archaeologist (Judd 1950). The flavor of the field-trip experience can only be captured by a student on one of Cummings's great expeditions. Neil Judd (1950:11–13), who was one of Cummings's student assistants from 1907 to 1909, gives an account of these "three glorious summers, crowded with adventure!" that also provides insight into Cummings's personality:

The country was wild and untamed; the trails we traveled were mostly Indian trails. There were no maps. . . .

For vacation time, 1907, a visit was planned to the White Canyon natural bridges, in San Juan County. . . . Two newspaper men and four university students constituted the Dean's party, plus a guide added at Bluff City. I was taken along either because I had failed in Latin the previous semester or because I could pack a mule and wash dishes.

Overnight by train from Salt Lake City to Thompson's Spring, a water stop on the D. and R.G.; thence by four-horse freight wagon a day and a half to the cable ferry at Moab; thence two more days to Monticello—the mere approach to our summer's work was an experience in itself.

At Monticello horses and mules were saddled for the trip down Montezuma Creek and thence to Bluff City. En route we thrilled at sight of cliff dwellings and promontory ruins [which] had been visited and described in 1895 by W. H. Jackson and W. H. Holmes, of the Hayden Surveys. The playful young Utes that stampeded Jackson's pack train were still present albeit somewhat sobered. In 1907 they were content merely with ordering the Cummings' party out of the valley. But the tone of that demand aroused the Dean's Irish blood. He told them quite positively he would leave early next morning and not before; invited the disputation to share our supper and, at least outwardly, dismissed the subject. The Dean's Dutch-oven biscuits always have had a way of melting opposition.

In 1915, there were troubles at the University of Utah, and a number of professors, including Cummings, resigned in protest (Fowler 2000: 260). Cummings was immediately offered, and accepted, a position with the UA, where he established the Department of Archaeology and became director of the ASM. Tanner (1954:7) recalls that the university president introduced Cummings to a pile of stone implements, "a jumble of some ethnological material, and several cases of bird skins" housed in the agriculture building. "This is your museum," the president said, "go to it." Although the prospect must not have been alluring, Cummings tackled the job with energy.

In 1919, Cummings's expedition offered university credit, marking the beginning of the Arizona field school (Brace 1986). This "Summer Course Among the Cliff Dwellers," as it was advertised, reflected the indefatigable Cummings's compulsion to explore the northern Southwest and his tireless efforts to expose students to natural and past cultural marvels. In this first expression of the Arizona field-school tradition, archaeological investigation was conceived almost exclusively as exploratory fieldwork. Cummings's clear purpose, although not articulated in his writings, was consistent with the prevailing objectives of the era— to explore, to collect, and, if fortunate enough to be first, to name the wondrous things of nature and prehistory. These objectives were a natural fit with Cummings's training as a classicist, his eclectic humanism, and his sense of service to students and the broader public.

Cummings's only continuous field school in the same locality was part of his excavation program at Kinishba, a large, fourteenth-century pueblo ruin near Whiteriver, on the Fort Apache Indian Reservation. In 1934, after three years of incorporating students into the work, he began to offer credit for their participation. This ceased after 1937, when Cummings retired as head of the Department of Archaeology.

The program at Kinishba was unique. Not only a teaching and research program, it was also one of public outreach. Cummings worked tirelessly to reconstruct important archaeological sites that could be admired by countless visitors and to build museums that would benefit Native Americans' understanding of their own past. His efforts resulted in the establishment of Tuzigoot National Monument, and he attempted similar programs at several other sites. One of these was Kinishba, where he envisioned a monument to the American Indian created through excavation, restoration of a portion of the pueblo, and the building of a museum. Cummings (1940:116–18) describes his plan in the conclusion of the Kinishba report:

> Visitors will then be able to climb over the rock piles representing the remains of the ancient apartments that still lie undisturbed . . . sit on the bench in the old patio in the shade of the walls of the restored portion, and repeople Kinishba with its happy, industrious throng. . . . The people of

Kinishba will still seem much like a dream, something intangible and unreal. But let the student and the visitor then pass on into the Museum and examine the things these people wrought—the implements and utensils of their everyday life—note carefully their skillful mastery of stone, bone, and clay, and the beauty of their patient handiwork, then these primitive men and women come alive. Their day and age ceases to be a vision, a dream; it becomes a reality—a real and a profitable chapter in the life history of man.

It is hoped that the Museum displays will include, also, a picture of the arts and crafts of the Apache who now occupy this region.

What is to hinder Kinishba from becoming a clearing house of ideas, information, and trade that will be profitable both to Apaches and white people? It is sure to become an educational center which will be recognized as valuable in the general scheme of progressive uplift of native Indians and white immigrants.

It is profoundly sad that Cummings's vision for Kinishba never reached fruition. All of his attempts to secure national-monument status and funding for Kinishba failed. The restoration—probably doomed by the methods and materials Cummings used—is in ruins once again, and so, too, is the museum. The White Mountain Apache have in recent years begun a program of stabilization and interpretation at Kinishba as part of cultural revitalization and tourism encouragement.

Southwestern archaeologists traditionally lament that Cummings committed little of his early explorations to print. His publication record as a measure of his archaeological research must be placed in historical perspective. Colleagues such as Douglass (1950), former students such as Judd (1950), and special people who were both (Tanner 1954) are compelled by prevailing academic values to address his seemingly spare publication record. Judd (1954:155) expresses the recurrent sentiment and the standard rationalizations:

It is an incalculable loss to Southwestern archaeology that much of his field work remains unrecorded as to details. Cummings never found the necessary leisure for writing. Teaching and administrative responsibilities crowded every daylight hour and diverse other obligations constantly intervened. . . . When failing sight brought its warning in 1946 he returned to Tucson determined to put all else aside but the writing. And then, while awaiting completion of a new home, his notes, his library, and other treasured possessions temporarily stored in the garage were all lost when fire destroyed garage and contents in the spring of 1949. Undaunted, he continued on the trail he had marked for himself and completed a number of manuscripts two of which have since been published: *Indians I Have Known*

(1952) and *First Inhabitants of Arizona and the Southwest*, issued September 19, 1953, on the eve of his 93rd birthday.

Cummings's record must be placed in perspective rather than rationalized. Importantly, he was no youngster when he came to Arizona in his *fifty-fifth year*. Compared to academic administrators, his record is substantial; compared to professors emeriti, his record is nothing short of phenomenal. One must marvel at his productivity, his energy, and his profound optimism in his own immortality.

As a pioneer archaeologist, Cummings must be measured against such peers as Frank Hamilton Cushing, Jesse Walter Fewkes, and Walter Hough, none of whom held academic appointments. Cummings's lack of formal training in archaeology has caused comment and concern. In truth, although Cummings indeed was self-trained, he believed strongly in the academic rigor of the discipline, which in those days maintained little formal training whatsoever (Willey 1988:7–8). Moreover, as Gordon Willey, who accompanied Cummings to Kinishba and later profiled his mentor (Willey 1988), points out, Cummings did have an academic background, although it was in classics. In addition, according to Willey (1988:13), Cummings tended to be uncomfortable with professional argument. This, in addition to his unquestionably kind and patient nature, led him to avoid disputes with a more vocal professional community. In Cummings's writings, we see the thoughts of a Victorian humanist instead of insights into the prehistoric peoples of the Southwest. His fate was to have been a pioneer archaeologist, selfless professor, and inveterate Victorian humanist writing long after such pioneer times and people had disappeared.

In the early part of the twentieth century, a time of many unknowns, archaeology was synonymous with fieldwork, and fieldwork was exploration. Although Cummings's fieldwork habitually engaged students for university credit, he sought to intrigue students with the past, rather than to train them in its systematic investigation. Willey (1988:20) points out that a younger generation would hardly consider excavation methods to be Cummings's forte: "Niceties of fine stratigraphy, seriation, or contextual associations had not been the Dean's primary interests in those days when he was making his explorations and discoveries or in the days which followed in which his central objective was to develop a public and a general academic interest in archaeology, and particularly Southwestern archaeology." It might be noted that such concerns were likewise unimportant to most of his contemporaries. But as Willey goes on to say, Cummings was a man of vision who encouraged

Willey to write a master's thesis on "Methods and Problems in Archaeological Excavation, with Special Reference to the Southwestern United States."

Cummings's legacy is that he was a remarkable person whose influence can be seen most obviously in the students who followed in his footsteps. In this regard there is continuity with his successor—Emil Haury.

Research, Teaching, and the Mogollon Controversy: Emil Haury's Archaeology

Haury succeeded Cummings as head of the Department of Archaeology in 1937 and as director of the ASM in the following year. From this vantage, Haury directed the course of Arizona archaeology for the next quarter century and infused the field-school tradition with the strong sense of research and scholarship that survives today.

Relative to Cummings, Haury was a "new" archaeologist. The disjuncture between his fieldwork and that of Cummings was far greater than the later unconformity between culture history and processual archaeology. Haury was trained much more rigorously than Cummings and in archaeology rather than classics. Haury believed in fieldwork as the cornerstone of the discipline, as we will see, and his fieldwork was not exploration and discovery in the Cummings tradition, but rather, the rigorous and systematic investigation of ideas about the past. Most important, it was fieldwork directed by an overarching research program and often designed to resolve controversial issues. Haury's methods of answering his critics through fieldwork would reemerge in the Field School during Jefferson Reid's tenure as director.

Haury had studied, worked, traveled, and taught with Cummings, receiving his A.B. in 1927 and his M.A. in 1928. He accepted Cummings's offer to teach in the Department of Archaeology during the 1928–29 academic year, but because of mounting uneasiness at suddenly becoming faculty to his peers, worked the following year with Douglass on the developing science of dendrochronology. With Douglass, he was further exposed to the rigors of scientific investigation.

Following the Douglass year, Haury spent seven years as assistant director of the Gila Pueblo Archaeological Foundation, a private archaeological research institution in Globe, Arizona, established by Harold Gladwin and Winifred Gladwin. During this time, Haury surveyed, excavated, and published at an exhausting pace. Haury conceived the concept of Hohokam with Gladwin, constructed the Hohokam chronology,

A. V. Kidder (left) and Emil Haury at Point of Pines in 1948.

and posed the original definition of the Mogollon culture, which also served to refine the concept of Anasazi (Dean 1988). By the time he returned to head archaeology at the UA, he was a research figure of national prominence conditioned by the Gila Pueblo schedule to year-round fieldwork and publication (Haury 1988).

Historians of southwestern archaeology have tended to denigrate the years postdating 1930 through the 1950s as mere "filling in the gaps." According to Taylor (1954), for example, the broad outlines of regional culture history were known by that time, and archaeologists focused their attention on unknown regions to discover how they fit into the overall scheme. Although there was certainly a good deal of "phase plugging," there was also directed research, hypothesis testing, and attention to processes of culture change, exemplified by Haury's research program at the Arizona field schools.

By 1939, Haury was in a position to give expression to his established research interests in the Hohokam and the Mogollon. He knew that the Arizona desert was not a congenial environment for fieldwork during the summer, the period of maximum field activity for university archaeologists. During the school year, therefore, he mounted his Papaguería project within striking distance of the university. This multidisciplinary, long-term effort was directed toward understanding the history of the Papaguería and the relationships between its prehistoric and historical-period peoples. Some of its monumental contributions were the investigations at Ventana Cave (Haury 1950). Haury took the summer field school to the high country—the Forestdale Valley on the Fort Apache Indian Reservation. The stated purpose was research into the prehistory of the Forestdale Valley as it bore directly on the mounting controversy over the concept of the Mogollon culture (Haury 1936, also in Reid and Doyel 1986). With subtle skill, Haury would maneuver his field schools at Forestdale (1939–1941) and Point of Pines (1946–1960) to validate the Mogollon. The "Mogollon problem" gave an immediate research purpose to the field school while simultaneously embroiling it in heated controversy.

The Field School at Forestdale and the Problem of Mogollon Cultural Identity

Haury had initially surveyed the Forestdale Valley in 1931 as part of an intensive reconnaissance of east-central Arizona and west-central New Mexico for Gila Pueblo. He knew the valley had a variety of sites, some of which displayed the brown pottery characteristic of the Mogollon tradition. The survey also demonstrated the widespread distribution of brown, plain ware pottery and pit-house village sites throughout the mountain region. During the 1931 survey, Haury located the Mogollon and Harris Villages, to which he later returned and excavated in 1933 and 1934, respectively, leading to his definition of the Mogollon culture. From today's vantage, *The Mogollon Culture of Southwestern New Mexico* (Haury 1936) appears as one of the most provocative publications in the history of southwestern archaeology, although this controversial aspect has largely been forgotten by younger archaeologists. Haury's well-reasoned, articulate description of two pit-house villages and material culture should have been an innocuous contribution to the prehistory of western New Mexico, but it was not. Instead, it generated a polarization of southwestern archaeologists that lasted for more than twenty years and a disdain for the Mogollon concept that lingers to this day.

In the monograph, Haury argued that the Mogollon should be recognized as a third culture distinct from Anasazi and Hohokam. He maintained further that the Mogollon culture was at least as old as Basketmaker culture, had developed pottery containers earlier than the Anasazi, and, late in its development, was submerged by the Anasazi. In Haury's view, Mogollon ended with the shift from pit houses to pueblos around A.D. 800, an end date later revised to A.D. 1000.

It took little time for a critical response to *The Mogollon Culture of Southwestern New Mexico* to enter the literature (Kidder 1939:315–16; Nesbitt 1938). Two questions marked the initial phases of the Mogollon controversy. First, were the mountain people so distinct from the Anasazi that a new label was required, and, if so, were these Mogollon to be viewed as a culture equivalent to the Anasazi and Hohokam? Second, regardless of the cultural status of Mogollon, how old was the ceramic tradition? Pottery was the hallmark of prehistoric southwestern cultures and the principal ingredient of archaeological reconstruction. Anasazi archaeologists did not warm to the prospect of a backward mountain people making pottery before their Anasazi.

Haury always was a firm believer in the notion that controversies must be solved by a reasoned consideration of the evidence, and the best way to obtain evidence was with the shovel. By 1939, it was apparent that more fieldwork was required if archaeologists were to accept the Mogollon concept, and Haury was ready to start a field-school program in the mountains. In 1936, Gladwin had suggested to Earl Morris, a highly respected Anasazi expert, that Morris should tackle the Mogollon problem with excavations in the Forestdale Valley (Haury 1985:139). Haury must have had faith that Morris would arrive at the same conclusions, and as an independent observer, would provide strong testimony for Mogollon distinctiveness. But Morris was occupied with his own early sites near Durango. Haury therefore proposed to Morris that the UA carry on the work (Haury 1985:139), and in 1939, Haury began his first field school in the Forestdale Valley.

The field schools of 1939, 1940, and 1941 combined students and Apache workmen in the pursuit of Haury's personal research goals. Haury sought to enhance the impact of the evidence they were obtaining through conferences and invitations that brought prominent archaeologists to view the record firsthand.

At Bear Village, Haury (1940, also Haury 1985) defined a pit-house occupation dated between A.D. 600 and 800. This site corroborated the antiquity proposed for the Mogollon and Harris Villages with additional tree-ring dates. Haury also made a substantial claim that Bear Village was distinctive in its complex of material remains, although he believed that the Mogollon of that time also displayed some Anasazi characteristics. Bear Village demonstrated that the Mogollon traits found in the Mimbres and San Francisco River valleys were not aberrant but also extended into the mountains of east-central Arizona.

In 1941, the last year at Forestdale, Haury began excavation at the

Bluff site, a pit-house village that would produce strong evidence for the association of pottery in pit houses dated by tree rings to around A.D. 300. Before this evidence would be accepted, years of controversy ensued. This story will be told elsewhere, so suffice it to say that no lesser figures than A. V. Kidder, J. O. Brew, Erik Reed, Paul Martin, and John McGregor would argue the distinctiveness and validity of the Mogollon concept.

The summer of 1944 was Haury's last season in the Forestdale Valley. He returned with E. B. "Ted" Sayles to supervise an Apache crew in completing the work at the Bluff site. With the end of the war in sight, Haury began to plan the revival of the field school. The early pit-house sites of the Forestdale Valley had been studied and reported; the Bear Village report had been issued in 1940, and the Bluff report would be available shortly (Haury and Sayles 1947). Although personal communication had made the interpretations of Bluff widely available, there was no general consensus concerning the separateness and antiquity of Mogollon, and the controversy that had begun in 1936 showed no signs of abating as archaeologists began to reorganize after the war. Haury had heard of ruins in the Point of Pines region of the San Carlos Apache Reservation. Point of Pines was a mountain location ideal for a summer field school. Perhaps it would have the quantity and diversity of sites needed for student training and further documentation of the Mogollon.

The Field School at Point of Pines: Consolidation of Mogollon Culture History

In the summer of 1945, Haury and Sayles surveyed Point of Pines, a cattle station on the San Carlos Apache Reservation. As at Forestdale, Haury was looking for a long sequence of prehistoric occupation as revealed in a range of sites. At Point of Pines, he found them in abundance—more than two hundred sites ranging from pit-house villages like those he had dug in Forestdale and New Mexico to small, medium, and large pueblos. It was an ideal situation for training students and for fleshing out the Mogollon story. At Point of Pines, with "a half-dozen satellite ruins and three pueblos with twelve or more rooms on top, it struck us as a possible focal place where field training of students could involve a variety of problems and where work could be carried out for a number of years" (Haury 1989:8). Tired of wrestling tents in the violent winds of mountain storms, Haury was also looking for a pleasant spot to establish a well-constructed, comfortable camp. He found that, too, at Point of Pines. Haury envisioned that fifteen years would be ample time to explore the cultural history of the region, and he kept to that schedule.

The field school at Point of Pines ran from 1946 through 1960, during which time it solidified Haury's considerable contribution to the field-school tradition and laid to rest most of the objections to his concept of Mogollon. Point of Pines was a rare and memorable experience to all who shared its moments, and only Haury (1989) himself could chronicle that experience with authority and authenticity.

At Point of Pines, Haury initiated a dramatic shift in the field-school program. Whereas at Forestdale he had shouldered responsibility for the analysis and publication of the excavations, at Point of Pines he gave this responsibility to graduate students who had supervised excavations as part of their staff duties. Haury published on only one Point of Pines site, Cienega Creek. In part, this shift was necessitated by Haury's increasing administrative load. It was also a product of the amount of work being done each summer. The data produced by the field school had become too much for one person to handle. Whereas other directors might have hoarded the data for a time in the distant future when they would be able to write it up, Haury permitted access and sole authorship to the enterprising student. In retrospect, this involvement of graduate students in the research process is one of the most significant features of Arizona archaeology in the field-school environment.

Haury evidently ran Point of Pines with a firm hand. His approaches to camp life, research, and teaching were along similar lines. He was methodical, rigorous, and ordered. His own words (Haury 1989:26) give a sense of Haury's field-school philosophy:

> My view of operating a camp successfully was that a reasonable schedule had to be developed, but, more importantly, that it had to be adhered to, barring unforeseen difficulties. Briefings, therefore, were in order so that what I expected of the students and what their obligations were to the program were clearly understood from the start. This applied equally to the camp routine and to the archaeological studies we were to undertake. . . . I was thoroughly convinced that our little society thrived best under a reasonable, but governed, structure that resulted in personal happiness and gains.

This is not to say that Haury was a martinet. As a teacher, Haury expressed great kindness, concern, and took extraordinary care with his teaching responsibilities. In later years, he would spend hours in discussion over particular problems or events that a student was attempting to puzzle out, and his graduate student seminars were treated to his and wife Hulda's hospitality in their home. Little wonder that he was fondly called "Doc" by all who knew him.

These qualities also are represented well in Haury's approach to grading. As he recalls (Haury 1989:122–23), he was uncomfortable with quantitative assessments. The real qualities for success at the field school were less definable—enthusiasm, dedication, the ability to relate socially to one's peers, and "the necessary willingness to operate within the rigors of scientific guidelines." In the end, Haury thought, reaching a decision about whether archaeology was to be a student's life endeavor or not was the ultimate "grade."

Point of Pines served as a venue for responses to the continuing attack on the Mogollon concept. Haury hosted the Pecos Conference at Point of Pines in the late summer of 1948 to show dubious colleagues what the Mogollon looked like in an archaeological context. The event served as subtle persuasion to a suspicious archaeological community always more inclined to believe in evidence that was inspected personally (see Woodbury 1993:167–87).

In 1950, Reed, who had long argued in support of the Mogollon concept, completed his summary of the traits that set it apart from the Anasazi. He also suggested the term *Western* (or *Southern*) *Pueblo* to label the pueblo-building Mogollon after A.D. 1000 and distinguish them from the Anasazi. This concept was the centerpiece of the Friday afternoon roundtable at the 1951 Pecos Conference, again held at Point of Pines (Woodbury 1993:204–12).

It is clear that, throughout these years of continued controversy, the Mogollon debate loomed large at Point of Pines. It is no coincidence that Point of Pines produced the synthetic statement resolving the twenty-year debate—Joe Ben Wheat's (1955) *Mogollon Culture Prior to A.D. 1000*. According to Wheat, the book synthesized all that was known about the Mogollon and in the process, though he does not avow it, validated the Mogollon concept. Although "it does not purport to be a final 'answer to the Mogollon problem'" (Wheat 1955:vi), in retrospect it was the answer to the problem as it was then posed.

Wheat was a student at Point of Pines in 1948. From 1949 through 1951, Wheat directed excavations at Crooked Ridge, a large pit-house site in the Point of Pines region believed to have been occupied between A.D. 100 and the late 900s. The report on this site and the Mogollon synthesis were combined in Wheat's 1953 dissertation. Wheat held the second Ph.D. in anthropology to be awarded by the UA, Charles Di Peso having received the first by virtue of alphabetical order.

The impact of Wheat's work was enhanced by its unparalleled distribution as a site report and a memoir of two major scholarly societies. In 1954, the Crooked Ridge Village section of the dissertation was published by the UA as a Social Science Bulletin (Wheat 1954a). The synthesis of Mogollon was published in 1955 *jointly* as a memoir of the Society for American Archaeology (SAA) and an American Anthropological Association (AAA) memoir (Wheat 1955), ensuring that Wheat's validation of the Mogollon concept was received by every member of the SAA *and* every member of the AAA. Few if any other pieces of American archaeological scholarship have received such a wide distribution.

In the Mogollon synthesis, Wheat addressed all of the contentious issues surrounding Mogollon—antiquity and chronology; relation to the Cochise, Anasazi, and Hohokam; and the priority of Mogollon pottery over Anasazi pottery. The persuasiveness of his presentation stemmed from three elements of the book: (1) a map showing the widespread geographic distribution of Mogollon branches, (2) a period-phase chart insinuating time depth and phase contiguity, and (3) a thorough comparison of pottery, architecture, and village plan. Wheat's work was a model of archaeological argument in the cultural-historical school. Haury's (1989:53) rather terse recollection of Wheat's work belies the enormous impact of this prodigious synthetic argument: "Most importantly, the work on Crooked Ridge Village represented the solid beginning of the Point of Pines chronology and clear evidence that the initial pottery-making and agricultural people of the region were those of the Mogollon culture."

For all intents and purposes, the Mogollon controversy had been annihilated by a thorough compilation of extensive excavation data distributed free of charge to every anthropologist and archaeologist in North America. The Mogollon problem had effectively ceased as a public topic of intellectual debate. Later controversies embroiling Grasshopper would not be erased so easily.

With Wheat's dissertation published widely and well accepted, Haury and his field school were freed from the immediate constraints of the Mogollon question to explore other problems of regional culture history. Throughout the 1950s, Haury's research program, as stated in his 1989 recollections, was to fill in the gaps in the Point of Pines cultural sequence and to groom his successor—Raymond Thompson.

The record hints that, by the mid-1950s, Haury's attention may have been diverted from the field school. The 1954 season, the year following the completion of Wheat's dissertation, was directed by Ned Danson while Haury stayed in Tucson. Thompson recalls that taking over the field school was to be one of his responsibilities when he was hired at the UA in 1956. Thompson was no stranger to Point of Pines. He was a student there in 1947, along with a number of others who would gain prominence in archaeology, and there he met Molly Kendall, the future Mrs. Thompson. The Thompsons returned to Point of Pines in 1948, joined Brew's Upper Gila Expedition in 1949, and then, after a brief interlude in Mesoamerica, went back to the pines in 1952 and 1954. Thompson was there each year from 1956 until the Point of Pines field school closed in 1960, either as assistant director or, in Haury's absence during the 1957 and 1960 seasons, as director. The last years of Point of Pines cannot be appreciated fully without mention of the role played by Thompson nor can Thompson's archaeological career be fully appreciated apart from Point of Pines.

Thompson arrived at Point of Pines a year after he was discharged from the Navy, having spent the closing years of World War II as a Seabee stationed in the Pacific theater. The elemental contrast in scenery would have made indelible impressions in the mind of a young man recently returned from jungle war, not to mention the ambience of people, place, and mission to meticulously uncover the past. Thompson's position as Haury's successor must have been obvious during the late 1950s, even though it would not be formalized until later.

The fifteenth and last season of Point of Pines arrived in 1960. Fifteen years had been the original estimate of time needed to work out the sequence of local prehistory, and it was almost complete. As Thompson always recalled around the campfire at Grasshopper when discussing the history of Point of Pines, Haury felt a lessening of research excitement as the information from each new excavation became redundant. Some of the camp buildings needed repair, and the Apaches were anxious to take over the camp for programs of their own. The culture-history program for archaeological research had been fulfilled. "There was nothing new to learn," as Thompson would later tell us. Haury stayed home that final season while Thompson directed a frenetic summer of tying up the inevitable loose ends of archaeological fieldwork and filling in the last major gap in the chronology, the Stove Canyon phase, with excavations at the Stove Canyon and Lunt sites (Neely 1974).

Haury returned at the end of the season to assist in the last camp closing and to say goodbye to a field school that in the nostalgic recollections of its participants had taken on a mythic aura rare in the annals of archaeological fieldwork (Haury 1989).

Point of Pines in Retrospect

The field school at Point of Pines, isolated as it was from normal channels of information and remote to all but the most persistent, nevertheless was a sensitive barometer of contemporary southwestern archaeology, and to some extent, American archaeology as a whole. As Wheat's synthesis of the Mogollon epitomized the structure of archaeological argument at the time, so, too, did the research program at Point of Pines exemplify the prevailing structure of archaeological investigation. Taylor (1954) referred to this structure as "filling in the gaps," a viewpoint he believed to characterize southwestern archaeology beginning in the early 1930s. Filling in the gaps was a research program for adding cultural-trait information to the blank spots or gaps in the time-space chart. Time-space systematics expressed in the map of branches and the chart of phases was the research program and the form of argument for southwesterners of the 1950s. Taylor's (1954:567) disparaging appraisal of this program was in part the result of merging the program with some of the byproducts of its application.

Taylor's (1954:566–70) psychoanalysis of this research program recognizes an "expedition" or "pioneering attitude" and an "archeological restlessness" that combined with the culture-area point of view to provide only a superficial view of prehistory. Taylor (1954:566) writes, "We have some knowledge of the cultures of many areas but only a shallow perception of the culture and cultural relationships of any one of them. Warrant has been given to extensiveness at the expense of depth, and the archeologists have been given an acceptable excuse for moving to fresher fields, whether or not the old ones have been fully exploited, fully described, or fully understood." To our ears, Taylor's appraisal sounds much more like he is describing new archaeologists than culture historians.

Taylor (1954:567) goes on to write:

> the hallmark of Southwestern archeology has been field work and descriptive accounts of specific sites, their specimen rosters and their relationships in time and space. The synthesizer, the theoretician, and "armchair" archeologist have been alien to the tradition. The stereotype of the Southwesternist is the field man, the "man of action," the pioneer. He is a factual man, dealing with concrete objects such as specimens, not much given to what is disdained as "speculation." Hypotheses, when he makes them consciously, are usually concerned with taxonomic and temporal relationships, seldom with more intricate cultural inferences. Strictly cultural problems and projects set up for the testing of theoretical and methodic premises

have been all but nonexistent. The Southwesternist is typically oriented toward geographic areas, descriptive taxonomy, and material objects—not ideas.

All of this Taylor attributes to the extraterritorial, specifically eastern, dominance of the southwestern field and to the expedition, or pioneer, attitude (Taylor 1954:567). Even as he wrote those words, the eastern dominance of southwestern archaeology was losing hold, and when the change came, it would go unremarked, because the difference Taylor assumed was always more chimeric than real. When Taylor said eastern influence, he meant Kidder. By the mid-1950s, Kidder's personal dominance had waned, but Haury continued the Kidder approach. Haury's orchestrated finale to the Mogollon controversy further diluted eastern influence in the archaeology of the Southwest. In so doing, however, he ratified the ground rules under which the scholarly community was to conduct archaeology.

Point of Pines research epitomized and in many ways made explicit the culture-history paradigm of archaeological investigation as it was expressed in the American Southwest, a version markedly different from other regions of North America (see Lyman, O'Brien, and Dunnell 1997). Survey and excavation were principal activities for acquiring data relevant to filling in the gaps of prehistory, architecture and pottery were the most informative categories of remains, and tree-ring dating provided a measure of chronological control unknown in the rest of North America. Kidder's (1931:6–8) initial expression of the field procedures best summarizes "the general method of attack upon any given archaeological problem" by culture historians:

> To indicate the precise bearing of the Pecos work it may be well to enlarge upon the remarks made earlier in this introduction regarding the general method of attack upon any given archaeological problem. The steps in such an attack are
>
>   1) Preliminary survey of remains in the region under consideration.
>
>   2) Selection of criteria for ranking those remains in chronological order.
>
>   3) Comparative study of the manifestations of the criteria to arrive at a tentative chronological ranking of the sites containing them.
>
>   4) Search for and excavation of sites in which materials may be found in stratigraphic relationship in order to check up on the tentative ranking and so to obtain a large number of specimens for morphological and genetic studies.
>
>   5) A more thorough resurvey of the area in the light of the fuller knowledge now at hand in order definitely to rank all sites and, if necessary, to

select for excavation new sites which may be expected to elucidate problems raised during the course of the research.

The degree to which Haury adhered to this "method of attack" is well documented in his own words (Haury 1989). A few points can be emphasized as they bear upon positioning Point of Pines in the succession of field-school research. Haury was able to translate the field procedures and expectations of culture history into a teaching-and-research program that became increasingly dependent on student involvement (see Gifford and Morris 1985). The labor of students moved dirt as well as explored uncharted analytical domains. Clearly, many projects, such as Wheat's research, pursued problems of personal research interest to Haury. Through time, however, graduate students developed their own research interests, some to be pursued in a broad, regional context well beyond the confines of Point of Pines.

A glance at the range of problems that were examined at Point of Pines indicates that culture history was not limited to issues of chronology building and artifact description. In addition to working out the phase sequence of a previously unknown region (Breternitz, Gifford, and Olson 1957) and validating Haury's construct of a Mogollon culture (Wheat 1954b, 1955), Point of Pines archaeologists investigated diverse problems ranging from the adoption of corn (Haury 1957; Martin and Schoenwetter 1960) and prehistoric agriculture (Woodbury 1961) to ceremonial architecture (Gerald 1958; A. Johnson 1961; Smiley 1952) and mortuary ritual (Bennett 1973; Merbs 1967; Robinson 1958, 1959; Robinson and Sprague 1965; M. Stein 1962). Haury's (1958; Lindsay 1987; see Thompson 1958b) documentation of a prehistoric migration is the example of a specific research problem most often cited by contemporary archaeologists. Multidisciplinary research was pursued through zooarchaeology (W. Stein 1962, 1963), ethnobotany (Bohrer 1973), palynology (Martin and Schoenwetter 1960), dendrochronology (Parker 1967; Smiley 1949), and geology (Heindl 1955; Morris 1957; Wheat 1952). These research problems of the 1950s are again in the forefront of southwestern archaeology in the 2000s. It was in matters of prehistoric social structure and organization that the investigations of the culture historians contrasted most sharply with the soon-to-appear processual archaeologists. Long after the close of the field school would students intent on examining features of past organization find Point of Pines data most compelling. As Lowell (1991) demonstrated, where else could one find a pueblo like Turkey Creek, with 314 of 335 rooms excavated, for studying the relationship between architecture and social groups in a large community?

Perhaps the most significant contributions to archaeological method, however, were in the arena of ceramic analysis. Haury had participated in the original definition of many southwestern ceramic types and, through his work in dendrochronology, was a major contributor to the development of ceramic cross dating. He had personally demonstrated the value of ceramics as markers of particular times, places, and peoples. Hohokam archaeology, for example, was dependent then and remains dependent to a large extent now—long after the invention of independent dating techniques—on the accurate identification of ceramic types. The presence of specific Hohokam pottery types permits an associated Hohokam structure or feature to be assigned to a phase. Little wonder that ceramics were a major focus of Point of Pines research and development.

This is not the place to chronicle the history of ceramic analysis at Point of Pines, other than to emphasize several points relevant to later work at Grasshopper. The type-variety method was developed at Point of Pines, along with the beginnings of a conceptual framework and vocabulary for analysis. Although the initial formulation of the type-variety method is credited to Wheat, Gifford, and Wasley (1958), it is clear that further development and clarification of the approach fell to Gifford. His contributions to ceramic analysis at Point of Pines are partially obscured by his investigation of caves and cliff dwellings (Gifford 1957, 1980) and his switch to Mesoamerican pottery. Minimally, he brought a higher degree of systematization to classification and encouraged a broad discussion of how best to interpret variability. It is tempting to suggest that Gifford had a greater impact on the direction of ceramic studies at Arizona than did the eminent ceramicist Anna Shepard. In the field, the Point of Pines archaeologists confronted extremely large quantities of highly variable ceramics—a problem of late prehistoric pottery in the American Southwest that archaeologists continue to confront today—and proposed the type-variety method as a means to order it. As Reid (1984b) notes elsewhere, this was less a solution and more a clarification of the problem.

The most widely known and perhaps most significant piece of ceramic research to emerge from this analytical atmosphere was David Breternitz's 1963 dissertation, published as *An Appraisal of Tree-Ring Dated Pottery in the Southwest* (Breternitz 1966). This classic discussion of ceramic cross dating is an indispensable text for all archaeologists working in the ceramic period of the central and northern Southwest. It evaluates the association of tree-ring dates with pottery types at archaeological sites to estimate the range of time during which a specific type was made. It is the basis of contemporary ceramic cross dating. Using Breternitz's compendium, a knowledgeable ceramicist can date a site in some areas of the northern Southwest at a higher resolution than can be achieved with radiocarbon analysis and at no cost. Although there is a need for revisions based on new and reevaluated tree-ring data (Mills and Herr 1999; Reid, Montgomery, and Zedeño 1995; Sullivan, Becher, and Downum 1995), Breternitz's work stands as a milestone (Blinman 2000).

Serving to broaden further the interest in ceramic studies at Point of Pines was Thompson's pioneering ethnoarchaeological study of Yucatecan Maya pottery making, which he completed as a dissertation at Harvard and published in 1958 as Memoir 15 of the SAA. In addition to the expanded definition of pottery analysis signaled by this work, there is Thompson's consideration of how archaeologists evaluate inferences about the past. Known as the "subjective element in archaeological inference" after the published paper (Thompson 1956), Thompson's model clarifies the role of the subjective element in generating hypotheses and codifies how most archaeologists at that time evaluated statements made about the past—they evaluated the archaeologist. The evaluation criteria emphasized academic training, background, and experience—essentially a scholar's pedigree and reputation. This seeming elitist model held no appeal for the archaeological scientists and intellectual populists of the 1960s and 1970s, who used it as a principal foil for promoting objective means of evaluating knowledge claims. Ironically enough, as the Grasshopper–Chavez Pass debate demonstrates (see chapter 8), subjective elements would come to dominate how "explicitly scientific archaeologists" would evaluate interpretations of late prehistory.

The success of Point of Pines must also be evaluated in terms of its contributions to the profession. Haury (1989:123) reported that one-fourth of Point of Pines students went on to distinguish themselves in archaeological careers. The success of the program, Haury maintained, was based on the involvement of its students in the research process. "They were made to feel that they had a stake in the larger effort of expanding our knowledge of the archaeological universe. The training went beyond the mere personal acquisition of technical skills" (Haury 1989:123).

Haury epitomized the southwestern archaeologist—he was a proficient fieldworker, explicit in his research, crisp in his interpretations of the past, and unafraid to announce a change of opinion when he thought the data required it, even when to do so must have been wrenching. Haury (1989:124) concluded his history of the Point of Pines field school by saying that "in spite of the many questions that remain to be answered, a large, previously unknown region of the Southwest has been brought into archaeological focus and mystery has been at least partly dispelled by fact." These idealized culture-history research goals would be taken up by another field-school director who assumed Haury's mantle in another venue—Grasshopper, Arizona.

4

Culture History, 1963–1965

It is in the practice of ethnography that the vitality of anthropology resides.
—**Nancy Scheper-Hughes** (1992), quoted in Kus (2000:166)

We begin Grasshopper's history in the 1960s, during a time that was turbulent socially and in American archaeology as well. In 1963, Raymond Thompson moved the field school to Grasshopper to begin excavation and training at a new venue following a short-lived experiment in southeastern Arizona. In so doing, he took on Emil Haury's mantle, and, as director, he began the Field School in Haury's footsteps, following the time-honored traditions of culture history and the field school as they were represented at Point of Pines. The Field School Thompson established would endure far longer than he envisioned, however, going beyond three brief years of culture history to encompass thirty seasons of fieldwork, two more directors, and two additional schools of archaeology.

This chapter chronicles the brief history of the culture-history years at Grasshopper, which lasted from 1963 to 1965. The period was not only short, it was also impure—that is, it had scarcely begun before it took on the character of processual archaeology, which emerged during that time. Therefore, the interlude may represent the culture-history approach less adequately than if viewed from other perspectives. For this reason, among others, we cannot use it as a criterion for evaluating the success of culture history at Grasshopper. We can simply catalogue these years and use them as a point of contrast for later periods in the history of Grasshopper.

First, however, we must discuss the transfer of directorship and the brief and poorly recorded experiment in which the field school abandoned the mountains of east-central Arizona. We also present how the camp itself was built, for the buildings and facilities that represented the Grasshopper camp not only were built under Thompson's tenure, but endured to the end.

A New Director Takes the Haury Mantle

The transition from Byron Cummings to Haury, as we have seen, was rapid and dramatic. There was only a one-year overlap, during the 1937–1938 academic year, when Haury was head of the Department of Anthropology at the University of Arizona and Cummings was still director of the Arizona State Museum. The transition was dramatic, in that each man exemplified a distinct perspective in archaeology. Cummings approached the record of the past as a pioneer, explorer, and collector, whereas Haury was among the first of the anthropologically trained culture historians.

The transition from Haury to Thompson was not so dramatic or well marked. Having left Point of Pines secure in the knowledge that the Mogollon had been validated at last, Haury turned the field-school reins over to a director who would continue in the same time-honored tradition of culture history but in an atmosphere free from the spurs of controversy and debate. Succeeding Haury would have placed incredible expectations and burdens on anyone, and attempting to duplicate Haury's archaeological contributions would have been folly. Moreover, to have rivaled Haury's fame would have required embracing a new paradigm while repudiating the old. Thompson could never have contemplated such acts.

It is an interesting sidelight that the Chicago Field Museum was charting a parallel course. Paul Martin and John Rinaldo, having left New Mexico in 1954, began anew in 1957 with a field camp at Vernon, near Show Low, Arizona, from which to investigate their hypothesis that the Pine Lawn Valley Mogollon had moved to Zuni. They pursued an excavation program and produced a laudable record of rapid publication. By the beginning of the 1960s, the Mogollon-culture concept had become so widely accepted that, at least at Vernon, it had become passé, and the fuss associated with it had become a quaint relic of a bygone era in southwestern archaeology, like the riding of a mule. The use of all cultural labels and attendant taxonomic controversies shortly would be abandoned in favor of examining anthropologically relevant questions according to what were perceived to be rigorous procedures of scientific investigation. Vernon would become a training camp for processual archaeologists; Grasshopper also would give birth to an emerging processual archaeology.

There was no field school in 1961, as Haury and Thompson pondered where to go next after Point of Pines ended. We turn next to the story of the transitional year before the field school settled at Grasshopper.

Transitional Year: The Field School at the Ringo Site

The end of Point of Pines must have been a signal event for Haury and his successor, for it left a gap that proved initially difficult to fill. Although Haury was interested in the Colorado Plateau of northern Arizona, this area had little appeal for Thompson, who wanted new data to interpret the late period represented by Point of Pines Pueblo. A solution appeared after Haury, Thompson, and Richard Harvill, then president of the UA, visited the El Coronado Ranch. This former guest ranch and boys' school, located on the western slope of the Chiricahua Mountains in the far-southeastern corner of Arizona, had been given to the UA. It had good camp facilities and was situated in an archaeologically unknown area. Research undertaken there would not infringe upon other investigators or institutions, most notably Charles Di Peso, who was at that time director of the Amerind Foundation, a private archaeological research institution in Dragoon, Arizona. Thus, the decision was made. In this way, 1962 witnessed a UA archaeological field school initiated and directed by Thompson forsaking the mountains for a program of research in southeastern Arizona for the first and only time in its history.

With Alfred Johnson as dig foreman, Wilma Kaemlein as laboratory supervisor, and seventeen students, excavations began at the Ringo site. A beginning was all that was to be, however, for the field school lasted just a single season. We can speculate on the reasons for this brief tenure. Although the southeastern corner of Arizona was indeed relatively unknown and certainly could have benefited from a sustained research effort, Ringo was not Point of Pines in archaeology, climate, or ambience. The Ringo site lacked the archaeological record of artifacts and features essential to research and student teaching, although the sparse remains may have provided the distinct advantage of amenability to rapid analysis and reporting. The climate surely must have been a factor. The Chihuahuan Desert grassland can be extraordinarily hot in summer. No doubt students, particularly those from greener, cooler climes, were slowed by the heat, and the work pace lagged. In southeastern Arizona, the ambience of pine-scented mountain air was an almost-forgotten memory.

By the next year, Johnson and Thompson (1963) had published a report on the Ringo site, a classic expression of exposition in the format of culture history. And that would be the end of the Ringo experiment. Thompson had become deeply interested in what is now called "aggregation" in late prehistory, especially as seen in late, large pueblos with plazas and great kivas. Such sites were concentrated along the Mogollon Rim. In moving the field school, Thompson evidently also had in mind Haury's patent formula for student training and research involvement—order, schedule, and rigorous adherence to scientific guidelines. We would wager that a certain longing for the pine trees and pueblos of the Arizona mountains also was involved.

The Founding of the Grasshopper Field School

Grasshopper began with a field trip and probably with a memory of good times and good archaeology, although we cannot be sure. In the fall of 1962, Raymond and Molly Thompson, along with Alfred and Ann Johnson, joined Haury's seminar class on one of his celebrated, overnight field trips. They camped at Grasshopper. Thompson remembers the cold and the whistling of elk, and we can imagine that, sitting around the campfire after supper and counting stars falling through the jet-black sky, these Point of Pines alumni reminisced about the good ol' days. They probably also dreamed about how they might rationalize returning the field school to its traditional mountain venue.

The fieldwork directive as set out by Kidder, which we discussed in chapter 3, was unambiguous—the archaeologist chose an unknown region or period for investigation by selectively excavating sites that would fill the gaps in knowledge. Grasshopper fit the bill in many ways. It represented an unknown region and the fourteenth century—a relatively little-known period, when a pottery tradition intermediate between the White Mountain Red Ware and Salado traditions promised "to shed light on the movements of Western Pueblo groups and on the origin of the Salado" (Thompson 1963:3).

Like the field-school locales the Thompsons and Johnsons had experienced, Grasshopper featured a large pueblo and numerous other ruins. Thompson remembers clearly, and the record supports him, that the principal reason for moving the field school was to provide the best-possible setting for student training, and the reason for selecting Grasshopper was for its research potential within a culture-history frame of reference. Like Point of Pines and unlike the El Coronado Ranch area, Grasshopper and the surrounding region had qualities holding great promise for training and research in the Arizona field-school tradition and, most especially, for comparisons with the Point of Pines data. Grasshopper also was located in the mountains on Apache land. The Apache had been good hosts at Kinishba, Forestdale, and Point of Pines.

As the group mused around the crackling campfire, the memory of El Coronado Ranch no doubt was fading. Thompson must have envisioned a field-school camp on the hill overlooking the pueblo ruin—a large, late prehistoric pueblo with several plazas and a great kiva. It was precisely what he wanted. The fates intervened during that winter to make the camp a reality. An anonymous benefactor provided twenty thousand dollars to enable a new field school to be established over the coming two years. Just like that, dream became reality, and memory came alive in the present.

A Field Camp Rises

Thompson took to the tasks of crafting a camp and archaeological program of his own design with energy, suggesting a long-term plan of personal involvement in the research. In the late spring of 1963, he began to build the kitchen and laboratory and fashion a shower house, which, according to knowledgeable observers, was a fair replica of the showers Navy Seabees had built during the war. In a few years, Thompson would construct a camp that was almost as comfortable as the one at Point of Pines. By then, however, Thompson would have handed over the keys to a new director and a new archaeology.

Thompson built the Grasshopper camp on a hill directly to the east of the ruin and across Salt River Draw, adjacent to the cowboy camp. Our romantic side envisions the building of Grasshopper on film, as a traditional barn raising with a host of happy campers wielding hammers and nails to a background of swelling music. Reality was no doubt more mundane. Although photographs document some staff members participating in the building efforts, most of the initial construction was by Thompson himself, assisted by a carpenter and a helper.

Longacre and Reid (1974:3) describe Grasshopper as "a self-contained field camp of 19 habitation, storage, and 'ceremonial' structures designed to accommodate 20 students, a staff of 14, and from 5 to 10 Apaches." This tongue-in-cheek appraisal described frame-and-plywood buildings that included a combination kitchen and dining room; laboratory and lecture hall with a ramada, darkroom, and director's office; conjoined shower house and laundry room; and two-seater outhouses.

There were two dormitories each for men and women students, a gas shed, a toolshed that housed the generator, and several prefabricated cabins for staff use. The buildings were roofed with roll roofing and, lacking insulation or air conditioning, could be rather warm when the temperature reached the nineties. Two house trailers, ancient relics from Haury's 1964 Snaketown camp, also were used to house staff. There is nothing louder in the middle of the night than a metal house trailer that is home to families of field mice, as we know from experience. In some years, tents would swell the number of dwellings in camp. When Apache workmen joined us, they maintained a separate tent camp north of the public buildings where they bunked during the work week, returning to Cibecue for the weekends.

Someone collected suitable stones from the camp area and aligned them to form walkways between the public buildings and staff cabins. This was a necessity where the sticky mud made walking, much less any other kind of travel, a hazardous experience after thunderstorms. Larry Agenbroad claims he was the walkway builder and insists it was hard labor, as it surely must have been. To accommodate the camp's social needs, a fire circle was built down the road from the director's cabin. The only other social facility was the tree house at the director's cabin, which Thompson built for his young daughters in the branches of a huge juniper. Abandoned by children, the tree house hosted parties in later years until it became too dilapidated.

The camp comprised a number of essential and more or less inter-related systems. Water came from a well at the base of a windmill at the cowboy camp by means of a submersible pump powered by a portable electric generator. Water was pumped daily into a nine-hundred-gallon tank that stood on the camp's highest spot. Initially, showers of dubious warmth were provided by filling fifty-five-gallon drums with water that was allowed to warm throughout the day. One of the first things that students were warned of was the necessity to keep showers brief, turning the water off after lathering, Army-style, and to use one tub of water only for laundry. Although the coldness of the water during the early years meant the former was no hardship, the requirement of the latter was stringent. One always began with the least-dirty clothes, but by the time the dig clothes were washed, the water had turned the terra cotta red of Grasshopper's dirt, and a fine silt had collected at the bottom of the tub.

Waste was accommodated the traditional way. Two gender-specific outhouses served sanitation needs. The women's outhouse was usually the first thing that visitors to Grasshopper noticed, as it overlooked the road into camp. Waste water was piped into the ground some distance beyond the shower house and kitchen. Garbage was burned to keep the bears away, and this could be hazardous duty should empty aerosol cans or other potentially explosive debris be included. In the early years, a backhoe was used to move the outhouses each summer to fresh, new locations and to dig a new garbage pit.

There was, of course, no electricity, Arizona Public Service having never extended its lines west of Cibecue. The Thompson camp produced electricity for its own use by means of a World-War-II–vintage, two-kilowatt, direct-current generator inherited from Point of Pines that has been described as having the size and weight of a small German automobile (Reid and Whittlesey 1999). Housed in the toolshed not far from the kitchen, the immobile generator remained at Grasshopper over the winter when the rest of the camp was boarded up and winterized. The main buildings were electrified, but the staff cabins and dormitories were not. This necessitated the use of candles and lanterns, which ultimately proved disastrous. The DC current ran an old-fashioned, wringer washing machine in the laundry–shower house and an evaporative cooler for the kitchen, where the temperature reached uncomfortable heights when the oven was on.

Staff members were tasked with keeping the generator running healthily and became concerned when it sputtered and coughed. No electricity meant no mixer to whip the potatoes or mix the cake batter. When the ancient slide projector was needed for a lecture, the AC generator that pumped water was moved temporarily into service.

The kitchen was the vital core of the camp, and every means was taken to ensure that the cook was well supplied and happy. Gas refrigerators and freezers in the pantry relied on propane, as did the gas water heaters. A tanker truck from Show Low periodically refilled the tank. To complete the kitchen system, a root cellar would be constructed in 1966.

This old-fashioned, partly underground facility was used to store fruits, vegetables, and eggs. The cooks and camp aides became creative in developing storage containers that were mice-proof. The constant battle against nocturnal rodents would later give us new insights into the reasons for the development of ceramic-container technology in the Southwest.

Most students arrived at Globe, where staff members met them in the lobby of the old Dominion Hotel, now demolished. Students and their belongings were hauled across the Salt River Canyon, onto the high plateau of the Fort Apache Indian Reservation, and through the village of Cibecue to Grasshopper. Leaving behind the real world, they were immersed in the tiny world of an archaeological field camp.

Camp organization was derived directly from Point of Pines. The cook stood at the apex of the camp hierarchy. Thompson, like Haury, understood that a field camp is only as good as its food. Kitchen assistants, later called camp aides, were an invaluable component of the well-tuned camp. Usually two young men, their primary responsibility was to wash dishes and do the heavy cleaning and fetching for the cook. They were also the principal camp gofers, who pumped water, cleaned and stocked the outhouses and showers, filled the tanks for showers, and burned garbage.

The daily schedule also was borrowed from Point of Pines (see Haury 1989:26), and one of a student's first duties was to become conditioned and inured to it. Beginning at 6:00 a.m. until lights out at 10:30 p.m., the day was completely orchestrated in the best Haury manner, as follows:

Daily Schedule of Activities

6:00 a.m.	First wake-up bell (slow beat)
6:20 a.m.	Second wake-up or ten-minute bell (fast beat)
6:30 a.m.	Breakfast bell (continuous beat)
7:30 a.m.	Start-for-the-field bell
9:30 a.m.	Coffee break
11:50 a.m.	Ten-minute bell (fast beat)
12:00 p.m.	Lunch bell (continuous beat)
1:00 p.m.	Back-to-the-site bell (fast beat)
3:30 p.m.	Leave site and return to camp
5:50 p.m.	Ten-minute bell (fast beat)
6:00 p.m.	Dinner bell (continuous beat)
8:00 p.m.	Lecture bell
10:30 p.m.	Lights out (generator off) and camp quiet

The schedule was governed by "the bell," a length of cast-iron pipe hung outside the kitchen. Like so much else at Grasshopper, this communication system was inherited from Point of Pines. An important camp-aide duty was to ring the bell energetically with a metal rod to call the camp for wake-up time, meals, and the arrival of the grocery run. We cannot speak to the hatred that may have developed in the Thompson years, but by the time we arrived at Grasshopper, the bell was universally loathed. Each summer, students would steal it and eventually return it for some ransom, often ice cream, in a ritual designed to show disdain for camp authority. The distinction in how the bell was struck was established later, in the early 1970s, by Stanley Olsen, who recognized the importance to sleepy students and staff of differentiating the first bell of the morning from the last bell calling them to breakfast.

Groceries and supplies were procured at Show Low, "the town named by a turn of a card," located fifty-five miles northeast of Grasshopper. Thompson initially instituted the Point of Pines routine of going into town every two weeks. This lasted until 1976, when it was realized that someone actually went to Show Low every week regardless. A staff member undertook the Show Low run, loading a truck with coolers and driving to town to pick up the food ordered on the previous trip and spend a day shopping for camp, staff, and student items. The latter was such an onerous, all-day chore that students were later pressed into accompanying staff members to do the student shopping.

When the Show Low run returned to camp, usually after the field day was over, the bell called everyone to help unload the truck and transfer food to the pantry and root cellar. Pharmaceuticals, cosmetics, and beverages of choice were piled for pickup on the wide porch of the cook's cabin. Often, it was an impressive, even monumental, sight.

Medical needs were met in camp. After a frightening experience in 1948 with a steer-riding incident in which a student was injured, Haury (1989:22) had vowed to have a resident doctor at Point of Pines. Doctors from Tucson and elsewhere were invited to camp with their families for a "vacation." Grasshopper never enjoyed this luxury because of changes in economic conditions. Instead, the ill and injured were ministered to in camp or driven into Show Low to the clinic when necessary. Haury (1989:122–24) was pleased to report that there were no outbreaks of epidemic proportions, births, or deaths during his tenure at Point of Pines, and happily, Grasshopper can boast the same record.

The most onerous tasks for the Grasshopper staff involved setting up the camp at the beginning of the season and disabling it for the winter when fieldwork was over. This meant arriving in camp at least a week before students arrived and remaining for a similar time after they left. Although it was hard work, in later years, we cherished this time to re-acquaint ourselves with Grasshopper before the student horde arrived and decompress when the summer was over. It was necessary to put all of the systems—electricity, water, plumbing, gas, and so on—into operating order and make the cabins habitable. The reverse was done to winterize the camp. Artifacts, samples, and field notes were brought to Tucson at the end of each season, and students and their belongings were dispersed to various airports and bus stations. In the beginning, closing the camp for the winter was simple. We sprayed the wooden buildings liberally with shingle oil, locked the doors, and boarded up the windows. In subsequent years, vandalism put an end to this practice, and we began boarding up and nailing down the doors and barricading them with milk lugs full of ground stone artifacts. If the summer had been a good one, the last glimpse of camp as we left on an August morning was as poignant as when we arrived in early June.

With the camp in place, the organization and schedule in operation, and the first season's students selected, fieldwork at Grasshopper began. We turn to cataloguing these culture-history years. Because the record of the early work is sparse, and we were not personally involved, we present the work of each field season, following the general outline provided by Thompson and Longacre (1966), and augmenting it as additional information permits.

The 1963 Season

The Field School was in session for eight weeks, from June 21 to August 16, with an enrollment of eighteen students—ten men and eight women, who represented five graduate and thirteen undergraduate students.

Fieldwork was concentrated in Room Block 1 of the main ruin (East Village). Rooms 1, 2, 3, 4, 5, 6, and 7 were excavated, and the trash deposits on the east side were tested extensively, exposing a number of burials and a row of thirteen masonry-lined ovens. Years later, similar sets of ovens were uncovered beneath the floor of one of the rooms in Room Block 3 and at the southern end of Room Block 2.

Twenty-eight test trenches and one large broadside exposure along the west bank of Salt River Draw were excavated to investigate the geological and cultural deposits. This work quickly established the presence of widespread secondary refuse in the form of sheet trash, trash mounds,

The 1963 Season

Research and Teaching Staff	Support Staff	Students	Family
Raymond Thompson, Director	James Williams, Cook	David Acton	Margaret Thompson
Marion Parker, Dig Foreman	Geoffrey Cross, Kitchen Assistant	William Barrera	Mary Thompson
Ernestene Green, Laboratory Assistant	Barrett Hamlink, Kitchen Assistant	Lilita Bergs	
	Molly Thompson, Camp Hostess (volunteer)	Michael Clark	
		William Dean	
		Gail Gibbons	
		Kathleen Godel	
		Sandra Hansen	
		Margaret Hardin	
		Clifford Hickey	
		Clyde Homen	
		Ellin Richardson	
		Robert Schuyler	
		Richard Warren	
		Joann Weber	
		Cheryl White	
		John Wilson	
		Jon Young	

and postoccupational alluvial deposits. In addition, the trenches revealed a realignment of Salt River Draw from its prehistoric channel between Room Block 1 and Room Block 2 to its current channel on the east side of Room Block 1. With no screening of fill dirt, students classified and recorded more than 75,000 potsherds, 393 permanently catalogued specimens, and 232 stone artifacts.

The 1964 Season

The Field School was in session for eight weeks, from June 12 to August 7, with an enrollment of twenty—ten men and ten women, divided among twelve undergraduate and eight graduate students. The Advanced Science Seminar Program, National Science Foundation (GE-4601), provided support for the teaching program. Students received full support, including tuition and fees, board, housing, and local travel.

Two events of 1964 would have a major impact on the future of the Field School. The first event was the beginning of NSF support from the Advanced Science Seminar Program, Division of Graduate Education, which would continue through 1971. This period coincided with the expansion of processual archaeology throughout North America and more specifically in the American Southwest and at Grasshopper.

Field School staff and students in 1964. Seated, left to right, are Richard Davis, Frank Santen, Marion Parker, Michael Bell, Anna Bennett, Margaret Thompson, Tao (cat), Mary Thompson, Tzotzim Pek (dog), Molly Thompson, Raymond Thompson, James Ayres; middle row, standing, Jim Williams, Mark Leone, Robert Fry, Carol Hoffman, Dudley Varner, Geoffrey Clark, Janet Fairbanks, Stella Grobel, Susan Adams, Robert Hommon; back row, standing, Fletcher Cosby, Valda Farris, Charles Hoffman, Barbara Stark, Edwin Slatter, David Ohmart, Carole Oshry, Elaine Griff, Patricia Lynn, Valdmyra Micpovil.   ·

The 1964 Season

Research and Teaching Staff	Support Staff	Students	Family
Raymond Thompson, Director	James Williams, Cook	James Ayres	Margaret Thompson
Marion Parker, Assistant Director	David Ohmart, Kitchen Assistant	Michael Bell	Mary Thompson
Robert Hommon, Dig Foreman	Frank Santen, Kitchen Assistant	Anna Bennett	
Susan Adams, Laboratory Assistant	Molly Thompson, Camp Hostess (volunteer)	Geoffrey Clark	
		Fletcher Cosby	
		Richard Davis	
		Janet Fairbanks	
		Valda Farris	
		Robert Fry	
		Elaine Griff	
		Stella Grobel	
		Carol Hoffman	
		Charles Hoffman	
		Mark Leone	
		Patricia Lynn	
		Valdmyra Micpovil	
		Carole Oshry	
		Edwin Slatter	
		Barbara Stark	
		Dudley Varner	

NSF support would play a prominent role in establishing a Grasshopper image and persona. It juxtaposed Grasshopper as the graduate training camp with the Chicago Field Museum's undergraduate training camp at Vernon, also supported by the NSF.

Grasshopper's NSF funding made it possible to attract excellent students from throughout the United States and many foreign countries. The downside was that this brief period of support for instruction fostered the illusion of Grasshopper research being heavily subsidized by the NSF. It also had the negative result of weaning the Field School from well-established sources of local funding. Although these factors worried Haury and Thompson, they opted for NSF support. The difference between funding for instruction and funding of research would bedevil Grasshopper when the Advanced Science Seminar Program of the NSF came to an end in 1971.

The second major event of this year was Thompson's appointment to succeed Haury as head of the UA Department of Anthropology and director of the ASM. His days as field-school director were numbered, for academic administration had become too complicated in the 1960s for one person to do both well. No longer was it feasible, as in Haury's day, to close the museum for the summer, reduce the department's functions, and move to the mountains of east-central Arizona to run a field school.

In December 1963, at Thompson's urging, Haury hired William Longacre to join the faculty in the fall of 1964 and the field-school staff in the summer of 1965. In only the second year of culture history at Grasshopper, the transition to a new director and a new archaeology was initiated.

The 1964 excavations were carried out in Room Blocks 1 and 2. Rooms 8, 9, 10, 11, 12, 13, 14, 15, and 16 were excavated, and Room 17 was trenched. Additional testing was done in the trash deposits east of the ruin. The Great Kiva–Plaza 3 complex in Room Block 2 was excavated with the help of Alan Olson, who operated the Museum of Northern Arizona's backhoe and dump truck. To enable removing the Great Kiva fill without damaging the walls or floor, students first excavated trenches, defined walls, and exposed the depth of the fill. After the backhoe removed the fill, students cleaned the floor by hand and excavated the features they uncovered.

Excavation revealed the Great Kiva to be a large (12 by 15 m), rectangular structure. Two rows of postholes for roof supports were exposed, remains of the juniper posts were removed, and the postholes were excavated. Also uncovered was a masonry-lined vault that was probably a foot drum—a log-covered trench that produced a hollow, booming sound when tramped upon. Four bird burials, at least one of which was a macaw, were found just beneath the floor. Room 16, which was a small, featureless room adjacent to the southeastern corner, may have served as the entrance to the Great Kiva. Below the kiva floor was an occupation surface that had been used before the Great Kiva was constructed over Plaza 3. A large, slab-lined hearth, a number of smaller hearths, several stone-lined boxes, a metate set into the floor, and a large central fire area may have been associated with Plaza 3.

William Robinson and Jeffrey Dean of the Laboratory of Tree-Ring Research at the UA collected tree-ring samples from Red Rock House, a cliff dwelling just off the western edge of the Grasshopper Plateau. The objective was to obtain dates to strengthen the regional chronology. Research at Red Rock House would continue in the 1980s.

The 1965 Season

The Field School was in session for eight weeks, from June 11 to August 6, with an enrollment of twenty students—fifteen men and five women, who represented fourteen graduate and six undergraduate students. NSF's Advanced Science Seminar Program (GE-7781) supported

The 1965 Season

Research and Teaching Staff	Support Staff	Students	Family
Raymond Thompson, Director	Mabel Rucker, Cook	Kenneth Adkisson	Margaret Thompson
William Longacre, Field Director	Marshall Grayson, Kitchen Assistant	James Bellis	Mary Thompson
James Ayres, Assistant Director	Edward Kauffman, Kitchen Assistant	Joanne Dombrowski	
Larry Agenbroad, Dig Foreman	Molly Thompson, Camp Hostess (volunteer)	Mary Dowden	
Lilita Bergs, Laboratory Assistant		Gerald Eck	
		Ernest Hemmings	
		John Henderson	
		Charles Hertz	
		Lynda Bird Johnson	
		Gerald Kelso	
		Lucille Lewis	
		David Libbey	
		Thomas Quick	
		Charles Rippey	
		Michael Simmons	
		Beve Lea Teasley	
		David Tuggle	
		William Waltman	
		Robert Welke	
		Lorraine Williams	
		Morton Womack	

the teaching program for the second year. Students received full support for tuition and fees, board, housing, and local travel.

The 1965 season was one of quick transition. It was Thompson's last summer at Grasshopper and Longacre's first. Longacre had an immediate impact on data collection and recording. Students were required to take daily notes on their excavation activities and observations as a basis for writing a report on their room or Great Kiva–Plaza 3 test unit at the end of the season. Expanding the documentation of field and laboratory observations would become one of the hallmarks of processual archaeology at Grasshopper. And, as if to highlight important personnel changes, Lynda Bird Johnson, the U.S. President's eldest daughter, attended the first ten days of the season as a special student, which she clearly was, with Secret Service guards, mobile field camp, and sophisticated communications apparatus.

The most prominent piece of research to emerge from this season's work was the Apache wickiup study by Longacre and Ayres (1968). At Martinez Ranch, an abandoned homestead about two miles east of Grasshopper, that summer's kitchen aides discovered a wickiup that had been occupied until recently. It would become a much-cited study in the resurgence of ethnoarchaeology during the processual revolution.

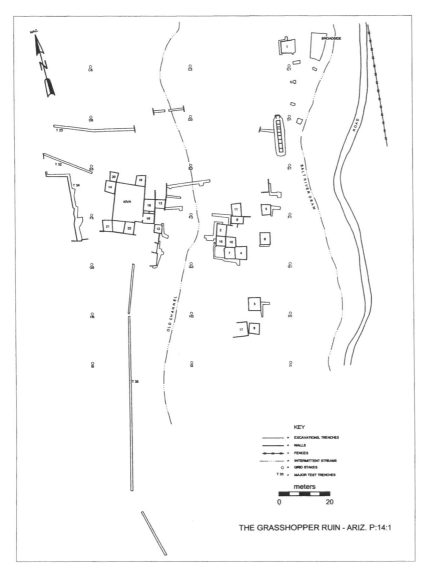

THE GRASSHOPPER RUIN - ARIZ. P:14:1

Excavations in 1965 again concentrated in the Great Kiva–Plaza 3 complex and consisted mainly of subflooring, or digging below the floor level to culturally sterile layers. These investigations confirmed use of the area as an unroofed plaza (Plaza 3) prior to the construction of the ceremonial structure. Hearths and other plaza features were uncovered underneath the floor and walls of the Great Kiva. A number of burial pits intruded into the layers underlying the plaza surface.

Four rooms adjacent to the Great Kiva were excavated, at least two of which had evidence of a second story. Excavators found additional evidence of the Plaza 3 surface underlying these rooms. The surface contained hearths and other cultural features, including a row of ovens similar to those discovered on the eastern flank of the ruin during the 1963 season. Clearly, Plaza 3 had grown smaller over time as rooms were constructed within its space.

Room 18, which was located adjacent to the east wall of the Great Kiva, was a rectangular, small kiva with a bench at the southern end and a number of kiva architectural features. These included a ventilator; a large, rectangular, slab-lined hearth; and a large floor pit. After this ceremonial structure was abandoned, the room was used for trash disposal. The resulting layer of trash, rich in cultural items as well as floral and faunal remains, was screened carefully using a mechanical shaker with a quarter-inch mesh. In addition, the entire layer was hand-screened employing eighth-inch mesh screen, and portions of the layer were additionally processed through window screen. These recovery techniques instituted by Longacre produced quantities of materials. Seeds, as well as bones from small fauna such as fish, reptiles, and amphibians, were recovered for use in reconstructing the local paleoenvironment and the resources that were exploited.

The large, enclosed Plaza 1 adjacent to the Great Kiva was trenched. The plaza floor, which contained a number of hearths and other features, was identified. We would determine later that the plaza had been covered through natural processes of water and wind deposition (see Whittlesey, Arnould, and Reynolds 1982).

A roofed corridor between Room Blocks 2 and 3 that connected Plaza 1 to the southern exterior of the pueblo was discovered. The charred remains of the roof produced a number of tree-ring specimens that would date the construction of the corridor, and thus also the joining of Room Blocks 2 and 3, as having occurred in the early- to mid-1320s (Dean and Robinson 1982; Graves 1991; Riggs 1999a, 2001).

The large, flat areas south and north of the pueblo were excavated mechanically to expose more than 250 linear meters of trenches that were two meters deep and slightly more that one-half meter wide. The trenches revealed the natural and cultural strata underlying the site and found no evidence of architecture or other indications of permanent habitation. Thin trash deposits were delimited, and a number of burials were uncovered.

By that time, 120 human burials had been recovered, and they appeared to be located in cemetery areas. One possible cemetery was found underneath the Great Kiva–Plaza 3 in Room Block 2. Other possible cemeteries were located on the eastern side of the ruin and in the north and south flats. The burials excavated in the Great Kiva–Plaza 3 were accompanied by generally greater quantities and varieties of goods than those located elsewhere. Not until the following year would the discovery of Burial 140 in this area provide the key to understanding Grasshopper social organization. A number of burials also were found beneath the floors of habitation rooms, and these tended to be of infants and young children and often were not accompanied by grave offerings. Most burials were fully extended or semiflexed.

This season would be the last under Thompson's direction and under the culture-history research program. Haury had established the field-school tradition and put it into practice at Forestdale and Point of Pines. Thompson had experimented with the model at a dude ranch in southeastern Arizona to find the pedagogical quality of that area sorely wanting. At Grasshopper, Thompson had discovered an archaeological context fully within the expedition tradition of exploration, adventure, and self-sufficiency in the backwoods of the American Southwest. After only three years of fieldwork under Thompson, archaeology at Grasshopper would undergo a dramatic change in language and practice as Longacre took over the Field School.

5

Processual Archaeology, 1966–1973

We view archaeology as an integral part of the larger discipline of anthropology (Long-acre 1964). It shares with the other fields of anthropology the aim of understanding culture and cultural process. Culture can be viewed as the systemic mechanism by which human populations adapt to their total environment. Changes in cultural systems can be viewed as adaptive changes and, as such, basic clues to an understanding of cultural evolution. —**Raymond Thompson and William Longacre** (1966:272)

William Longacre assumed the directorship and full control of Grasshopper research in 1966 and immediately infused the program with the direction and energy of the "new" or processual archaeology. The conceptual shift from culture history to processual archaeology is chronicled best in the review article by Thompson and Longacre (1966:270), in which they enumerate their research questions, goals, and philosophy:

> Our primary research goal is to describe and analyze the extinct cultural system reflected in the material remains of the site. Implicit in that statement are two important assumptions that must be made clear at this point. First, we view culture as systematic and thus composed of various highly interrelated subsystems such as the social system, the technological system, and the religious system. This approach to culture by the archaeologist has recently been discussed and described by Lewis Binford (1962, 1965). It is our job to infer the nature and interrelations of the sub-systems of prehistoric cultural systems within an ecological frame of reference. Our aim is to isolate and understand the workings of cultural processes, the means by which cultures change or remain stable.

To attain our research goals it is necessary to make another primary assumption. This is that all of the material remains in an archaeological site are highly patterned or structured directly as a result of the ways in which the extinct society was organized and the patterned ways in which the people behaved. Thus, our first task is to define the archaeological structure at the site and then from that infer the organization of the society and aspects of behavior.

Thompson and Longacre (1966) also listed a number of specific research questions. Although the first three questions represent the culture-history objectives discussed in chapter 3—investigating an unknown region, a poorly known time, and an area of sufficient ceramic variability to make sense of both—the last five questions are quintessential processual archaeology as it was then expressed in the American Southwest. These research questions were so basic, so necessary to write the ethnography of ancient Grasshopper that they continued to guide research throughout the history of the program. This is indicated by the temporal breadth of the published research tackling these questions. After each of Thompson and Longacre's (1966:257) major research questions, we list the papers and publications that addressed the question.

1. To "test the hypothesis of a slight climatic shift at about A.D. 1300" (Dean and Robinson 1982; Holbrook 1982a, 1982b, 1983).
2. To "understand better the processes of population aggregation that culminate during the 14th century in [the Grasshopper region] and many [other] areas of the Southwest" (Ezzo and Price 2002; Graves, Holbrook, and Longacre 1982; Graves, Longacre, and Holbrook 1982; Griffin 1969; Longacre 1975, 1976; Reid 1973, 1978, 1989; Reid and Shimada 1982; Riggs 1994, 1999a, 1999b, 2001; Tuggle 1970).
3. To attempt to define and analyze "the nature of social groups, residence and inheritance patterns, and means of achieving social integration at [Grasshopper] in an effort to understand the processes responsible for the cultural system of the modern western Pueblo peoples" (Ciolek-Torrello 1978, 1984, 1985, 1986, 1989; Ciolek-Torrello and Reid 1974; Clark 1967, 1969; Griffin 1967, 1969; Reid and Whittlesey 1982, 1990; Whittlesey 1978, 1984, 1989; Wilcox 1982).
4. To "delimit the economic basis of this extinct society" (Ezzo 1991, 1992a, 1993, 1994; J. Olsen 1980, 1990; Sullivan 1982; Triadan 1989, 1997; Tuggle, Reid, and Cole 1984; Welch 1991, 1996; Welch and Triadan 1991; Whittaker 1984, 1986, 1987a).

5. To investigate "the implications of the stylistic blending evidenced in the ceramics in an attempt to understand the nature of the interaction with adjacent regions" (Crown 1981; Graves 1982b, 1984; Mauer 1970; Montgomery 1992b; Sullivan 1984; Triadan 1989, 1994, 1997; Tuggle 1970; Van Keuren 1994, 1999, 2001; Whittlesey 1974; Zedeño 1991, 1992, 1994, 1995).

On a more abstract level, we note that the concise expression of the core principles and philosophy of processual archaeology seen in the Thompson and Longacre coauthored article suggests that, at this early moment in the development of processual archaeology, culture history and processual archaeology were not perceived as incompatible, at least in the Pueblo Southwest. At other times and in other places, the two paradigms would be seen as uncongenial, even conflicting. We discuss the broader implications of this conceptual change and the relation between these two archaeological programs in chapter 8. In summarizing the yearly research activities from 1966 to 1973, we draw again upon the published record (Longacre and Reid 1974) and amend it as appropriate.

The 1966 Season

The Field School ran for eight weeks, from June 10 to August 5, with twenty enrolled students—ten women and ten men, who represented eleven graduate and nine undergraduate students. The teaching program received support from the Advanced Science Seminar Program of the National Science Foundation (GZ-22).

The 1966 season was essentially a continuation of excavations begun the previous year, accompanied by a revolution in data-recording procedures. Recording forms were used more frequently, more forms were employed, and new attributes were recorded, as research objectives began to be built into the recording format. Although pottery was sorted according to the standard southwestern type-variety system developed at Point of Pines, it also was classified in terms of a typology of containers to record quantitative data on vessel function. This typological experiment stressed variation in shape and size of ceramic containers to augment recording of traditional data. In addition, all students were required to take notes and to write a descriptive and interpretive account of their excavation unit. The room report, which had been born the previous year while most students were excavating relatively small

The 1966 Season

Research and Teaching Staff	Support Staff	Students
William Longacre, Director	James Judd, Cook	Regina Alvino
James Ayres, Assistant Director	Henry Gulick, Kitchen Aide	Donald Dickson
Stephen Hayden, Dig Foreman	Jonathan Ingersoll, Kitchen Aide	Nancy Foster
Lilita Bergs, Laboratory Supervisor	Joyce Ayres, Hostess (volunteer)	Ingrid Gram
Geoffrey Clark, Archaeological Assistant		Paul Grebinger
		Vera Green
		Bion Griffin
		Pamela Horner
		Janet Karon
		Lawrence Manire
		Stephen Mann
		Frank Mikeleit
		Helen Phillips
		William Rathje
		Susanne Rothstein
		Charles Seastone
		Jonathan Taylor
		John Thatcher
		Penelope Whitten
		Sabra Woolley

and shallow Great Kiva–Plaza 3 units, would become pervasive and all consuming, as the size of excavation units and amount of data grew exponentially.

We can glimpse the magnitude of this revolution in the volume of the records. Whereas the notes and forms for *all sixteen rooms* excavated in 1963 and 1964 fill one three-ring binder, at least one separate binder was required for *each* room excavated in 1966 and thereafter. The immediate effect was to have students go sleepless much of the last week as they rushed to finish excavating their room—usually only to the last-occupied floor—complete the processing of the recovered material, and write the room report. The longer-term effect was to increase the corpus of observations and information on Grasshopper by several orders of magnitude. Not only was it most difficult for new staff, much less students, to get up to speed quickly, the corpus of data that could be used to prepare a site report in the traditional manner was growing by leaps and bounds. Each room typically produced an enormous quantity of material culture. The rapidly increasing data would soon strain available means of storage and retrieval and further separate Grasshopper from the simpler archaeological contexts of the Hay Hollow Valley, where processual archaeology had proved so encouraging.

Excavations were completed in the Great Kiva and in four adjacent rooms (16, 19, 21, 22) begun the previous year. Two new rooms (23, 24) were begun. The Great Kiva subfloor investigations, which probed down into Plaza 3 surfaces, produced additional information on plaza activities and the remarkable Burial 140 (J. Brown 1969; Griffin 1967), a Mogollon male between forty to forty-five years old at death who would later provide the key to Grasshopper leadership.

It was serendipitous that during this season the students participated in a dramatic event of experimental archaeology. Don Crabtree had been in camp demonstrating flintknapping techniques and the use of stone tools, when one evening after dinner, according to Stephen Hayden's journal, a black bear pursued the aroma of freshly baked banana bread into camp. Initially a nuisance, the lonely bear persisted and soon became a threat to a camp dependent on free access to outdoor facilities. Gene Seeley, the local stockman and an experienced hunter, dispatched the animal. Next morning, as Seeley was preparing to skin the bear, someone suggested that he try to use stone tools. With obsidian blades and other tools made by Crabtree, Seeley skinned the bear in half the time it normally took him with a steel knife. He was so impressed by the sharpness and efficiency of the stone tools that he persuaded Crabtree to make him a tool kit for future use. This incident has been retold in several popular books (Claiborne et al. 1973; Pfeiffer 1972).

The 1967 Season

The Field School ran for eight weeks, from June 9 to August 4. Twenty students were in residence — ten women and ten men, divided among fifteen graduate and five undergraduate students. The teaching program again received support from the Advanced Science Seminar Program of the NSF (GZ-397).

The season saw the beginning of the cornering project, which was envisioned as a long-range project to map and measure rooms for constructing what was called a "scientifically valid sampling design" (Thompson and Longacre 1966:270):

> At the Grasshopper Ruin then, our first task is to define the archaeological structure of the site. Since, by definition, the structure cannot be homogeneous and because the site is too immense to be completely excavated, we are immediately faced with a problem of sampling. Because we want to control the mutual variation of all the data in the site, we must have a sample that accurately reflects the nature of the total site. To draw that

The 1967 Season

Research and Teaching Staff	Support Staff	Students
William Longacre, Director	Mary Brooks, Cook	Steven Amesbury
James Ayres, Assistant Director	John Cundiff, Kitchen Aide	Adrienne Anderson
Bion Griffin, Dig Foreman	Gerald Porter, Kitchen Aide	Judith Connor
Lilita Bergs, Laboratory Supervisor	Joyce Ayres, Hostess (volunteer)	Robert Conrad
Sharon Urban, Archaeological Assistant		Peggy Davis
		Paul Donahue
		Robert Edwards
		Janet Ford
		Rand Foster
		Birute Galdikas
		Gayle Harrison
		Meade Kemrer
		Francis Lees
		Leslie Lischka
		Shela McFarlin
		James Mueller
		Joyce Rehm
		Judith Riley
		Jerry Williams
		Robert Wulff

sample from the site requires a delicate balance between statistically valid sampling procedures and the knowledge and experience of the archaeologist.

Initial work was in Room Block 1. After clearing away the surface brush and trees, the objective was to excavate a minimum of two diagonally opposite corners in each room and record wall bonding and abutting relationships. A map of the entire room block showing the sequence of room construction, as well as variations in room size and shape, could then be drawn. These data were intended to be used in constructing a typology of rooms and to define major architectural divisions of the room block, which in turn would permit selecting a stratified random sample of rooms for excavation. A similar procedure had been employed at Broken K Pueblo (Hill 1970; see Wilcox 1982 for a history and critique).

Seven rooms (28, 31, 37, 42, 40, 108, 121) of various types were excavated to floor. Two rooms (26, 27) adjacent to the Great Kiva that were not selected by sampling procedures were begun and excavated completely. In addition, two rooms (23 and 24) cleared to floor in 1966 were subfloored.

The thesis research of Geoffrey Clark (1967, 1969) completed in 1967 focused on testing the possibility of status differentiation at Grasshopper as represented by differential treatment of burials. In his analysis of 197 burials and associated grave goods, Clark defined two different kinds of cemeteries. One was composed of "low-status" individuals located in trash mounds peripheral to the pueblo, and the other was an area of "high-status" individuals associated with Plaza 3 and the Great Kiva. The most impressive of these was Burial 140, the individual with the greatest quantity and quality of grave goods at Grasshopper (J. Brown 1969; Griffin 1967). Clark concluded that social stratification was the operating principle at Grasshopper Pueblo and suggested that status was associated with membership in kin groups and ascribed at birth.

The 1968 Season

The Field School was in session for eight weeks, from June 7 to August 2, with twenty-one students. Eleven women and ten men, all graduate students, participated. The teaching program continued to receive support from the Advanced Science Seminar Program of the NSF (GZ-745).

The 1968 season was a benchmark year for processual archaeology at Grasshopper. A shift in the sampling unit from individual rooms to sets of rooms would reorient work on the architectural signature of social groups for years to come (Wilcox 1982). It also became clear that, if the sampling design was to be completed, it would be necessary to augment the cornering project with additional personnel. To do so, in the fall, Longacre would submit the first research grant to the NSF that essentially proposed to complete the cornering project and to reconstruct the paleoenvironment. In addition, interaction with Paul Martin's field school at Vernon, Arizona, reached a new level of intensity, student research projects were required for the first time, and Bion Griffin completed the fieldwork for the first Grasshopper dissertation in processual archaeology.

The cornering project begun during the 1967 season was extended to Room Block 2, where seventy rooms were added to the growing site map. Staff members Griffin and David Tuggle were instrumental in shifting the sampling emphasis from single rooms and size categories, as at Broken K Pueblo, to sets of rooms probably used by socially significant groups. This critical conceptual change formed the foundation of subsequent work by David Wilcox (1975, 1982) in refining architectural criteria for identifying social groups, and it would contribute to a recon-

The 1968 Season

Research and Teaching Staff	Support Staff	Students
William Longacre, Director	Illa Mai McFarlin, Cook	Wendy Arundale
Bion Griffin, Assistant Director	Chuck Brice, Kitchen Aide	Sharon Burnston
David Tuggle, Dig Foreman	John Phillips, Kitchen Aide	Janet Chernela
Sharon Urban, Laboratory Supervisor	Mary Ellen Griffin, Hostess (volunteer)	Ingrid Christensen
John Cundiff, Archaeological Assistant	Vivian Tuggle, Hostess (volunteer)	Sandra Crafton
		Virginia Donlon
		Susan Furer
		John Hanson
		Peter Hemingway
		Michael Jacobs
		Janet Johnson
		Alexandra Klymyshyn
		Raymond Leicht
		Patricia Linskey
		Bruce Moore
		Mario Navarrete
		Susan Newgreen
		William Potts
		George Thomas
		Gerald Tuggle
		Richard Von Schmertzing

struction of pueblo growth based on architecture (Reid 1973; Reid and Shimada 1982; Riggs 1994, 1999a, 2001).

Excavations took place in Room Blocks 1 and 2 of the main ruin and in two of the outlying room blocks. Exploratory backhoe trenches were excavated in the north and south flats, and at intervals perpendicular to the exterior walls of the main ruin, permitting an outline map of the entire West Village to be drawn. Seventy-two human burials were uncovered, bringing the total population to 327 individuals.

The roofed corridor leading from Plaza 1 to the pueblo exterior was excavated, and Room 153, adjacent to the Great Kiva, was excavated to floor. Another room in this area was subfloored to sterile soil.

An important event of the season was an expansion of the competition between the graduate field school at Grasshopper and Martin's undergraduate field school at Vernon, both supported by NSF education programs. In previous years, the schools had exchanged site visits and held a generally friendly, but highly competitive, volleyball game known as the Mogollon Bowl. In 1968, an informal gathering to exchange research papers was added. Anticipation of this intellectual exchange was a factor in Grasshopper students being required for the first time to design and complete a research paper in addition to the room report. (Read Wood-

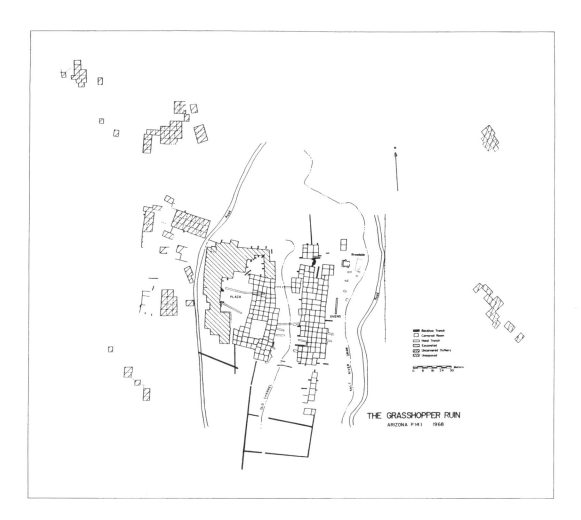

THE GRASSHOPPER RUIN
ARIZONA P:14:1 1968

Grasshopper Pueblo
as of 1968.

bury's [1993] account of the 1968, 1969, and 1970 Pecos Conferences to appreciate the furor created by Vernon student papers.)

In the fall, Longacre, who perhaps was weary of the slow pace of students mapping a five-hundred-room pueblo ruin and surely anxious to bring in specialists to reconstruct the past environment, prepared a research proposal to the NSF simply entitled "Archaeological Research at the Grasshopper Ruin, Arizona" (Longacre 1969). The following abstract summarizes the proposed research:

> The research is designed to investigate the nature of the environment and the nature of the extinct cultural system reflected in the archaeological remains. Man's use of the environment and a major cultural readaptation as the environment changed slightly are the major problems areas of our research. We hope to shed some understanding on the prehistoric background of the modern western Pueblo societies through an analysis of this

late prehistoric puebloan cultural system. More generally, we are interested in the nature of cultural processes in systems undergoing major cultural readaptation.

Funds are requested to support environmental research such as the identification of floral and faunal remains found in the archaeological excavations and interpretation of them from an ecological point of view. Funds are also requested for laborers and some supervisory staff to help implement the sampling design. The proposed project is designed to last two years, June 1, 1969–June 1,1971.

A more detailed view of the type of research questions being asked at the time also can be gleaned from the proposal (Longacre 1969), as follows:

> Our research at this site is designed to investigate the nature of cultural evolution in the Mogollon area after A.D. 1250. Of special concern is the late Mogollon readaptation involving the aggregation of populations into increasingly larger units and the identification of the selective pressures leading to this readaptation.
>
> We are attempting to identify changes through time in such systemic variables as residence unit size, nature of the task performing groups, mechanisms of social integration, and the nature of status differentiation.
>
> More specific goals of our research are: to delimit the economic basis of this extinct society; to test the hypothesis of a slight climatic shift at about A.D. 1300 (Schoenwetter and Dittert 1968); to determine the causes for the failure of this cultural system at about A.D. 1400; and where the people went after the abandonment of Grasshopper; to define and investigate the nature of interaction among the extinct societies in the Grasshopper area and between that region and those further to the north and south.

The questions in these excerpts are less interesting than the jargon, which clearly reflects the tenets and language of processualism. Culture is viewed as a system, one particularly designed to adapt humans to the environment. People are curiously scarce in these statements; instead, there are residence units, task-performing groups, and extinct societies. The perspective is heavily ecological, emphasizing adaptation to the environment, cultural ecology, and the human response to environmental change. The quaint use of the politically incorrect "man" and the puzzling and vague term "readaptation" ("reorganization" in contemporary usage) further mark the chronological age of these statements as clearly as bell-bottom pants, gold chains, and big hair.

The research proposal sought a larger staff, an Apache crew to expand the cornering project, and a team of environmental specialists. Longacre may have realized at this early date a fact of Grasshopper research that would play a critical role in later years—the information requirements of the teaching and research programs were too big for the traditionally small staff and large number of students. If a Vernon-type teaching-and-research program was to be maintained, along with the overwhelming demands of Grasshopper fieldwork, then the number of staff would have to increase dramatically. An additional requirement that would emerge later was that of staff continuity from season to season.

It was also the first year that alcoholic beverages—beer, wine, and distilled spirits—officially were sanctioned in camp for those of legal drinking age. According to informants, however, Grasshopper never was a truly dry camp.

The 1969 Season

The Field School was in session for eight weeks, from June 13 to August 8, with an enrollment of twenty students. Eight men and twelve women, who represented one undergraduate and nineteen graduate students, were in residence. The teaching program continued to be supported by the NSF Advanced Science Seminar Program (GZ-1113), and the research was enhanced by the first research grant from the NSF (GS-2566).

The 1969 season celebrated the fiftieth year since the beginning of formal student field training in archaeology by the University of Arizona (Brace 1986; Gifford and Morris 1985). The event was marked by a brief ceremony at Grasshopper on July 24 attended by the UA president, Richard Harvill, and Mrs. Harvill; H. D. Rhodes, dean of the Graduate College; Emil Haury; and Raymond Thompson, head of the Department of Anthropology and director of the Arizona State Museum (ASM).

Excavations concentrated on a cluster of eight rooms (33, 35, 39, 40, 41, 43, 44, 45) in the north end of Room Block 1 that were selected on the basis of size, shape, and room-set criteria. Two additional rooms (116 and 195) were excavated in the small, detached Room Block 5 immediately north of Room Block 1. Rooms 143 and 197, adjacent to the Great Kiva, also were excavated to floor by Wilcox and the Apache crew.

A backhoe and dump truck were used to expose exterior portions of the ruin as well as to define Plaza 1, located in the West Village. In the course of these excavations, the small Plaza 2 was discovered, along with a short passageway connecting it with Plaza 1 and a corridor leading from Plaza 2 to the outside.

The 1969 Season

Research and Teaching Staff	Support Staff	Apache Crew	Students
William Longacre, Director	Illa Mai McFarlin, Cook	Dewey Case	Janet Brashler
Bion Griffin, Co-assistant Director	Chuck Brice, Kitchen Aide	Andy Enfield	Robert Buettner
Gwinn Vivian, Co-assistant Director	John Phillips, Kitchen Aide	Dallas Gregg	Richard Effland
David Wilcox, Dig Foreman	Mary Ellen Griffin, Hostess	Norbert Josay	Shirley Greiff
Meade Kemrer,	(volunteer)	Elliot Mason	Allison Helfgott
Archaeological Assistant	Patricia Vivian, Hostess	Alvin Murphey	Margaret Houston
Ingrid Christensen,	(volunteer)	Dudley Patterson	Candace Johnston
Laboratory Supervisor		Wilford Peaches	Lydia Kelley
Susan Furer,		Hickson Pina	Cheryl
Laboratory Assistant		Lansford Quay	Kronenwetter
		Glendale Tessay	Michael Mauer
		Leo Tessay	David Potter
			James Rock
			Daniel Seligsohn
			Susan Speier
			Linda Stacy
			Marilyn Steely
			Jennifer Taschek
			Barry Thompson
			Robert Vierra
			Polly Wiessner

The cornering project initiated in 1967 was expanded with NSF support for a large Apache crew, with Wilcox as the full-time staff supervisor. Room Block 3 was brushed, and corners were excavated to permit interpretation of bonding and abutting patterns as well as to add to the map of the main ruin. These investigations led to more rigorous cornering methods and the initial formulation of "construction unit" as a meaningful architectural category and sampling unit (see Wilcox 1975, 1982).

A significant achievement was Griffin's completion of the first Grasshopper dissertation, titled "Late Mogollon Readaptation in East-Central Arizona" (Griffin 1969). He expressed the prevailing research emphasis of processual archaeology in investigating the responses of social organization to environmental factors by attempting to test two mutually exclusive hypotheses: (1) as the need for efficient utilization of energy increased, redistribution and ranking systems developed; and (2) as a horticultural adaptation was emphasized, egalitarian social units controlled energy resources. Griffin rejected the first and tentatively retained the second, which was a blatant contradiction of Clark's (1967) inference of social stratification. Although recognized as "an alternative interpretation of some social organizational principles at Grasshopper" (Longacre and Reid 1974:19), these countervailing interpretations of the same phenomena coexisted until almost a decade later, when Whittlesey (1978) exposed a fatal flaw in processual archaeology.

The most important piece of new research in 1969 was an add-on to the Field School. Tuggle initiated a systematic site survey of the Grasshopper region, which would form the basis for his doctoral dissertation, "Prehistoric Community Relationships in East-Central Arizona" (Tuggle 1970). A grant from the Wenner-Gren Foundation for Anthropological Research and an NSF Dissertation Improvement Grant supported the fieldwork. The latter was the only grant of its kind to be awarded to the UA during the thirty years of Grasshopper fieldwork. Tuggle examined the hypothesis of increased interaction among settlements between A.D. 1000 and 1400 in terms of two processes—the circulation of pottery-producing women and the distribution of pottery by economic mechanisms, such as trade. His analysis supported the hypothesis of increased interaction during the period and suggested that it was probably economic in nature. Tuggle's project began the systematic survey of the Grasshopper region and established many of the techniques that would be employed in later years as survey intensified.

A student project begun this season would be the second and, for the next twenty-three years, the only one to fulfill the plan of developing student summer projects into a master's thesis, because the Department of Anthropology at the UA would soon drop the thesis requirement for the master's degree. Michael Mauer's thesis, "Cibecue [sic] Polychrome: A Fourteenth Century Ceramic Type from East-Central Arizona" (Mauer 1970) analyzed the function and distribution of Cibicue Polychrome ceramics at Grasshopper. (Note: The pottery is Cibicue, the town is Cibecue. The pottery type examined by Mauer was actually what we now label Cibicue Painted Corrugated [see Hagenbuckle 2000; Zedeño 1994] and not the type Haury [1934] originally defined as Cibicue Polychrome and which he spelled that way.)

The 1970 Season

The Field School ran from June 12 to August 7, with an enrollment of twenty students—ten men and ten women, who were divided among nineteen graduates and a single undergraduate student, Izumi Shimada. The teaching program continued to be supported by the NSF through the Advanced Training Program of the Division of Graduate Education and Science (GZ-1493), and research was assisted by the second year of the NSF research grant (GS-2566) to Longacre as principal investigator.

The 1970 Season

Research and Teaching Staff	Support Staff	Apache Crew	Students	Family
William Longacre, Director	Illa Mai McFarlin, Cook	Bowman Beatty	Cynthia Bergstedt	Charles Collins
Jefferson Reid, Co-assistant Director	Michael Bilbo, Kitchen Aide	Dewey Case	Curtiss Brennan	Melinda Collins
David Wilcox, Co-assistant Director	Edward Read, Kitchen Aide	Jonathan Case	David Denison	
Michael Collins, Dig Foreman	Karen Collins, Hostess (volunteer)	Dallas Gregg	Michael Gregg	
James Rock, Archaeological Assistant	Karen Rock, Hostess (volunteer)	Norbert Josay	Mark Harlan	
Anna Bennett, Laboratory Supervisor		Elliot Mason	Carolyn Koehler	
Sandra Crafton, Laboratory Assistant		Peter Mason	Tony Luebbermann	
Martin Davis, Laboratory Aide (volunteer)		Alvin Murphy	Abdullah Masry	
Susan Luebbermann, Photographer (volunteer)		Amos Nagle	Phyllis McKenzie	
		Clarence Peaches	Karen McLeod	
		Glendale Tessay	Carol Meyer	
		Leo Tessay	Constance Piesinger	
		John Watt	Joyce Resnick	
			Gene Rogge	
			Izumi Shimada	
			Mollie Struever	
			Sharon Thomas	
			Ellen Tiger	
			Alexander Townsend	
			Michael Whalen	

This was Jefferson Reid's first season at Grasshopper. He had arrived as a doctoral candidate in anthropology at the UA the previous fall after having taught anthropology for two years at Baylor University in Waco, Texas. He was enthusiastic about adding a summer in the famous Southwest to his fieldwork experience, especially after the intellectual electricity of Longacre's fall seminar, "Archaeology as Anthropology," but in the beginning had every intention of returning to the Southeast upon completing his doctorate. Although he recalls no single event that would qualify as an epiphany, by the end of the summer Reid was hooked on southwestern archaeology, more specifically on pueblos in the pine forests of east-central Arizona, labeled tongue-in-cheek as the "coniferous neolithic." After six long seasons in the Southeast and one in Mexico, he found in the archaeological context of Grasshopper a variable and challenging set of whole artifacts neatly partitioned by stone-walled rooms and well dated by tree rings and ceramic cross dating. In addition, compared to the Southeast and the rain forests of Chiapas, Mexico, there was low humidity, few insects, and poisonous snakes that rattled and were rather small. Fortunately, there also were no alligators.

Excavations in eleven rooms focused on the nature of domestic activities and the use of space, but most of the work was simply completing rooms previously excavated to the uppermost floor, a procedure that had come to be called subflooring. Longacre and Wilcox probably selected this strategy, because the rest of the staff was new and without specific research interests. One team, under the supervision of James Rock, who had been a student the previous year, subfloored rooms in the north end of Room Block 1 that had been started in 1969. A second team, under Reid's direction, excavated one room (146) and subfloored three others (143, 153, 197) adjacent to the Great Kiva in Room Block 2. Room 146, which had been trenched the previous year, was excavated to the collapsed second-story floor. Although it was essentially clean-up work, this project also fit the long-term investigations into the sequence of change in activities in that area before and after the Great Kiva was constructed. For Reid, it was also a good, low-impact introduction to the archaeological record of a large, complicated pueblo ruin.

The third team, directed by Wilcox, began a new excavation project on a contiguous group of six rooms (205, 206, 210, 211, 215, 218) belonging to what was labeled "construction unit L" (CUL) in the southern part of Room Block 3. Wilcox undertook this project to formulate a methodological framework for testing the relationship between architectural units and social groups (Rock 1974; Wilcox 1975, 1982). Further, the construction units making up this large pueblo now formed significant analytical units as well as major sampling strata.

Under the direction of Michael Collins, the cornering project continued to identify construction units, sequences of room construction, and the general outline of the pueblo. Collins and Reid established a site-wide vertical datum on bedrock in the northwest corner of Plaza 1 at an arbitrary elevation of one hundred meters. They called it "Fred" so as not to confuse it with the individual-room datum points that continued to be used. Site-wide vertical measurements were expressed, therefore, in "meters Fred," or MF.

A backhoe excavated a series of long, deep trenches in the large, open flat north of the main ruin to explore the geological and cultural deposits. The objective was to gain a better understanding of the original Salt River Draw channel and collect further data on a prehistoric pond that had been speculated to be in this area (see Agenbroad 1982; Kelso 1982; S. J. Olsen 1982).

One weekend was spent at Chediski Farms, an abandoned Apache community northwest of Grasshopper, mapping structures and taking tree-ring samples. This work was a continuation of a study begun previously and partially reported by Griffin, Leone, and Basso (1971).

Paleoenvironmental research was the theme of an informal conference of specialists held at the Field School in July. Attending were Vorsila

Bohrer, palynologist; Jerry Greene, zooarchaeologist; Thomas Mathews, zooarchaeologist; Charmion McKusick, zooarchaeologist; Stanley Olsen, zooarchaeologist; and James Schoenwetter, palynologist. These individuals would form the nucleus of specialists participating in the all-day Grasshopper symposium at the 1972 annual meeting of the Society for American Archaeology (SAA) that eventually would be published in the multidisciplinary volume on Grasshopper (Longacre, Holbrook, and Graves 1982).

The 1971 Season

The Field School was in session for eight weeks, from June 11 to August 6, with twenty students. Ten men and ten women, all graduate students, were enrolled. The teaching program received the final year of support from the NSF through the Advanced Training Program of the Division of Graduate Education in Science (GZ-1924). There was no Apache crew leader or laboratory assistant, because the research grant supporting them had expired.

Much like 1968, the 1971 season marked another milestone in bringing Grasshopper research closer to the ideals of processual archaeology. Much of this was driven by Reid's zeal as a recent convert to processual archaeology and his own experience the previous year in trying to learn quickly everything necessary to survive and do research at Grasshopper. In the spring, the graduate-student staff began holding weekly meetings to plan the research and teaching programs and the organization and logistics of the camp and site.

Two immediate results were an increase in the material sent to student participants and the beginning of procedural manuals. Materials sent to students included summaries of dissertation- and master's-thesis research by Griffin, Tuggle, Clark, and Mauer, along with a little section on explanation in archaeology and hypothesis testing, the latter borrowing heavily from Fritz and Plog (1970). Also included were selected bibliographies on explanation ranging from Binford and Binford (1968) to Thompson (1958c) and on current directions in archaeology spanning R. Adams (1968) to Wheat (1955). Stephanie Whittlesey, whose introduction to southwestern archaeology took place that summer at Grasshopper, recalls being stunned not so much by the sheer volume of these materials as by the expectation that she would learn and practice this kind of archaeology.

Reid's own research interests were beginning to take form in a posi-

Field School staff and students in 1971. Seated, front row, left to right, are Peggy Powers, Susan Kus, Nancy Curriden, Stephanie Whittlesey, Tony Luebbermann, Karen Merrey; second row, Martin Davis, Sandra Kemrer, John Keane, Mark Grady, Tom Mulinski, Charles Borum, Glen Rice; standing, Susan Luebbermann, Jefferson Reid, Sharon Debowski, David Cleveland, Sandra Schultz, David Doyel, Illa Mai McFarlin, Alan Sullivan, Joseph Rawls, Caroline Bledsoe, Anthony Cooley, Susan Stankowski, William Reynolds, Nelve McFarlin, James Rock, Shirley Pettengill, Veletta Canouts, William Longacre.

The 1971 Season

Research and Teaching Staff	Support Staff	Apache Crew	Students
William Longacre, Director	Illa Mai McFarlin, Cook	Anthony Cooley	Caroline Bledsoe
Jefferson Reid, Assistant Director	Charles Borum, Camp Aide	Alvin Quay	David Cleveland
James Rock, Dig Foreman	Nelve McFarlin, Camp Aide	Ervin Quay	Nancy Curriden
Tony Luebbermann, Archaeological Assistant	Veletta Canouts, Hostess (volunteer)	Glendale Tessay	Sharon Debowski
Sandra Crafton Kemrer, Laboratory Supervisor		John Watt	David Doyel
Martin Davis, Laboratory Aide (volunteer)			Mark Grady
Susan Luebbermann, Photographer (volunteer)			Stephen Hynson
			John Keane
			Susan Kus
			Karen Merrey
			Thomas Mulinski
			Shirley Pettengill
			Margaret Powers
			Joseph Rawls
			William Reynolds
			Glen Rice
			Sandra Schultz
			Susan Stankowski
			Alan Sullivan
			Stephanie Whittlesey

tion paper presented at the first Southwestern Anthropological Research Group meeting in April (Longacre and Reid 1971). Although it was a ragged collection of buzzwords and loosely connected thoughts, the paper announced interest in population growth and response to conditions of environmental stress that would occupy later dissertation research—a topic of obvious interest at the Field School and one also deeply entrenched in processual archaeology.

The development of procedural manuals for the field and laboratory, which, in succeeding years, grew into dark and hairy monsters that would occupy inordinate amounts of staff time to develop, fix, and implement, began innocently enough. Forms and procedures developed in earlier years were systematized toward the laudable goal of seeking to inform students as quickly as possible about what they needed to know to survive and prosper in the high-information research environment of Grasshopper.

Student dig teams working on ongoing research projects excavated in fourteen rooms. In the north part of Room Block 1, one team, under Longacre's supervision, worked to complete subflooring of rooms that had been excavated to floor in 1969. Another team, under Rock's direction, continued work on the CUL Wilcox had begun in 1970, with a research objective of investigating the relationship between the architectural units and social groups (Rock 1974). A third team completed the excavation begun in 1969 of Room 146, a trash-filled room adjacent to the Great Kiva.

Reid began the growth project, essentially an expansion of the cornering project, to investigate community growth by means of room-construction patterns. To obtain tree-ring specimens that would date initial construction, Tony Luebbermann supervised the excavation of one room in each of the earliest construction units of the three room blocks in the main ruin (Rooms 47, 164, 270). Combined with existing dates for later construction, these new dates would provide estimates for the rate of pueblo growth and the chronological framework of Reid's (1973) dissertation research. As it turned out, Reid would later find it necessary to turn to behavioral archaeology for a solution to the chronological problem left unresolved by dendrochronology.

The cornering project, now subsumed by the growth project, continued under Reid's supervision with a five-man Apache crew. In addition to finishing work in the main ruin, we began cornering the outlying room blocks.

A backhoe was again employed to backfill rooms and outline exterior walls. As part of the paleoenvironmental research, additional backhoe trenches defined the pond in the flat just north of the main ruin and sampled the old channel of Salt River Draw for pollen, microfaunal remains, and gravels (see Agenbroad 1982; Kelso 1982; S. J. Olsen 1982).

One of the more exciting events of the summer demonstrated well the dangers and difficulties of conducting a field school in the wilderness. The Field School helped to battle wildfires that broke out across the reservation. We fought a small, nearby fire with excavation equipment— sprayers, shovels, and even enlisting the aid of the visiting backhoe and its operator, Dick Throp. Reid, student Glen Rice, and Apache workman John Watt battled the Carrizo fire north of Grasshopper. Reid recalls that his choice to become an archaeologist rather than a firefighter was wise. Larger, fiercer wildfires in 2002 would devastate the reservation and the rim communities.

Longacre was on leave the fall semester 1971 as a visiting professor in anthropology at Yale University, where he organized the Grasshopper symposium for the upcoming SAA meeting and enticed Gene Rogge, who had been a student at Grasshopper in 1970, to come to Arizona to finish his graduate work. Longacre had requested that Wilcox, Collins, and Reid prepare a joint paper on the cornering project and pueblo growth for the Grasshopper symposium. We were unable to merge our different viewpoints successfully and eventually had to go our separate ways (Reid and Shimada 1982; Wilcox 1982). Collins's paper on population estimates was superceded by later work and never made it into the published volume (Longacre, Holbrook, and Graves 1982).

In Longacre's absence, Reid was thrilled to participate in the exclusive 14th Annual Ceramic Conference at the Museum of Northern Arizona (MNA) and to use Longacre's office and books in studying for the UA preliminary examination, at that time an eight-hour, written examination spread over two days.

All was not roses that fall after the field season ended. As we analyzed the cornering data for growth studies, we found problems and raised questions that could only be resolved in the field. Unwilling to wait until the summer to answer these questions, Reid coaxed Alan Sullivan and Shimada to accompany him to Grasshopper over Thanksgiving for some autumnal cornering. The two-page report on this expedition, entitled "Toward Experimental Replicability in Archaeology: Reevaluation of Grasshopper Cornering Data, November 24–28, 1971" is so filled with hypotheses (H) and null hypotheses (Ho) that it hurts to read it. But that was the way archaeologists talked back then, of course, at least in formal presentations.

Discussions with Wilcox over the cornering project and the CUL demonstrated the need for additional fieldwork and initiated a long-term program of collecting diverse kinds of architectural information. The fall cornering expedition was the impetus that eventually resulted in Riggs's (1999a, 2001) dissertation, as well as other research (e.g., Graves 1991).

The 1972 Season

The Field School was in session for eight weeks, from June 9 to August 4, with twenty-one students. Nine men and twelve women, who represented nineteen graduate and two undergraduate students, attended. Although fieldwork was assisted by a research grant from the NSF (GS-33436), this was the first year without NSF support for students and the teaching program. There was no reduction in field and support staff, however, as the research grant supported these positions. The "Grasshopper Fellow" was an unpaid staff position we developed to increase the number of staff without adding to support costs. Selected from qualified applicants, the Grasshopper Fellow received experience and a research opportunity as partial compensation for lack of pay.

The research year began with a symposium organized by Longacre for

The 1972 Season

Research and Teaching Staff	Support Staff	Apache Crew	Students
William Longacre, Director	Ruth Scoggin, Cook	Allan Boni	Mark Aldenderfer
Jefferson Reid, Assistant Director	Joyce Kuntz, Assistant Cook	Joe Boni	Melody Brancato
James Rock, Dig Foreman	Tom Anderson, Kitchen Aide	Anthony Cooley	Curtis Buck
Izumi Shimada, Apache Foreman	Easy Barber, Kitchen Aide	Elliot Mason	Richard Ciolek-
Tony Luebbermann,	Dan Scoggin, Camp Aide	John Mason	Torrello
Archaeological Assistant		Wilford Peaches	Susan Ciolek-
Veletta Canouts,		Alvin Quay	Torrello
Laboratory Supervisor		Ervin Quay	Katherine Condliffe
Stephanie Whittlesey,		Lansford Quay	Deborah Dennis
Laboratory Assistant		Howard Taylay	Patricia Gilman
Alan Sullivan, Grasshopper		Chester Tessay	Karl Helmgren
Fellow (volunteer)		Delmar Tessay	Susan Howard
Susan Luebbermann,		Glendale Tessay	James Kelley
Photographer (volunteer)		John Watt	Elinor Large
Leon Prodon, Laboratory Aide			Linda Mayro
(volunteer)			James McDonald
			Robert Neily
			Ilene Nicholas
			Linda Popelish
			James Sheehy
			Frances Stier
			Spencer Turkel
			Toby Volkman

the thirty-seventh annual meeting of the SAA in Bal Harbour, Florida, entitled "Multidisciplinary Research at the Grasshopper Ruin, East-Central Arizona." Participants included the environmental specialists who had been working on various pieces of the research since the informal conference held at Grasshopper in the summer of 1970. The papers from this symposium would form the core of the UA Anthropological Paper (No. 40) edited by Longacre, Holbrook, and Graves (1982). Overall, the symposium was rather disappointing; there were always more people on the stage than in the audience, and little discussion was generated.

Disappointment with the symposium turnout, if any, did not linger and apparently did not affect the outcome of the grant proposal submitted to the NSF in late December 1971. Entitled "Archaeological Investigations at the Grasshopper Ruin, Arizona," with Longacre and Thompson as principal investigators, the proposal was essentially the same as that for the grant awarded for research in 1969 and 1970. Clearly, the driving force must have been the reputations of Longacre and Thompson and Longacre's implied promise in the proposal that, during his 1972–1973 sabbatical leave at the Center for Advanced Studies in the

Behavioral Sciences at Stanford, he would "prepare the first of what we hope will be a series of major studies on Grasshopper prehistory." Research questions remained essentially unchanged from the earlier grant proposal, as follows (Longacre and Thompson 1971:1):

> The research is designed to investigate both the nature of the environment and the nature of the extinct cultural system reflected in the archaeological remains. Man's use of the environment and a major readaptation as the environment apparently changed slightly are the major problem areas of our research. We hope to shed some understanding on the prehistoric background of modern puebloan societies as a result of our research. More generally, we are interested in the nature of cultural processes in systems undergoing readaptation or adjustment.
>
> Funds are requested to support environmental research such as the identification of floral and faunal remains found in the excavations and the interpretation of them from an ecological point of view. Funds are also requested for the support of twenty graduate student research participants, a team of Apache excavators, supervisory staff, and logistic maintenance costs. The proposed project is designed to last from June 1, 1972, to May 31, 1973.

The research grant was largely devoted to the continuation of logistical support, which had previously been funded by the defunct NSF teaching program.

Tuggle's dissertation research gave impetus to expansion of Grasshopper research as expressed in Longacre's NSF grant proposal: "to define and investigate the nature of interaction among the extinct societies in the Grasshopper area . . . and between that region and those further to the north and south." In addition, because Longacre was one of the prime movers in establishing the Southwestern Anthropological Research Group, Grasshopper research began to address the SARG question of "Why are population aggregates located where they are?" and the auxiliary questions of "Why do aggregates differ in size, why do the locations differ through time, and why does a single population aggregate grow or decrease in size?" (see Longacre and Reid 1971). It would take several more years, however, to actually put a survey project in the field.

The growth project provided the research questions and criteria of selection for new fieldwork in the 1972 season. Reid had presented a paper on the growth of Grasshopper Pueblo at the SAA symposium and had taken the empirical requirements of processual archaeology seriously. The 1972 growth project was outlined in an eleven-page research design. A hypothetical model of pueblo growth comprising five construction sequences also was proposed to coordinate the relationships between the main ruin and the outliers. Fieldwork disproved a number of hypothesized relationships, most notably that the outliers predated the main ruin.

Three of the earliest-constructed rooms had been excavated to floor in 1971 as part of the growth project. Unfinished subfloor excavations in two of these rooms (164 and 270) were completed. Four new rooms (183, 187, 216, and 231) in the main ruin were selected for excavation as part of the growth project. They were randomly chosen from groups of rooms (construction units) built during the early to middle periods of pueblo growth (see Riggs 1999a, 2001). The rooms also were in areas of the main ruin not represented in the excavated sample.

Excavation of rooms from the outlying room blocks was another focus of the growth project. Until 1972, little had been done in the outliers. Armed with the information provided by the cornering project as it progressed in the outliers, we randomly selected four new rooms (319, 341, 359, and 404) located in various outlying room blocks. The results of the growth project are discussed by Reid (1973, 1978, 1989), Reid and Shimada (1982), and Riggs (1994, 1999a, 2001).

Rock (1974) completed the excavation of CUL in Room Block 3, a project Wilcox had begun in 1970. The cornering project, under the supervision of Shimada, investigated most of the outlying room blocks, and new data on attributes of wall construction were recorded to expand the analytic potential of the analysis (see Scarborough and Shimada 1974).

The highlight of the summer was the visit by a crew from the children's television show *Make a Wish*. They filmed the field crews busily at work for an episode on "keys" to illustrate that archaeology is the key to the past. Whittlesey recalls this introduction to the world of film and television as sparking an interest in presenting archaeology to the public.

At the end of the summer, Longacre left to spend the year at the Center for Advanced Studies. He was supplied with cornering-growth data for several papers (Longacre 1975, 1976) that supported the inference of growth as a function of immigration. Gwinn Vivian and Reid participated in the annual, invitation-only ceramic conference at the MNA. Except for a brief gathering on Cibola White Ware ceramics (Sullivan and Hantman 1984), this would be the MNA's last annual ceramic conference.

The 1973 Season

Research and Teaching Staff	Support Staff	Apache Crew	Students
Jefferson Reid, Field Director	Ruth Scoggin, Cook	Gilbert Gooday	John Antieau
Michael Schiffer, Assistant Director	Joyce Kuntz, Assistant Cook	Frank Lee	Wendy Ashmore
Izumi Shimada, Senior Dig Foreman	Steve Silverman, Camp Aide	John Mason	Charlotte Benson
Alan Sullivan, Dig Foreman	Charles Zukoski, Camp Aide	Ramirez Patterson	Richard Brook
Stephanie Whittlesey, Archaeological Assistant	Annette Schiffer, Hostess (volunteer)	Alvin Quay	Sarah Campbell
Linda Mayro, Laboratory Supervisor		Delmar Tessay	Arlen Chase
Richard Ciolek-Torrello, Laboratory Assistant		Glendale Tessay	Kristy Ellis
James Kelley, Grasshopper Fellow (volunteer)		Leo Tessay	Polly Fahnestock
Margaret Thompson, Photographer (volunteer)			T.J. Ferguson
			Nancy Kays
			James Lockhart
			James Nolan
			Carol Poliak
			Konstanze Rahn
			David Siegel
			Constance Silver
			Gary Somers
			James Spain
			John Sparling
			Pamela Van Tassel

The 1973 Season

The Field School ran from June 8 to August 3, with an enrollment of twenty students. The ten men and ten women represented eighteen graduate and two undergraduate students. The fieldwork program was again assisted by an NSF grant (GS-33436) to Thompson and Longacre.

The 1973 season at Grasshopper signaled a shift in research orientation and initiated a period of overlapping research interests that would continue through the 1978 season. After a year at the Center for Advanced Studies, Longacre spent the summer of 1973 in the Philippines laying the groundwork for ethnoarchaeological research among the Kalinga of northern Luzon. Michael Schiffer joined Grasshopper as assistant director to form with Reid a dynamic duo of fresh Ph.D.s bombarding students with what was perceived to be a new and powerful research program. In addition, this year was characterized by changes in our permitting procedures with the White Mountain Apache tribe. When Thompson and Reid negotiated a new permit and lease agreement, Fred Benashly, who was then tribal chairman, and Wesley Bonito came to the UA to discuss and sign it.

While Longacre was away, but with his help, Thompson and Reid wrote the NSF grant proposal. The "Outline of 1973 Research Projects" was written by Reid in December 1972, as he was beginning his dissertation analysis. We quote it directly:

I. Research in the Grasshopper Region
  A. *Regional Site Survey Project*

Tuggle (1970) conducted a survey of a stratified sample of the Grasshopper Region. This survey is to be extended in the heavily dissected southwestern sector of the region and east of Canyon Creek where additional well preserved cliff ruins are suspected in the south-facing, sandstone exposures.

Additional data will be sought to test the hypothesis that site location during the Grasshopper period is the result of a diversified adaptive strategy for resource exploitation in response to conditions of environmental stress.

Pilot tests of the SELGEM program will be conducted. This program is an information storage and retrieval system designed by the Smithsonian Institution which is currently being developed for computerization of site survey information by the Arizona State Museum.

  B. *Canyon Creek Project*

Research will focus upon the relation between this community and Grasshopper. Initial investigation seeks to augment Haury's (1934) work by gathering data on construction sequence, room function, activity areas and resource potential of the immediate environment. The hypothesis is entertained that Canyon Creek began as a limited activity site occupied seasonally. This hypothesis is related to the contention that the edge effect (Odum 1959:278; Gumerman and Johnson 1971) should be greater in this region and should provide a superior collecting environment. Palynological and ethnobotanical samples and specimens will be collected. No excavation is planned for this phase of research. It is anticipated that these data will be collected from other cliff sites in the region.

  C. *Hill Top Ruin Project [mistaken for Chodistaas]*

This site (Arizona P:14:24 [actual site number of Chodistaas]) is a small masonry pueblo about 2 miles southwest of Grasshopper. It was first described by Hough (1935:9). Its importance to the regional research program lies in the fact that it was occupied during the period immediately prior to the establishment of Grasshopper. During 1973, research will concentrate on defining the walls and mapping the ruin, and plotting the distribution of refuse in preparation for future intensive excavation. Further sampling of the surface debris and limited test excavations will be conducted in both the masonry unit and in a nearby pit house village. [We did not get to Chodistaas until 1976.]

II. Research at Grasshopper Ruin

A. *Pueblo Growth Project*

This project will attempt to test the following hypotheses:

1. The main ruin expanded through normal population growth.
2. The main ruin expanded at a more rapid rate than can be accounted for by normal population growth.
3. The main ruin expanded initially as a response to rapid immigration.
4. The Great Kiva was constructed during maximum pueblo expansion.
5. The Great Kiva was constructed after maximum pueblo expansion.
6. The Great Kiva was built in response to increased population density and intensification of interaction.
7. The Great Kiva was built in response to social disequilibrium (possibly population dispersion) induced by environmental stress.
8. Rooms in the outlying room blocks represent seasonal activity areas.

A pilot test of the SELGEM program will be applied to the retrieval and storage of excavation data from two rooms. Because the SELGEM program is designed to solve inventory and retrieval problems in museum collections, its application to field research problems needs to be carefully explored.

B. *Construction Unit Project*

Over the past three years we have attempted to identify domestic groups and their corporate activity structure. In 1973 we will focus on changes through time and responses to environmental conditions. The following hypotheses are considered:

1. During periods of environmental stress, activity structure of domestic groups becomes less patterned.
2. Domestic group size decreased during the occupation of Grasshopper. We hope to relate this possible trend to what we tentatively perceive as a progressive decrease in domestic group size in other regions of prehistoric Western Pueblo culture.

C. Cornering Project

Early in the 1973 season we plan to complete the cornering project in the few outlying room blocks that remain to be tested. Upon its completion, we will have a reasonably accurate picture of the entire community as it grew from three detached core construction units to its final configuration of perhaps 500 rooms, kivas, and plazas over the 125 years of its existence.

By the beginning of the 1973 field season, Reid had completed his dissertation, "Growth and Response to Stress at Grasshopper Pueblo, Arizona," and with it found answers to many of the questions posed in the grant proposal. One result was to synthesize pueblo growth into establishment, expansion, dispersion, and abandonment periods and to account for the dynamics of growth as a product of immigration and the developmental cycle of domestic groups.

The excavation of new rooms in 1973 focused on further defining pueblo growth by examining the outlying room blocks on the low hills surrounding the main ruin. Preliminary excavation of outlying rooms in 1972 had indicated that some of these outliers were constructed late in the growth of the pueblo. In addition, the 1972 excavations permitted the formulation of a measure of relative room abandonment (Montgomery 1993; Reid 1973; Schiffer 1976), which, when combined with the construction sequence provided by the cornering project, would allow us to estimate the duration of room occupation. In addition, the outlying rooms contributed to our increasing understanding of household activities and their changing structure through time. The hypothesis that relative household size decreased during the occupation of Grasshopper was supported tentatively with a model employing measures of household facilities, such as size of rooms, cooking vessels, and cooking hearths (Ciolek-Torrello and Reid 1974). Rooms 349, 352, 371, 376, 425, 398, and 434 were excavated by crews directed by Sullivan and Reid.

Excavations in the main ruin included finishing rooms begun the previous year and completing excavations in two new rooms. Rooms 183 in Room Block 2, 187 in Room Block 2, adjacent to Plaza 2, and 231 in Room Block 3 were subfloored. Room 62 was chosen for excavation, because it was the core room (first constructed) of the East Village. Room 145 was one of two unexcavated rooms adjacent to the Great Kiva. It was selected because, as one of the latest-constructed rooms in that area, it would help us to bracket the construction of the Great Kiva. Whittlesey's investigations in these rooms also probed the produc-

KEY
- BACKHOE TRENCH
- CORNERED ROOM
- HAND TRENCH
- EXCAVATED
- UNCORNERED OUTLIERS

SCALE
METERS

THE GRASSHOPPER RUIN
ARIZONA   P:14:1

tion and distribution of trade goods and the role of regional trade as one mechanism for coping with environmental stress, later presented in her preliminary examination paper (Whittlesey 1974). The discovery of numerous burials in these rooms, some of which were under the water table and required excavation methods unique to Grasshopper, such as wet screening, piqued Whittlesey's interest in mortuary practices, social organization, and the life history of individuals.

Seven years after it began in 1967, the Apache crew under the direction of Shimada completed the cornering project. At last, we could begin constructing an accurate map of room relationships and growth patterns in all of the room blocks. Ironically, although we had obtained the necessary framework to devise sampling strategies for solving many important questions concerning past human behavior, there is no record of ever again selecting a room using random-sampling procedures.

Grasshopper Pueblo as of 1973.

In 1973, we progressed toward the total conversion of all data to computer storage by applying a pilot test of the SELGEM program to the retrieval and storage of data from four rooms. Sullivan and Richard Ciolek-Torrello directed the test under the overall supervision of Lawrence Manier of the Department of Anthropology. The test provided refinements to the annotation classes and free-form data language that were necessary to implement the program with the existing Grasshopper data and employ it in future data collection. The reality of SELGEM and its impact upon Grasshopper archaeology was long reaching and dramatic, as we will see in the following chapter.

Intriguing events in Grasshopper's social history also marked this summer and illustrate well how small-group dynamics affected the research agenda. The huge size of Room 62, which necessitated backfilling it at the end of the season with broken appliances, worn mattresses, and other nontraditional filler, sparked a minor student rebellion. The male students assigned to the room refused to complete the subfloor excavations, which they perceived as an onerous task. To finish excavations, backfill, and close down the camp, the staff remained at Grasshopper for two weeks after the official close of the Field School. Whittlesey recalls this time as the most pleasant fieldwork she has ever undertaken. She also cherishes the apology for the rebellion extended some years later by an older and wiser perpetrator.

Beginning the Transition

At the close of the field season in 1973, the days of programmatic hypothesis testing at Grasshopper in the mode that had become fashionable in the late 1960s and early 1970s were gone. We had identified the flaws inherent in processual archaeology, at least when used to investigate the rather complicated archaeological context of a large neolithic pueblo community in the Southwest (see chapter 8). Behavioral archaeology promised to provide the framework for resolving these problems, creating a heightened sense of optimism.

Longacre's absence in 1973 to initiate his ethnoarchaeological study of Kalinga pottery set the stage for the shift from processual to behavioral archaeology in the Grasshopper teaching and research programs. We have seldom seen anyone so excited about fieldwork in faraway places as Longacre after his reconnaissance visit (see Skibo 1999). As his interest in the Kalinga research increased, his enthusiasm for Grasshopper was transferred to others such as Ciolek-Torrello, Sullivan, Whittlesey, and Reid, all of us at different stages in our careers but all sharing a remarkable interest in the record of Grasshopper Pueblo and what it could tell us about the past.

The critical point of closure for processual archaeology was Schiffer's and Reid's completion of graduate studies. They spent the winter and spring of 1973 in hot pursuit of concepts and procedures that would rectify the inadequacies of processual archaeology and provide more accurate statements about the past. This, to Reid, was the beginning of behavioral archaeology (see Schiffer 1995a).

Pieces of this program were presented at the 1973 Pecos Conference in Tucson (Woodbury 1993:346–49). Along with Wilcox, Reid and Schiffer organized a session on "Provenience Concepts, Room-fill and Floor" to explore the implications for distinguishing behavioral spaces from recovery spaces. After suffering through the garbled transcript of the session, Woodbury (1993:349) concludes generously: "This unique and lively symposium was the final scheduled event of the 1973 conference. The rapid give-and-take, the questions and doubts, the explanations, and the search for areas of agreement might, with little stretching of the imagination, be thought of as echoing the vigorous and exploratory nature of the first Pecos Conference."

In retrospect, it is unclear to what extent these ideas and enthusiasm influenced the students, but the excitement of that season is firmly ingrained in Reid's mind. The three members of the 1973 staff who completed Grasshopper dissertations—Ciolek-Torrello, Sullivan, and Whittlesey—took up the program willingly, as Whittlesey recalls. These graduate students perceived a fresh, enthusiastic trend in direction that seemed lacking in previous seasons. Whittlesey suggests that the sense of excitement and shared passion for archaeology among the staff was no small factor contributing to the program shift. We cannot speak to whether this also was true of the previous years at the Field School, but the staff formed a cadre of like-minded individuals. All students at the UA and friends who shared the experiences of the field together, they had been indoctrinated similarly in the tenets of processual archaeology back in Tucson. Being involved in the generation of a new archaeology was at times exhausting, at times exciting—but certainly never the same old grind. Indeed, the subsequent research of these students would contribute substantially to the body of work demonstrating the efficacy of behavioral archaeology in reconstructing the past.

Behavioral archaeology, unlike processual archaeology, could not be done quickly, and therefore its effects on research did not show up immediately in the Grasshopper work. As we shall see shortly, there was no dramatic clash between paradigms. In this sense, the shift was no more remarkable than Thompson's assumption of the Haury mantle or the change from culture history to processual history at Grasshopper. Longacre's remaining years as director would continue the established research themes of ecology and sociology that would be pursued within the framework of behavioral archaeology.

6

Transition and Change, 1974–1978

The term "new archaeology" has been much used. In the absence of progress toward usable theory, there is no new archaeology, only an antitraditional archaeology, at best. I look forward to a "new archaeology," but what has thus far been presented under the term is an anarchy of uncertainty, optimism, and products of extremely variable quality.—**Lewis Binford** (1977)

The five years from 1974 through 1978 were a time of change and transition at Grasshopper, marked by shifts in personnel, funding, and research goals. The overlapping research emphases of these years are best described as transitional between William Longacre's processual archaeology and Jefferson Reid's behavioral archaeology. The basic questions of prehistory remained essentially unchanged. By the end of the 1978 season, behavioral archaeology had replaced processual archaeology in its purest nomological, hypothetico-deductive, Hay Hollow Valley expression, and the Field School would never be the same.

The 1974 season was a turning point in Grasshopper research. Three events signal the end of processual archaeology—the close of Paul Martin's Vernon field school, the beginning of Longacre's active fieldwork among the Kalinga, and behavioral archaeology's expanded research agenda emphasizing methodological research and middle-range theory.

Martin's death in January 1974 marked this year as the end of an era in southwestern archaeology. It brought to a close a remarkable archaeological career and the conclusion of the phenomenon that was Vernon. Although Martin's research program continued during the 1974 season, when it was based at the town of Snowflake and directed by John Fritz, the energy and excitement of the Vernon experience as a dynamic force of processual archaeology in the Southwest suddenly were gone. The field school and research station at Vernon had been the epicenter for the development of processual archaeology and certainly its most active laboratory in the Southwest. It had spawned or nurtured Longacre and James Hill, the first legitimizers of processual archaeology, along with Mark Leone, Michael Schiffer, Fred Plog, Stephen Plog, Charles Redman, and Norman Yoffee, among many more.

As in the annual volleyball contest to win the Mogollon Bowl, Vernon had been a friendly rival to the Grasshopper research and teaching program. The ties between Martin and Longacre fueled a close relationship between Grasshopper and Vernon staff and students. Longacre had persuaded Martin to move to Tucson in the fall of 1973 and take an adjunct appointment in anthropology at the University of Arizona. Martin's rapidly failing health kept him from his new office and from being a part of the changes then taking place at the UA, many of which he had initiated or encouraged. We cannot speculate on the effects of Martin's death and the closing of Vernon on Longacre's interest in Southwest prehistory or in Grasshopper research and teaching. Clearly what remained was waning, however, and his intellectual curiosity was increasingly directed toward ethnoarchaeology.

In 1974, Longacre returned to his director's chair at the Field School to find most of the staff with developed dissertation projects. Richard Ciolek-Torrello was exploring methods for identifying the household in the archaeological context; Stephanie Whittlesey was interested in public activities, social differentiation, ritual, and models of archaeological inference; Alan Sullivan was exploring the natural and cultural processes that formed small sites; and Reid, having completed his dissertation, wanted finally to expand research to sites that bracketed the peak occupation at Grasshopper. In addition, we were faced with the continuing conversion of data recording from the standard forms to the SELGEM computer format. The Grasshopper research program had developed a momentum of its own that could proceed with only light steering by the director.

Volume 40, nos. 1–2, of the journal *The Kiva* was devoted to Grasshopper research (Reid 1974). Titled *Behavioral Archaeology at the Grasshopper Ruin*, it contains a mixture of papers and research orientations that testifies to the transitional character of the times. The introductory article by Longacre and Reid (1974) takes up where Thompson and Longacre (1966) left off by describing the fieldwork for the years 1966 through 1973. They emphasize the multidisciplinary objectives of the research and teaching program. The focus of this work is clearly within the processual idiom, as expressed by Longacre and Reid (1974:10–11) (citations have been updated):

> All of these researches in concert are designed to describe and explain the processes of stability and change among the extinct cultural, behavioral and environmental systems operating in this relatively unknown region of the Southwest during the 14th century. The investigation of cultural and behavioral change focuses on the establishment, growth, and abandonment of the Grasshopper pueblo community. In this regard our work is designed to investigate three broad areas of potential "causality" utilizing an integrated multidisciplinary approach.
>
> First, the nature of the natural and social environment and the effects of environmental change in the Grasshopper region are being examined as selective pressures responsible for population aggregation and the ultimate abandonment of the pueblo (Longacre 1975; Reid 1973; Reid and Shimada 1982).
>
> Second, we are greatly concerned with the possibility of systemic change in the economic sector of cultural and behavioral systems in this area of the Southwest during the 13th and 14th centuries, especially in the possibility of major involvement in large-scale trading enterprises. The pressures for aggregation and relocation of populations may involve social and economic interaction with other communities in a network of trading relationships (Tuggle 1970; Whittlesey 1974). And, third, we are looking at the possibility that the cultural and behavioral changes we observe during this period reflect a major adaptive shift in ecological patterns that results in a more efficient utilization of available energy and not triggered exclusively by environmental pressures (Griffin 1969). Population pressure may be a key variable in explaining this kind of behavioral change (Boserup 1965; Longacre 1975; Netting 1971).

We can see the concerns of behavioral archaeology in the discussion of methods, measurements, and middle-range theory represented in the majority of these papers.

In 1976, Reid again took over as acting director while Longacre executed his first extended period of research with the Kalinga. Longacre's last two years at Grasshopper in 1977 and 1978 paralleled the departure of Reid and Whittlesey to direct the fieldwork phase of the Cholla Project, a six-year contract project to mitigate the impacts of a transmission line along the western edge of the Grasshopper region, for the Arizona State Museum. In the final two transitional years, during which processual archaeology gave way to behavioral archaeology, Grasshopper took on a radically new look. Personnel shifted, field projects expanded, and an adjustment of the teaching program took place. In the spring of 1977, Reid also received an NSF grant to support writing a monograph on Grasshopper, to be based largely on the dissertation research of Reid (1973), Whittlesey (1978), and Ciolek-Torrello (1978). We discuss the relation of the Cholla Project to Grasshopper research and the impacts of Cholla and the NSF grant at the end of this chapter.

The 1974 Season

The season ran for eight weeks, from June 7 to August 2, with an enrollment of twenty students—ten men and ten women, who represented eighteen graduates and two undergraduates. The Field School received support through a research grant by the National Science Foundation to Thompson and Longacre as principal investigators (GS-33436, Amendment No. 2). The grant supported the staff, the Apache crew, the student research participants, the use of a backhoe at the site, and environmental research. Sullivan, who had broken his leg that spring, was the first Grasshopper staff member to negotiate Grasshopper's environs on crutches.

The season targeted four projects: (1) defining the earliest, indoor domestic activities; (2) investigating community activities and ritual in public places; (3) surveying the Grasshopper region; and (4) converting laboratory recording to a computer-based, data-management system. The first three projects resulted in dissertations (Ciolek-Torrello 1978; Sullivan 1980; Whittlesey 1978) and the last in disaster.

Ciolek-Torrello supervised the study of domestic activities within early rooms. To reconstruct late domestic activities, previous work had concentrated on late-abandoned habitation and storage rooms. By providing information for the reconstruction of early domestic activities, the 1974 work sought to develop a framework for comparing changes in household organization through time. An earlier analysis (Ciolek-Torrello and Reid 1974) had indicated that household size decreased with the growth of the community and development of community integrative mechanisms, and it was possible that other changes took place. More information on early domestic activities within rooms was needed.

The core construction unit of Room Block 3 (Rooms 246, 269, 270, 278, 279) was the smallest and best defined of the core units in the main pueblo, and Room 270 had already been excavated as part of the 1971 growth project. We selected three rooms (246, 269, 279) from

The 1974 Season

Research and Teaching Staff	Support Staff	Apache Crew	Students
William Longacre, Director	Ruth Scoggin, Cook	Gilbert Gooday	Therese Adams
Jefferson Reid, Associate Director	Joyce Kuntz, Assistant Cook	Ramirez Patterson	Steven Ahler
Stephanie Whittlesey, Senior Dig Foreman	John Agosta, Camp Aide	Alvin Quay	Patricia Beirne
James Spain, Dig Foreman	Michael Wendorf, Camp Aide	Glendale Tessay	Steven Brandt
Alan Sullivan, Dig Foreman			Gordon Bronitsky
Richard Ciolek-Torrello, Archaeological Assistant			Thomas Cinadr
Linda Mayro, Laboratory Supervisor			Pamela Easter
T.J. Ferguson, Laboratory Assistant			Laura Gerwitz
James McDonald, Laboratory Assistant			Michael Graves
			David Groenfeldt
			Julie Hewlett
			Kenneth Jones
			Bonnie Kranzer
			Gadi Mgomezulu
			Thomas Pilgrim
			Cherie Scheick
			Brian Sheehan
			Ann Smith
			Julie Stein
			Julie Wizorek

the core unit, along with Room 280, which was a later addition to it. This project would be completed during the 1975 season and form a major component of Ciolek-Torrello's (1978) dissertation, as well as his subsequent work on the Grasshopper household and the use of space for domestic activities (Ciolek-Torrello 1984, 1985, 1986, 1989; Reid and Whittlesey 1982). Room 246 proved to be a large, unusual storage-and-manufacturing room with numerous bird burials and evidence for manufacture of large bifaces. Early domestic activities were more difficult to define, because the room floors had been severely altered by changes in room function and the recycling of tools and facilities. This problem would not be solved until 1976, when we decided to look elsewhere for evidence of early activities and began excavations at Chodistaas Pueblo.

Rooms 279 and 280, adjacent to Plaza 2, fitted neatly into Whittlesey's research to investigate community activities in public spaces, which was the second research objective of the season. Whittlesey reasoned that information on plaza activities was heavily biased toward Plaza 3, which was unique in having been converted into the Great Kiva. In addition, mortuary analyses (Clark 1967, 1969; Griffin 1967) had shown that Plaza 3 interments were accompanied by more artifacts than those in any other area. If we were to understand the use of public space

East and West Villages of Grasshopper Pueblo, showing excavated one- and two-story rooms.

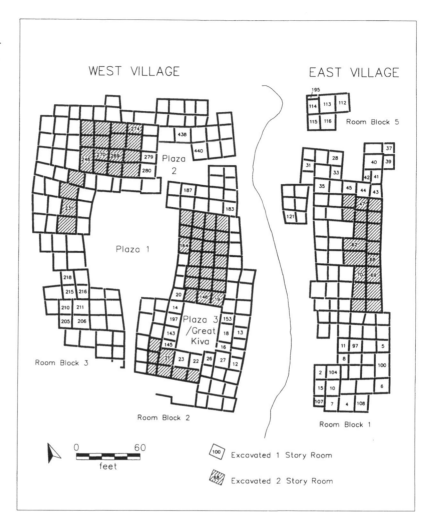

and begin to distinguish household activities from community activities, then Plazas 1 and 2 would have to be investigated.

Whittlesey directed test excavations in Plaza 2 and would continue the following year by investigating Plaza 1. About 50 percent of Plaza 2 was sampled by 2 × 2 m squares, and three previously unrecorded rooms (438, 439, 440) were discovered along the northern edge of the plaza. Stratigraphy revealed the presence of three main plaza surfaces, layers of trash and silt, and considerable mixing of deposits. It might be more than just coincidental that Julie Stein, who would become an authority on geoarchaeology and archaeological sediments, was a student that summer. A number of interments were discovered in Plaza 2, which indicated the multifunctional nature of outdoor areas at Grasshopper

Pueblo. Differences in mortuary treatment among the burials found in the three plazas began to emerge during this project.

The third project was the beginning of a long-term survey of the Grasshopper region. Nick Spain was slated to supervise an Apache crew in this effort, but the project was delayed by extreme fire danger that mandated closing the west end of the reservation. The project finally got off the ground during the last two weeks, when the beginning of monsoon rains opened the reservation to travel. Surveyors identified sites and features within a Grasshopper catchment area initially defined as a two-mile radius that in later years was extended to three miles.

The fourth project was the conversion of recording procedures to the SELGEM computer format that had been pretested on a sample of rooms in 1973. At this writing, a quarter century later, we still cringe when we read again the naive optimism and blind faith placed in main-frame computer technology of the mid-1970s. It infuriates us to recall the amount of time the staff spent in developing the computer-based recording system and the manuals that had to accompany its implementation in the field—all for a system that eventually proved to be unworkable. The staff would continue to use and tinker with the system until Reid took over as director in 1979.

As if to mark ceremonially the end of processual archaeology, Reid and other staff helped to decommission the Vernon field camp. Equipment was distributed among the Snowflake and Grasshopper camps. We received gas incinerators that proved hopelessly inadequate and several excellent tetrapod screens.

The 1975 Season

The Field School ran for eight weeks, from June 6 to August 1, with an enrollment of twenty-two students. The ten men and twelve women represented twenty graduate and two undergraduate students. Support was received through a research grant from the NSF to Longacre and Thompson (SO72-05334-DO3). Again, this grant supported staff and the Apache crew, the student research participants, the use of a backhoe, and environmental research.

Research projects continued many of the objectives of the 1974 season, including investigation of community activity areas and survey of the Grasshopper region. Excavations focused on outdoor areas; remarkably, not a single new room was opened. Reid and Ciolek-Torrello super-

The 1975 Season

Research and Teaching Staff	Support Staff	Apache Crew	Students
William Longacre, Director	Ruth Scoggin, Cook	Gilbert Gooday	Hamilton Ahlo
Jefferson Reid, Associate Director	Joyce Kuntz, Assistant Cook	John Mason	Eric Arnould
Sally Holbrook, Research Ecologist (volunteer)	Steve Bilbo, Camp Aide	Ramirez Patterson	Frank Bayham
Stephanie Whittlesey, Senior Dig Foreman	Steve Kozak, Camp Aide	Alvin Quay	Catherine Brandon
Richard Ciolek-Torrello, Dig Foreman		Aaron Tessay	Evelyn Caballero
Alan Sullivan, Dig Foreman		Glendale Tessay	Cheryl Claassen
Michael Graves, Archaeological Assistant			Haree Deutchman
Timothy O'Meara, Archaeological Assistant			Stanley d'Entremont
T.J. Ferguson, Laboratory Supervisor			Michael DiBlasi
Constance Silver, Laboratory Assistant			William Fash
Michael Wendorf, Laboratory Assistant			Ingrid Herbich
William Reynolds, Grasshopper Fellow (volunteer)			Terry Klein
			Diane McLaughlin
			Vikuosa Nienu
			John Olsen
			Sue Powell
			Doug Rautenkranz
			John Robertson
			Patricia Crown Robertson
			Elizabeth Skinner
			Sandra Sobelman
			Rebecca Storey

vised subflooring operations in Rooms 438 and 440 in Plaza 2 and Rooms 246, 269, 279, and 280 in Room Block 3.

Contrasts between Plaza 2 and Plaza 3 discovered during the previous season dictated that we test Plaza 1, the largest at Grasshopper. Whittlesey supervised excavations of sixteen test units, mostly 2 × 2 m squares, and the reopening of two backhoe trenches dug in previous years. These excavations revealed extremely complicated stratigraphy, the product of frequent and varied activities and the natural slope of the prehistoric surface from northwest to southeast—the inexorable play of cultural and natural formation processes. Experimental studies into the role of natural and human agents in the formation of plaza sediments were undertaken (Whittlesey, Arnould, and Reynolds 1982). The plaza explorations led to Whittlesey's interest in explaining variability in mortuary ritual and ultimately to the methodological study that would become her dissertation (Whittlesey 1978).

The survey was supervised by a healed, crutchless Sullivan and assisted by Michael Graves, and it was oriented to the investigation of methodological questions related to Sullivan's dissertation (Sullivan 1980). Sullivan began working on the Pinnacle Flats locality, which we labeled rather pejoratively as "Pitiful Flats." The flats locale was situated midway between Grasshopper and Cibecue. Sullivan's summary of this work in the 1975 report for the Bureau of Indian Affairs provides one of the best accounts of the changes in language and thought that accompanied the beginnings of behavioral archaeology at Grasshopper.

> Although some of the work of the past summer [1975] was exploratory, the survey effort was directed toward the solution of several problems of archaeological methodology. The survey area was selected on the basis of data requirements specified by these research problems.
>
> One archaeological problem was generated from work done by archaeologists in the vicinity of nearby Snowflake, Arizona [epicenter of processual archaeology in the Southwest]. At this location, inquiries about the nature of prehistoric carrying capacity by Ezra B. W. Zubrow and of culture change by Fred Plog were based on the assumption of systemic equivalence between sites. This assumption implies that the behaviors or sets of behaviors inferred to be responsible for the deposition of a class of remains, a lithic scatter for example, could be extended to all other representatives of that class of remains. For analytic purposes, then, these workers conclude that the systemic context of lithic scatters are the same. This assumption, however, obscures much behavioral variability that is potentially retrievable from archaeological deposits.
>
> It seems difficult to assume that sites observed to be similar in the present represent material transformations of similar ranges of activities performed in the past. The main reason for conducting a survey in the [Pinnacle Flats] area described above, then was to gather data necessary to demonstrate the inadequacy of the equivalence assumption. This phase of the research had to be accomplished before testing behaviorally significant hypotheses.

While Sullivan was surveying, Sally Holbrook, a paleoecologist, was studying modern rodent distributions in the vicinity of Grasshopper as a guide to reconstructing botanical characteristics of the paleoenvironment. The first season of a three-year project supported by an NSF research grant was spent trapping rodents and recording their habitats within a five-mile radius of Grasshopper. This study, presented in Holbrook (1982a, 1982b) and Holbrook and Graves (1982), constituted the last project at Grasshopper oriented specifically to paleoenvironmental reconstruction as a principal research goal.

At some point during the season, Longacre became "Uncle Willy." Another memorable event, and in many respects the most frightening, was Bill Fash's twenty-first birthday party. Further exposition must await the Grasshopper social history.

The 1976 Season

The Field School was in session for eight weeks, from June 11 to August 6, with twenty students. Ten men and ten women, who represented fifteen graduate and five undergraduate students, were enrolled. Support was provided by the remnants of the last NSF grant (SOC72-05334-DO3) awarded to Longacre and Thompson and the patchwork of local accounts and student fees that would take the Field School through the next seventeen years.

Longacre spent the year in the Philippines, leaving Reid as director once again. Field projects continued some graduate student research, but principally filled in descriptive gaps in our knowledge of Grasshopper Pueblo and accomplished a few tasks that had long interested Reid, such as an architectural analysis of Red Rock House and Canyon Creek cliff dwellings and finally beginning the excavation of Chodistaas Pueblo.

In June, Sullivan completed the fieldwork for his dissertation study at Pinnacle Flats. A crew led by Whittlesey defined and mapped the extent of trash on the surface of Grasshopper and tested the low trash mounds south of the main ruin. Graves began his surface collections of sites dated to the preceramic and pit-house periods. The catchment survey around Grasshopper continued under the supervision of T. J. Ferguson. Holbrook continued her NSF-supported reconstruction of the paleoenvironment from rodent-species distributions.

William Reynolds had become interested in the cliff dwellings of the region during the previous year. With his crew of three, Reynolds hiked daily into Red Rock House and later to Canyon Creek Pueblo. The crew cored construction timbers not sampled by Haury and gathered architectural information that would form the basis of Reynolds's (1981) dissertation research.

Patricia Crown Robertson, who had excavated plaza sections while a student in 1975, supervised excavation of three rooms (395, 397, 411) in the outlying room block on the hill between the women's dorm and privy. This work was designed to extend the sample of rooms from outliers and provide excavation experience preparatory to digging at Chodistaas Pueblo, which was projected as her dissertation venue (Crown 1981).

Chodistaas had long been slated for investigation (see Longacre and Reid 1974:26), but we were unable to begin excavation there until 1976. Although there may have been discussion among the staff (see Crown 1981) as to which early pueblo to excavate—Chodistaas or Grasshopper

The 1976 Season

Research and Teaching Staff	Support Staff	Apache Crew	Students
Jefferson Reid, Acting Director	Illa Mai McFarlin, Cook	John Mason	Lacy Atkinson
Sally Holbrook, Research Ecologist (volunteer)	Mary Bayham, Assistant Cook	Alvin Quay	Karen Barnette
Stephanie Whittlesey,	David Emory, Camp Aide	Aaron Tessay	Christine Eckels
Assistant Director	John Wysham, Camp Aide	Glendale Tessay	Tirzo Gonzalez
T.J. Ferguson, Senior Dig Foreman			Claire Gordon
Alan Sullivan, Senior Dig Foreman			Douglas Hanson
Michael Graves, Dig Foreman			John Hildebrand
William Reynolds, Dig Foreman			Yusef Juwayeyi
Timothy O'Meara,			Kathryn Kamp
Archaeological Assistant			Amy Marcum
Patricia Crown Robertson,			Joan Mathien
Laboratory Supervisor,			Michael McCarthy
Apache Foreman			Samuel Mild
Michele Aubrey, Grasshopper			Barbara Mills
Fellow (volunteer)			Patty Neuhaus
			Michael Pool
			Glenn Russell
			Susan Spencer
			Christopher Stevenson
			Meredith Weber

Spring—there was never doubt in Reid's mind. There had been no doubt since the winter of 1972, when students in the UA southwestern archaeology class taught by Longacre and assisted by Reid went to Chodistaas for a field trip and class-research project. The same winter, Thompson and Reid put together the NSF grant that targeted Chodistaas, at that time misidentified as the Hilltop site, for exploratory excavation in 1973.

The work at Chodistaas was designed primarily to illuminate household activities, particularly those at the early stage of occupation. Field School research had relentlessly pursued households—identifying them, defining variation among them, and seeking changes through time in household organization. Although sought first in architectural units (see Wilcox 1975, 1982), the household subsequently had been perceived better in fixed features, such as hearths (Ciolek-Torrello and Reid 1974), and in floor artifacts (Ciolek-Torrello 1978). With the completion of Reid's (1973) dissertation and the Ciolek-Torrello and Reid (1974) study, it was apparent that artifact-rich room floors at Grasshopper Pueblo represented households and activities at the end of the occupation. Ciolek-Torrello's work in the core rooms of Room Block 3, targeted to illustrate the early household, confirmed that early households and their activities at Grasshopper Pueblo only could be reconstructed from sherds and fragments, not a fully satisfying data set for comparison with the whole pots and numerous tools found on late-occupied room floors (see Reid, Schiffer, and Neff 1975). We knew that we could approximate the early Grasshopper household most easily from nearby settlements occupied immediately prior to Grasshopper. This was the principal reason for going to Chodistaas Pueblo.

The other avenue of research that directed the shift from Grasshopper Pueblo to Chodistaas was the expanding investigation of regional growth and settlement, including stepped-up site surveys and the reexamination of Red Rock House and Canyon Creek cliff dwellings.

Sullivan and the Apache crew brushed the site, and on July 4, the entire camp blazed a road into Chodistaas Pueblo. Tim O'Meara and Reid drew the first contour and pueblo-outline map, estimating that there were approximately forty rooms, only to discover after beginning to excavate Rooms 1, 2, 3, and 4 that the rooms were twice as large as those at Grasshopper. Excavation ceased on Rooms 1 and 4. Rooms 2 and 3 were excavated to floor to reveal a rich ceramic inventory of whole and reconstructible vessels apparently frozen in time by a catastrophic fire, precisely the archaeological context we were hoping to find.

At that time, Ciolek-Torrello was defining functional room types, their distribution throughout the pueblo, and change through time as a background for a sophisticated, computer-assisted household investigation. His dissertation research was related closely to the emphasis on early households at Chodistaas. Whittlesey, by contrast, had come to focus on archaeological approaches to the reconstruction of social organization and life histories of individuals as revealed in mortuary practices. Often misrepresented as a study of Grasshopper social organization, Whittlesey's dissertation was a methodological examination of models used by archaeologists to infer features of structure and organization. She sought to account for the contradictory interpretations of Clark (1967) and Griffin (1969). The dissertation illustrates well the behavioral archaeologist's concern with concepts and procedures for reconstructing past social organization.

Our flop of the summer was an experiment in teaching. At the end of the 1975 season, there had been rumblings among the students concerning the amount of time devoted to teaching basic field and laboratory techniques, Southwest prehistory, and Grasshopper research. Because no major, deep-room excavation projects were planned, the 1976 summer would be ideal for decreasing field time and increasing teaching. We rearranged the weekly schedule to devote all of Tuesday and Thursday mornings to seminars and workshops and Tuesday and Thursday afternoons to laboratory processing. We would go into the field full days only on Mondays, Wednesdays, and Fridays and half days on Saturdays.

We thought students would be overjoyed at this reallocation of vital resources to teaching. They hated it, and after three weeks we returned to the old system of being in the field five and one-half days a week.

The 1977 Season

The Field School was in session for eight weeks, from June 10 to August 5. Twenty students—eleven men and nine women, representing sixteen graduates and four undergraduates—were enrolled. Although, according to the annual report for 1977, there was money left in the final NSF research grant (SOC72-05334-DO3), it could not have amounted to much.

Although Longacre was back as director, most of the design and supervision of the field program was in the hands of Graves, who had been a staff member each summer after his student year in 1974. In 1977, he served as assistant director. Reid and Whittlesey had departed to direct the Cholla Project for the ASM. As when any new administration takes over, there was a radical shift in the teaching and research program. New recording forms were implemented, and following the failed experimental program of 1976, teaching continued in the traditional format. Behavioral archaeology's stress on formation processes and middle-range theory, which had been increasingly placed in the forefront in 1974 through 1976, also was deemphasized.

None of the fieldwork begun during the 1977 and following 1978 seasons developed into dissertation projects, in part because of the change in staff and a lack of direction. Longacre's research interests had clearly shifted, and by that time, Graves also had altered his dissertation research to focus on Kalinga ethnoarchaeology. Although it may be hindsight, we can see the importance of graduate students pursuing dissertation research on Grasshopper in imbuing the Field School with energy and enthusiasm and encouraging student interest and excitement in Grasshopper's past.

Grasshopper alumnus David Tuggle, at that time on the anthropology faculty at the University of Hawaii, was a visiting professor for the summer continuing the regional site survey. With his wife, Myra, and the occasional student or two, he initiated a survey of the lower Salt River Draw and mapped a number of isolated, large pueblos that otherwise would have gone unrecorded. Graves, who was assisted by Madeleine Hinkes and James Dodge, continued the catchment survey—the intensive survey to record all sites within a two-mile radius of Grasshopper—

The 1977 Season

Research and Teaching Staff	Support Staff	Apache Crew	Students
William Longacre, Director	Ruth Scoggin, Cook	Arnold Beach	Jerry Barnett
Sally Holbrook, Research Ecologist (independent)	Leslie Finnerty, Assistant Cook	Jonah Beach	Cynthia Bates
David Tuggle, Research Archaeologist (volunteer)	Charles Brown, Camp Aide	Labert Beach	Roderick Brown
Michael Graves, Assistant Director	Kurt Dongoske, Camp Aide	Timothy Nachu	Brian Byrd
Patricia Crown Robertson, Dig Foreman		Aaron Tessay	Suzi D'Auria
Michael Wendorf, Dig Foreman		Glendale Tessay	Susan Dobyns
Madeleine Hinkes, Archaeological Assistant			Daniel Farslow
Anna Urizar, Photographer			Michael Faught
James Dodge, Grasshopper Fellow (volunteer)			Sonia Guillen
			Hiram Henry
			Janine Hesch
			Dorothy Hosler
			Kathleen Martin
			Timothy Maxwell
			Craig Montgomery
			Khoach Ba Nguyen
			Ann Roth
			Mark Stromdahl
			Alison Wylie
			Fernando Zialcita

begun in 1974. Graves also conducted controlled experiments in surface collecting on six sites to solve general problems of site disturbance and to estimate site potential for management and research purposes.

Excavation at Grasshopper focused on early-constructed rooms in Room Block 1, a room block and construction phases poorly represented by previously excavated rooms. Two core rooms (68 and 69) and the later-constructed Room 70 were excavated under the supervision of Michael Wendorf. At Chodistaas, Crown Robertson continued her dissertation research by excavating four rooms (5, 8, 9, and the extension of Room 2) and testing outdoor activity areas, including the enclosed plaza. Holbrook continued her study of the rodent community in the vicinity of Grasshopper begun in the 1975 season.

The 1978 Season

The Field School was in session for eight weeks, from June 9 to August 4, with nineteen students. Twelve men and seven women, representing eight graduates and eleven undergraduates, were enrolled. Grasshopper received a small grant for site survey from the Arizona State Historic Preservation Office (SHPO) through Arizona State Parks.

This was to be Longacre's last year as director and Graves's final stint

The 1978 Season

Research and Teaching Staff	Support Staff	Apache Crew	Students
William Longacre, Director	Milton Rogers, Cook	Alvin Quay	Alexander Adelman
Sally Holbrook, Research Ecologist (independent)	Susan Granger, Assistant Cook	Roy Quay	Mark Calamia
	Paul Harris, Camp Aide	Aaron Tessay	Ronald Douglas
Michael Graves, Assistant Director	Bruce Porterfield, Camp Aide		Kimberly Fenner
Brian Byrd, Dig Foreman			Polly Haessig
Madeleine Hinkes, Dig Foreman			Thomas Hogue
Patricia Crown Robertson, Dig Foreman			Laura Kersten
			Anthony Lane
Mark Baumler, Survey Foreman			Peter Locavara
Michael Faught, Archaeological Assistant			Robert MacBride
			Robert Markens
Rebecca McSwain, Archaeological Assistant			Mary Mundahl
			Daniel Nelson
Clara Gualtieri, Archaeological Assistant			Marilyn Samore
			Kenneth Sassaman
John Whittaker, Photographer			Chester Shaw
			Karen Spradling
			Karen Swanekamp
			Michael Woods

as assistant director. Four rooms (1, 11, 16, and 15) were excavated at Chodistaas Pueblo, completing the ceramic data that Crown Robertson would use for her dissertation analysis (Crown 1981). She would return for one month in 1979 to finish excavating below the floor level in these four rooms. At the close of the field season, excavation of Chodistaas, except for subflooring several rooms, was judged to be complete.

Michael Faught began excavations at Grasshopper Spring Pueblo. Room 1 would be completed in 1980, and we would return frequently thereafter to excavate additional rooms. In addition, a rock ring identified as an Apache wickiup circle (see Reid 1998b) was excavated. Brian Byrd conducted excavations at a pit-house site (AZ P:14:176 [ASM]) in the woods below Chodistaas Pueblo. Hinkes initiated a salvage research program to collect human skeletal remains exposed by pot hunters at sites in the Grasshopper region, such as Spotted Mountain Ruin. Mark Baumler completed the two-mile-radius survey surrounding the main ruin and began a second survey project.

These projects contributed to the inventory of sites, and the material culture accumulated during surface collections and excavations constitute research collections for future comparative studies on earlier occupation in the Grasshopper region. In 1979, the salvaging of vandalized human remains Hinkes had begun as a dissertation project on the regional population would be redefined as a reburial project, and she would go on to write her dissertation on the subadult population of Grasshopper Pueblo (Hinkes 1983).

The Cholla Project and Grasshopper Research

The final two years of the transitional period at the Field School coincided with Reid's and Whittlesey's first venture into cultural resource management (CRM), or contract archaeology, at that time in its infancy. It was a turbulent time in Arizona archaeology. The legislation mandating CRM work had only recently been enacted, and archaeologists and federal land managers were beginning to work out the bugs in the bureaucratic compliance system that would eventually come to dominate field archaeology in the American Southwest. At the same time, Phoenix and Tucson began to grow by leaps and bounds, necessitating building new infrastructure. Importantly, the Central Arizona Project (CAP) was initiated. It was to prove the largest long-term archaeological project in Arizona history and one of the largest in the nation (Whittlesey 2003). Arizona universities, museums, and the private sector began to jockey for position in obtaining pieces of the well-funded research pie. These factors collided to create a fragile, vulnerable, and overworked young CRM archaeology.

The Cholla Project took place within this context. In early 1977, Lynn Teague, a longtime friend and head of the Cultural Resource Management Division (CRMD) of the ASM, asked Reid to direct the Arizona Public Service (APS) Cholla-Saguaro Transmission Line Mitigation Project. The APS Cholla-Saguaro transmission line stretched from the Little Colorado River across the Mogollon Rim to the Sonoran Desert northwest of Tucson. The project was initiated to mitigate impacts to sites along a 135-mile section of the corridor.

The survey phase of the project, which had been directed for the ASM by Linda Mayro, a former Grasshopper student and staff member, had come under considerable criticism from Dee Green and Fred Plog. Green, then a supervisory archaeologist with the National Forest Service, Southwestern Region (NFS), was overseeing the project. Plog was at that time on the faculty at Arizona State University (ASU), and the long-term rivalry between ASU and the UA was beginning to take on a less friendly tone as Plog battled to strengthen ASU archaeology and build a CRM program. Because of the criticism and continued close scrutiny of the Cholla survey, the ASM was required to hire an archaeologist with a Ph.D. to run the mitigation project, and there were none on staff in the CRMD. Of the available archaeologists with a doctorate, Reid was probably the nearest, perhaps the cheapest, and certainly the most familiar with the project area. In this way, Reid became project director of the Cholla Project, a position equivalent to that of a principal investigator in most modern contract situations. The Cholla Project ran for six years (1977–1983) and had an enormous impact on Grasshopper research.

The research attraction and academic promise of the Cholla Project was the mountain portion of the transmission line that skirted the western edge of the Grasshopper region (see map). The project area crossed the three major environmental zones of Arizona, representing a unique transect from the Colorado Plateau (Chevelon Region), through the mountain transition zone (Q Ranch Region), and well into a good-sized chunk of Lower Sonoran Desert region on both sides of Theodore Roosevelt Lake (Tonto-Roosevelt Region). The 248 sites along this corridor presented an excellent opportunity to carry out the macroregional exploration necessary to understand population movement in the mountains and its relationship to developments on the adjacent Grasshopper Plateau.

Furthermore, the project seemed well funded at more than six hundred thousand dollars, a veritable fortune to any field-school director just barely managing a program with salary savings, year-end leftovers, and student fees. It would be possible to hire an experienced crew and not worry about a time-consuming and labor-intensive training component. It would be archaeology in its purest form, the kind that Haury had carried out during his celebrated return to Snaketown in 1964–1965.

With Whittlesey and Ciolek-Torrello, each busily working on a dissertation, Reid hurried during spring break to produce a research proposal for the Cholla Project. It was quickly approved, far more quickly than any of us had expected, given recent relations between the ASM and the NFS, and along with approval came immediate pressure to put a large crew into the field well ahead of the construction schedule. Undaunted by these pressures and ignorant of the field conditions that would confront us—we had visited only a few of the sites, mostly lithic scatters in the Theodore Roosevelt Lake area—we set about planning for a six-year project.

In the midst of feverish planning for the Cholla Project, we learned that our NSF grant proposal had been awarded against all odds and expectations. Our initial excitement was tempered with the realization that overlapping personnel and obligations on both projects could potentially create difficulties, particularly because Whittlesey and Ciolek-

Torrello had not yet completed their dissertations, which were integral to the NSF project. We anticipated no coordination problems, however, because Ciolek-Torrello and Whittlesey were critical personnel in the NSF and Cholla projects. We were young, we were smart, and we could do both. Reid fully expected their dissertations would be completed during the first year of the Cholla Project, when most of the activity would take place in the field, and, indeed, both were finished in the spring of 1978. Looking back, our naiveté and boundless optimism seem unbelievable.

Crews were put into the field under the supervision of field directors. Reid, Ciolek-Torrello, and Whittlesey remained in Tucson, administering the project and burdened with its voluminous paperwork — budgets, monthly administrative reports, preliminary field reports, National Register of Historic Places nomination forms, and more — and completing dissertation research. The extraordinary allure of the Cholla Project faded when we were in the field. Some of the problems we endured with this project — unusual logistical challenges, primitive living conditions at the field camps, torrid weather, imploding water tanks — were unavoidable products of conducting archaeology in the Arizona desert in the summer. Others, including personnel difficulties and monumental volumes of paperwork, stemmed from the unformed nature of the infant CRM, which was still struggling to develop workable procedures for implementation. It should be noted that Cholla was one of the largest projects of the early CRM years and certainly the first big data-recovery effort the ASM had undertaken.

The Cholla Project was completed on time and under the $635,000 budget, which should have given it exalted status in the annals of ASM contract projects. The project ran from March 1977 through March 1983, its allotted six years, with one additional month to ensure that all invoices cleared accounting. Reid made a partial escape from tenure-irrelevant departmental duties by remaining in the department half-time as undergraduate adviser and devoting the other half to the ASM as project director. Reid's funded position as project director for the ASM lasted for only three of the project's six years. This is to point out that, for the last three years of the project, Reid received absolutely no monetary compensation for supervision and editing of the five volumes of the final report (Reid 1982). Whittlesey also contributed uncompensated time to the report writing. Oddly, the standard burden of academic research — completing analyses and writing monographs on one's own time — had infected the CRM world.

Not unlike childbirth, the horrors were soon forgotten. When the worst of the fieldwork was over, the important connections between the Cholla Project and Grasshopper came into focus once more, and we were able to build upon three positive aspects. First, the research questions of both projects were similar, emphasizing population movement, settlement behavior, and environmental adjustments. The specific questions we were investigating at that time have only recently returned to occupy archaeological attention. When other southwestern archaeologists diligently pursued managed mercantilism and the scant traces of social complexity, we were expanding our long-term Grasshopper interests in population movement, aggregation, abandonment, macroregional behavior, ethnic identity, and ethnic coresidence.

Cholla provided an unparalleled venue for answering these questions. It encompassed a stretch of central Arizona commensurate with the potential range of the prehistoric inhabitants, rather than the little valleys investigated by most archaeological projects of the day. We compiled an extraordinary database of 172,000 sherds and 94,000 lithic artifacts collected from 248 sites (Reid 1982). Cholla provided the hard evidence for the broad-ranging movement of prehistoric peoples over a vast landscape that we had suspected but only glimpsed at Grasshopper.

Second, the methodological issues of a nascent behavioral archaeology were similar. With Cholla, we were concerned first with estimating settlement occupation parameters, such as residential stability, to categorize sites accurately into more meaningful groups than the standard dichotomy of habitation and limited-activity sites (Reid 1982; Whittlesey and Reid 1982b). In addition, we were interested in adjusting ceramic classifications to specific research needs, such as chronology building and measuring directionality in regional interactions and shifts through time (Reid 1982; Tuggle, Kintigh, and Reid 1982). We also sought to test the degree to which lithic analysis could inform on interesting past behaviors of village farmers (Graybill and Reid 1982; Reid and Graybill 1982; Whittlesey 1982). As always, additional questions cropped up as we proceeded.

The third and most critical positive connection between the Cholla Project and Grasshopper research was in expanding regional survey to map past behavior on a macroregional scale with high-quality data in which we had confidence, because we had collected it ourselves. Much of this survey expansion involved Tuggle, who had conducted the first systematic survey in the Grasshopper region in 1969 for his dissertation (Tuggle 1970). He returned in 1977 to survey on the Grasshopper Plateau, and in 1978 he supervised the Q Ranch survey for the Cholla Project. Tuggle joined the Grasshopper staff for the 1979 and 1980 seasons to direct a stepped-up survey effort and to oversee much of the fieldwork carried out as part of management and planning grants funded by the Arizona SHPO.

It was heartening to discover that the historical, behavioral, and methodological concerns of behavioral archaeology could be implemented as readily and have as positive results in a CRM context as in the traditionally academic field-school situation. Its broad usefulness as a programmatic research tool was demonstrated well during Cholla. Moreover, we are pleased to think that the often-cited split between academic archaeology and contract archaeology was, even at that early time, more mythic than real. From 1979, when Reid took over Grasshopper, until the end of the Cholla Project, the research was integrated into the Grasshopper work through a free exchange of questions, procedures, and personnel.

7

Behavioral Archaeology, 1979–1992

The validity of the initiative, or of the philosophical/methodological positions adopted, will not be judged by *a priori* epistemological arguments, but by what can be discovered, constructed, reconstructed or otherwise informatively asserted about the past.
—**Colin Renfrew** (1994:5)

The 1979 season began fourteen years of teaching and research at the Field School under Jefferson Reid's direction. It was a time of unparalleled optimism that sprang from three directions—the research potential of the ongoing Cholla Project, a National Science Foundation grant to synthesize Grasshopper research, and Reid's tenure-track position at what was the largest, and also widely perceived as the best, anthropology department in the Southwest.

It was also a time of unprecedented change in virtually all aspects of the research and teaching programs at Grasshopper—personnel, funding, staff organization, research projects, conceptual framework, relationships with the Cibecue Apache, and teaching methods. The camp and physical plant also altered radically, as years of weather and deterioration took a toll on buildings not designed to last for thirty years. The camp slowly deteriorated throughout the 1980s in accord with the immutable laws of nature and culture, forming in time an archaeological record of its own. This necessitated changes in the allocation of staff research and teaching time. The ongoing Cholla Project, which lasted until 1983, and the Grasshopper–Chavez Pass debate that was initiated

133

in 1982 impacted further the direction and conduct of Grasshopper research.

The end of this era witnessed the permanent closing of the Grasshopper Field School and the shifting of the University of Arizona Archaeological Field School to another director and another location.

We must place the research program of the behavioral archaeology years in the context of normal science, and, as with all science, evaluate it in terms of the constraints of budget, personnel, and equipment. As in the chronicle of the preceding sixteen years, the matrix of people and decisions surrounding the research was critical to its history, and we begin with this framework.

Background to Behavioral Archaeology at Grasshopper

What began in 1979 as a massive reconfiguration of the research program turned quickly into a restructuring of the teaching agenda with a stronger emphasis than ever before on providing basic training in fieldwork. This shift was necessitated by changing student attendance and elimination of student financial support. Fewer students attended the Field School, and more of them were undergraduates and inexperienced students. Their lack of training mandated an increase in instruction, and the reduced numbers of students made enhanced teaching possible with a compact, highly trained staff. Whereas during the 1960s and early 1970s, students were fully subsidized, including travel to the Field School, by 1979, they were required to pay all of their expenses. This fact may account in part for their demands for instruction. These problems and areas of concern were inextricably woven into Grasshopper research of the 1980s. Camp maintenance was related closely to such budgetary and personnel issues. In addition, our relationships with the Cibecue Apache and the conceptual framework for research had changed radically from the processual-archaeology and transitional years.

Teaching and Research Personnel

The initial task facing us was that of personnel recruitment. New graduate students were needed to take pieces of a database that had become enormous. It was apparent that the bulk of the research would have to be done by graduate students as part of their dissertation work. The master's thesis in anthropology at the UA had been eliminated to speed students through the program and was not reinstated until the waning days of the Field School. The downside of eliminating the thesis was to remove the small, master's-level project from the research agenda and to rely exclusively on large, dissertation-level projects. Unlike Point of Pines, we lost the opportunity to employ master's-level students regularly in the program and to benefit from the master's project in examining the kinds of small-scale questions that often combine to answer big questions. A rough gauge of lost research productivity is that a twenty-three-year drought separated Michael Mauer's (1970) thesis from that of Leon Lorentzen (1993). The potential extent of this loss is illustrated by the insightful thesis work of Charles Riggs (1994) that developed into his dissertation (Riggs 1999a) and by Scott Van Keuren's (1994) thesis, which was later published (Van Keuren 1999) and further developed into his dissertation (Van Keuren 2001).

Our practice of recruiting fresh graduate students who could remain in the graduate program and complete a dissertation on a Grasshopper topic was fraught with risk and uncertainty. Its only real advantage was that it was cheap. One tactic for enhancing research and spreading risk was to make Grasshopper data available for dissertation research to students enrolled in other doctoral programs. Dissertations based exclusively on Grasshopper data were completed by Joseph Ezzo (1991), University of Wisconsin–Madison; John Olsen (1980), University of California–Berkeley; William Reynolds (1981), Arizona State University; Daniela Triadan (1994), Freie Universität–Berlin; and Nieves Zedeño (1991), Southern Methodist University (SMU). Doctoral research that incorporated Grasshopper information into a larger analysis included studies by Ronna Bradley (1996), ASU; David Berry (1983), University of California–Los Angeles; and Masashi Kobayashi (1996), UA. Despite the risk, Grasshopper had produced no fewer than twenty-four doctoral dissertations by 2003.

A personnel strategy that developed later was to rely on postdoctoral research interests of ex-staffers such as Ezzo, Triadan, Zedeño, Julie Lowell, Barbara Montgomery, and David Tuggle. Without the efforts of these and the many other graduate-student staff members who were overworked, underpaid, and insufficiently acknowledged, the research and teaching programs of the Field School would not have been possible, much less successful.

The Teaching and Research Budget

The second problem to affect the Field School was money. In 1979, Grasshopper was broke. Years before, the NSF had departed as funding agent for staff, student support, and food. The Field School did not exist as a line item in any budget anywhere. There was some hope when Reid took over as director that Raymond Thompson and William Longacre would be able to secure funding in the Department of Anthropology through established university channels, but the combination of a new university administration unsympathetic to the social sciences and a period of legislative-induced budget cutting doomed those hopes.

Moreover, local support was waning. The Arizona State Museum experienced annual budget reductions of 10 to 12 percent during the mid-1980s. To protect its staff, the ASM gave up most of the capital, wages, operating, and travel funds—the sources from which the ASM's longstanding contribution to the Field School came. ASM support for Grasshopper ended in 1986. The budget was left in the hands of William Stini, a biological anthropologist with enthusiasm sufficient to maintain the Field School at a bare subsistence level. The budget situation did not improve when Longacre became department head in 1989.

From 1979 until the mid-1980s, our annual funding tactic was to submit a legislative decision-package proposal to the college dean, who would batch it with others for forwarding to higher levels of administration, where the proposals were sorted, prioritized, and shipped off to the next level of budget gods and goddesses. We never received a dime through this mechanism, and by the time we finally quit submitting requests, the Grasshopper package had been downgraded to second rank by the Department of Anthropology. A fund-raising campaign in 1984 collected the total sum of one hundred dollars. Our prospects looked bleak, indeed.

In 1985, an alumni letter-writing campaign had positive results in inducing the provost, Nils Hasselmo, to become our patron. Although Provost Hasselmo began to provide the bulk of the budget, this support ceased not long after he left to become president of the University of Minnesota. We have heard a partially apocryphal story of budgeteers in higher administration wondering, after Hasselmo's departure, why they should support insect research on grasshoppers by the Department of Anthropology.

Except for two years of grant funding for survey from the Arizona State Historic Preservation Office, the budget was cobbled together from various sources. Two attempts to bring the NSF back into narrowly defined portions of Grasshopper research were unsuccessful. The patchwork included salary savings; year-end leftovers in scattered accounts with varying amounts of travel, operations, or student-wage money; returns on registration fees; and direct student payment for food. Because most of these were State of Arizona funds, accounts had to be closed on June 30 at the end of one fiscal year and fresh ones begun the next day. Generally, if we could just make it through June, we could complete the season.

Budgetary constraints meant that the halcyon days of student subsidies for a summer in the piney woods of Arizona were gone. One result was that students, who were now paying for their tuition and food, began to demand more instruction than in previous years.

The Camp Falls Down

In almost every annual report submitted to the Bureau of Indian Affairs (BIA) summarizing each season's work is a paragraph, actually a secular prayer of sorts, that describes the field camp. As the facility built to last ten years slowly approached the age of thirty, that description's relationship to reality diminished geometrically. During the 1960s, the camp may have required little staff time for maintenance, but by the 1980s, duct tape, baling wire, and JB Weld were called into regular service to keep critical pieces of the camp functioning. As the years rolled by and the operating budget became leaner, buildings and systems had to be redefined, cannibalized, or decommissioned. Budgetary constraints also affected the support staff, and the research staff began to be recruited for successively more responsibility in dishwashing, cooking, and camp maintenance.

In the early 1980s, the bottom of the nine-hundred-gallon water tank began to develop big holes, which were plugged with pieces of inner tubing so that in time, the entire water system became a masterpiece of jerry-building. As the wartime-age generator inherited from Point of Pines became harder to repair and demand for electricity increased, the Field School converted to a 4-kilowatt AC generator only moveable with four people. Physical, fiscal, and esthetic factors compelled the final five years at Grasshopper to be conducted in relative darkness and silence without electricity in camp. The smaller, two-person generator for pumping water, however, remained in service.

Cooks were an invaluable part of the Field School, as were camp aides—when they could be afforded. During the last decade, we functioned without camp aides and rotated the tasks among staff-led student crews. We protected the cook's position fiercely during these years, however. Only in 1992, the final year, was there no full-time cook.

An experienced and youthful staff required a full, seven-day week to set up camp; closing at the end of the season could be done with student assistance in about three days. Setting up, maintaining, and winterizing a deteriorating field camp took an inordinate amount of staff time, energy, and practical knowledge, but the essentially rural skills needed to maintain the camp were becoming increasingly rare among urban-raised staff and students. At what point we decided to ride the camp into the ground is unknown, although every season brought with it the hope that all the critical systems would last just one more summer. And they did, with the appropriate application of duct tape and baling wire, along with a flexible definition of what was essential and what was not.

Grasshopper Research and the Cibecue Apache

One of the great ironies of Grasshopper research was the forced isolation of archaeologists from the Cibecue Apache, even though they had been part of the daily work force since 1969. This situation was largely because Keith Basso, longtime ethnographer of the Cibecue Apache (Basso 1970, 1979, 1990, 1996), enjoined us not to attempt ethnography. Item seven on the list of "Rules for Safety, Health, and Harmony" given to every student was "the privacy of the Apache must be respected; this is an archaeological, not ethnological, field school." Each summer, the first evening students were in camp was climaxed with a lecture listing the things to do and not to do for health, safety, and ethical concerns. It included an admonishment to stick to archaeology and avoid ethnography.

This prohibition was extended to the staff. Basso was the middleman between the Field School and the Apache in all matters, from recruiting the Apache crew to advising us on rumors circulating among the grandmothers of Cibecue. Longacre was fully satisfied to let Basso occupy this role as intermediary, but during Reid's tenure as director, his personality and the Archaeological Resources Protection Act (ARPA) of 1979 changed that relationship.

One irony in the early Apache avoidance policy is that Longacre always had strong ethnographic leanings, perhaps stronger than his interest in prehistoric archaeology. In 1965, he conducted the ethnoarchaeological study of an Apache wickiup (Longacre and Ayres 1968) and supported work at Chediski Farms, an abandoned Apache community along upper Canyon Creek (Griffin, Leone, and Basso 1971). A further irony would be revealed when Basso's (1996) award-winning book, *Wisdom Sits in Places*, became the principal reference of southwestern archaeologists concerned with cultural landscapes. Much of the fieldwork for the book was conducted during the years when Michael Graves was Basso's field assistant and was staying at Grasshopper.

The Conceptual Framework

Studies in archaeological method were a critical part of this period of research, illustrated best by Stephanie Whittlesey's (1978) dissertation using Grasshopper mortuary data to examine and refine models of archaeological inference and by Montgomery's (1992a) analysis of the formation of the ceramic record at Chodistaas Pueblo. Even in dissertation research not primarily directed to methodological issues, there was concern with data quality, quantity, and appropriateness for specific inferences about the past and for the resolution of specific problems.

Cholla Project laboratory work, analysis, and writing continued through the 1979, 1980, 1981, and 1982 seasons and played a major role in shaping the Grasshopper survey and settlement work. The Cholla Project was essentially an extension of Grasshopper research by Grasshopper researchers—Montgomery, Reid, Tuggle, Whittlesey, and Richard Ciolek-Torrello.

The conceptual framework underlying Grasshopper research during the 1980s is best recorded in the introduction to Reid's draft paper for the 1983 School of American Research Seminar, "Dynamics of Southwest Prehistory," and it is summarized here:

1. The marginal subsistence characteristics of the Southwest are well enough established to consider them a fact of prehistoric existence.

2. If any statement about the prehistoric Southwest has a high probability of being true, it is that people moved; they abandoned small and large communities continually and moved elsewhere. "Population movement was a recurrent response to conditions of life when natural and social environmental variables reached untenable values in areas where geographic circumscription was minimal." Prehistorians need to develop techniques and models for the study of past movements and their effects.

A related problem is the identification of settlements that were inhabited only part time. Misidentification of part-time occupations leads to inflated estimates of prehistoric population parameters.

Weak settlement-system reconstructions that are subsequently employed in higher level inferences are misleading and potentially detrimental to our understanding of exchange and organizational processes.

3. An implication of populations moving is that they do not always relocate in an uninhabited area; they may join an already existing commu-

nity that may not be of the same ethnic affiliation. There is evidence for ethnic coresidence—different ethnic groups living together in the same village as well as within normal interaction distances of the same region—in the mountains and it may have been more prevalent there than in other areas of the Southwest.

4. A consideration of ethnic coresidence introduces the bothersome problem of ethnic identification. There are important analytical contexts where different ethnic groups must be identified. These contexts involve situations of ethnic contact relevant to reconstructions and explanations of social continuity and change. There are research questions "that not only involve the use of ethnic labels but demand that these labels have analytical power relevant to real cultural boundaries of the past." There has been little research for establishing procedures by which ethnic boundaries or ethnic groups might be identified in the archaeological record. This critical problem must be resolved before one can have confidence in reconstructions of the past that potentially entail such situations.

5. There is concern for the analytical inappropriateness of partitioning archaeological variability according to traditional phase-period sequences. The apparent discreteness of phase-period schemes promotes a notion of independent, parallel developmental trajectories—one for Hohokam, one for Mogollon, and one for Anasazi. Although it may be temporarily advantageous for an investigator to make the simplifying assumption of behavioral continuity and developmental independence, such assumptions fail to approximate the archaeological record after A.D. 1150. I suggest that we think in terms of populations that were far more interrelated than conventional schemes imply.

6. The information we possess on the archaeological record throughout the Southwest is not strictly comparable at all levels of discussion or analysis. This condition is an obvious result of contextual characteristics and research activity.

Within the mountain transition zone, the data are not comparable at all levels of inference because of variable information and differences in occupational characteristics. Grasshopper, Q Ranch, Forestdale, and Point of Pines are nonequivalent data points in the Mogollon landscape.

7. Regions are simply geographic units, carrying no information pertaining to subcultural variability comparable to that of cultural branches, even though some of the region labels are the same as published branch labels.

With this prelude concluded, we begin the yearly chronicle of the behavioral archaeology years.

The 1979 Season

The Field School ran for eight weeks, from June 8 to August 3, with an enrollment of twenty-one students. Eight men and thirteen women, who were nine graduate students and twelve undergraduates, were enrolled.

Terry Banteah, a Zuni student, spent two weeks at Grasshopper as part of a program initiated by T. J. Ferguson to involve Native Americans in archaeological training.

The beginning of the season was filled with great enthusiasm for the moment and optimism for the future. The summer also was marked by a significant change in our relationship with the Apache. Reid persuaded the staff to begin two weeks early to tidy up a camp that had undergone a few years of neglect and to improve the facilities. We had bold plans for winterizing the staff cabins for extended research seasons, for building a fireplace in the dining room like the one at Point of Pines, and generally for upgrading all the critical systems. It did not take us long to discover that a camp built to last ten to twenty years of use was not going to tolerate these improvements. In fact, it was a minor miracle that the camp worked at all, an observation that led to the formulation of the principle of molecular familiarity—molecules that have always been together will tend to stay together. Some structural upgrades were possible, however, and permitted us to expand our research emphasis. The student dormitory closest to the laboratory was appropriated for staff research. It was wired for electric lights and furnished with work tables, providing a permanent place for staff research for the first time.

Freshly infused by Cholla Project fieldwork, the Grasshopper research program concentrated on survey funded by the SHPO for the purpose of developing a management plan. In 1978, a small grant supporting completion of the inventory within a two-mile radius of Grasshopper Pueblo had been labeled Phase I of a proposed five-year project. The 1979 Phase II survey included an expanded regional survey of varying intensities, the continuation of the pit-house identification project begun the year before by Brian Byrd, the redefinition of the human remains project supervised by Madeleine Hinkes to mitigate effects of vandalism, and the initiation of studies to estimate and monitor adverse impacts to cultural resources. Tuggle, who had led the Cholla Project Q Ranch survey in 1978, took full responsibility for directing the Grasshopper survey, which was to incorporate a strong teaching component. We were finally getting around to defining the range of site variability in the region.

In addition, Patricia Crown returned for the month of June to com-

Field School staff and students in 1979. Seated on ground, left to right, are Terry Mazany, Pamela Chester, Felipe Jácome, Mona McGuire, Mary Dohnalek; seated, Jefferson Reid, Stephanie Whittlesey, Erin Reid, Diane Grund, Julie Lowell, Cathy Stokes, Laura Greig, Michael McComas, James Ingraham; first row standing, Orlando Tessay, Nancy Orton, Michael Johnson, Clare Yarborough, Jay Enstad, Kristin Cheronis, Katherine Wright, Mark Elson, Daphnia Tuggle; back row standing, Robert Cole, Carolyn Orth, Andreas von Romdohr, James Vreeland, Jane Dierking, Brian Byrd, Robbie Baer, Maya Tuggle, Valerie Griffin, Jeannette Fox, Elizabeth Pate, David Tuggle, Travis Tessay.

The 1979 Season

Research and Teaching Staff	Support Staff	Apache Crew	Students	Family
Jefferson Reid, Director	Daphnia Tuggle, Cook	Alvin Quay	Kristin Cheronis	Erin Reid
David Tuggle, Associate Director	Valerie Griffin, Assistant Cook	Roy Quay	Pamela Chester	Maya Tuggle
Stephanie Whittlesey, Research Archaeologist (volunteer)	Jane Dierking, Camp Aide	Orlando Tessay	Robert Cole	
Patricia Crown Robertson, Dig Foreman	Jeannette Fox, Camp Aide	Travis Tessay	Mary Dohnalek	
Brian Byrd, Dig and Apache Foreman	Elizabeth Pate (volunteer)		Jay Enstad	
Robbie Baer, Archaeological Assistant			Laura Greig	
Mark Elson, Archaeological Assistant			Diane Grund	
Terry Mazany, Archaeological Assistant			James Ingraham	
Michael McComas, Archaeological Assistant			Felipe Jácome	
			Michael Johnson	
			Julie Lowell	
			Mona McGuire	
			Carolyn Orth	
			Nancy Orton	
			Steve Schweizer	
			Cathy Stokes	
			Andreas von Romdohr	
			James Vreeland	
			Helen Wheeler	
			Katherine Wright	
			Clare Yarborough	

plete the excavation of Rooms 1, 11, 15, and 16 at Chodistaas Pueblo for her dissertation research.

Perhaps the most significant outcome of the season was the negotiation of a human remains and burial excavation policy for the Field School. Although no burials had been excavated during the 1976 season when Reid was acting director, he was not in a position to set policy. Upon taking over as director, however, Reid began to discuss what we were doing in the field with tribal authorities.

In 1979, Ronnie Lupe and Reid met in Lupe's office in Whiteriver to discuss what might be an appropriate experimental policy for dealing with human remains in an archaeological context. We agreed on some rather vague wording that stressed an attempt to reduce the impact to human remains as much as possible. In practice, however, we pursued a no-excavation policy whenever possible, and subsequently, no intact, primary human burial was disturbed during Reid's directorship. Scattered, disarticulated remains encountered during the course of room excavation were reinterred. These agreements preceded the passage of the Native American Graves Protection and Repatriation Act (NAGPRA) by eleven years. The irony of this has gone unnoticed by all save ourselves.

Reid also began to establish a close working relationship with the tribal chairman, Ronnie Lupe, and members of the Cibecue community, especially Nashley Tessay Sr., the tribal policeman who was in charge of renting us the old Cibecue jail we used to store our equipment over the winter. Following the passage of ARPA in 1979, an annual appearance before the White Mountain Apache Tribal Council was required to obtain a resolution to conduct the Field School's research and teaching activities. In this way, the tribal council under the leadership of the chairman became the principal authority overseeing the operation of the Field School. Later, the passage of Arizona State laws ARS sec. 41-844 and ARS sec. 41-865 protecting human remains and associated artifacts placed the ASM in the position of mediating burial policy with concerned tribes.

The 1980 Season

The Field School was conducted for eight weeks, from June 13 to August 8, with an enrollment of eighteen students—five men and thirteen women, who represented ten graduate students and eight undergraduates.

Reduced funds required us to alter the long-term research strategy of expanded regional survey coverage. The anticipated Phase III grant from Arizona State Parks through the SHPO was unavailable. Sufficient funds to complete the third phase of the proposed five-year survey and planning work were lacking, but scaled-down research continued during the 1980 season under Tuggle's direction. The 1980 work was compelled to target survey and data collection that were not labor intensive. This included a continuation of light-intensity surveys; limited, medium-intensity surveys; tree-ring sampling of cliff dwellings; and monitoring sites for effects of pothunting.

Research priorities were adjusted to fill critical gaps in our knowledge of Grasshopper Pueblo, ultimately resulting in excavations in Room Block 5, two three-walled structures in the outliers, and a third room south of the main ruin. During the spring of 1980, analysis had led to the realization that our household reconstructions were incomplete. Most of our household inferences had been drawn from information gathered from noncontiguous rooms. Additional information was required to

The 1980 Season

Research and Teaching Staff	Support Staff	Apache Crew	Students	Family
Jefferson Reid, Director	Daphnia Tuggle, Cook	Orlando Tessay	Barbara Ayers	Erin Reid
David Tuggle, Associate Director	Valerie Griffin, Assistant Cook	Travis Tessay	Theresa Bauer	Mary Mims Reid
Stephanie Whittlesey, Research Archaeologist (volunteer)	Bruce Ashby, Camp Aide		Charles Bello	Maya Tuggle
	John Leavitt, Camp Aide		Lida Bilokur	
Michael McComas, Senior Dig Foreman			Ralph Cavallaro	
Mark Elson, Dig Foreman			Debbie Chason	
Gary Funkhouser, Dig Foreman			Laurel Cooper	
Barbara Klie, Laboratory Supervisor			Christian Downum	
			Douglas Elson	
Julie Lowell, Archaeological Assistant			Paul Freidel	
			Dawn Harvey	
Karen Wright, Archaeological Assistant			Eleanor King	
			Carole O'Leary	
Clare Yarborough, Archaeological Assistant			Nancy Rosoff	
			Lisa Senior	
Elizabeth Pate, Grasshopper Fellow (volunteer)			Denise Shay	
			Nina Tannenwald	
Kristin Cheronis, Grasshopper Fellow (volunteer)			Bonnie Wisthoff	

provide a more accurate reconstruction of organization and change in domestic activities of households occupying contiguous rooms.

Investigations at Grasshopper Pueblo had shown, however, that as households expanded in the three large room blocks, they often renovated and occupied adjacent, abandoned rooms. The task of isolating discrete households was difficult, unless a large number of rooms were excavated. This problem had been encountered in the investigation of construction unit L (CUL) in Room Block 3, where Room 216 appeared to have been reused by the inhabitants of the construction unit as they expanded (Rock 1974). In seeking an economical solution, we looked at room blocks and smaller groups of rooms that were isolated architecturally and thus limited in the number of renovation-reoccupation options available to past inhabitants. In other words, we needed to be efficient in excavating an architecturally distinct set of contiguous rooms. Room Block 5, with its six contiguous rooms, fit this criterion nicely. Its fit was made more comfortable by the fact that three of the rooms (114, 116, 195) had been excavated. Furthermore, previous excavation had provided information on the nature of room function and change that

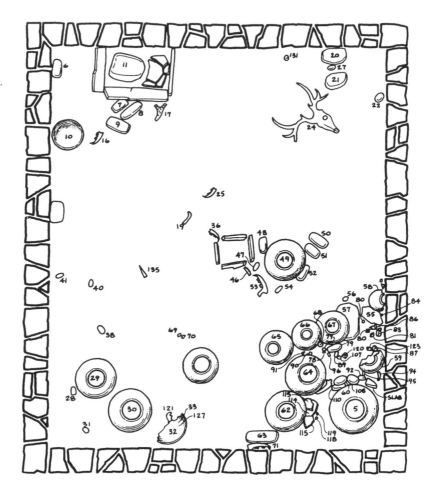

Room 216, a typical specialized-habitation room at Grasshopper Pueblo.

indicated the existence of sufficient temporal variability to inform on household modification.

In 1980, Room 115 of Room Block 5 was excavated completely under Gary Funkhouser's supervision, and Room 113 was excavated to floor and then sealed for completion at a later date. Room 113 would be completed in 1981, along with Room 112.

During analysis, we also had discovered that we had not excavated the full range of architectural forms used for domestic structures. There were four architectural forms: (1) two-story, masonry rooms with full-standing walls and typical pueblo roof construction; (2) single-story, masonry rooms with full-standing walls and typical pueblo room construction (see map); (3) single-story, masonry rooms with low walls and superstructures made of poles and brush, jacal, or a combination (see map); and (4) three-walled rooms constructed of either masonry or cobbles (or a combination) with superstructures of pole and brush

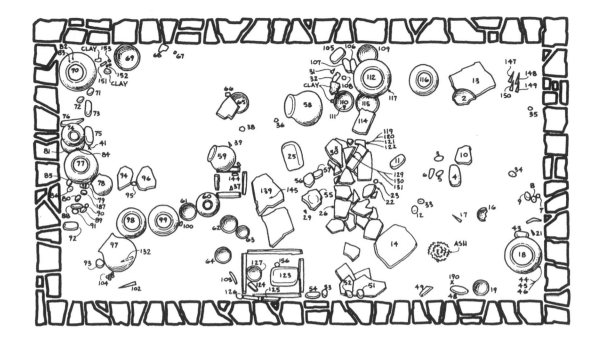

Room 359, a typical low-walled, generalized-habitation room at Grasshopper Pueblo.

or jacal, or both. Our inventory of excavated rooms included a reliable sample of the first three forms but none of the fourth, although several three-walled rooms had been tested. In two other instances, rooms were excavated without locating a fourth wall, but it could not be asserted whether the fourth wall was clearly absent.

Review of the three-walled rooms surrounding the main ruin led us to select for excavation two rooms located at the southwestern edge of the site. The rooms were likely to have floor-artifact arrays undisturbed by earlier cornering-project excavations. They also could antedate the main ruin and thus provide information on the earlier occupation. We also were interested in the character of households using three-walled structures and the potential for identifying seasonal occupation. Excavations in Room 309 were supervised by Kristin Cheronis, and Room 312 was overseen by Mark Elson.

Investigating household organization and excavating three-walled structures formed the basis for excavating Room 25, located south of Room Block 1, under Karen Wright's direction. Along with the contiguous and previously excavated Room 24, Room 25 constituted a detached, low-walled structure indicated by prior excavation to have expanded from an original three-walled structure. This architectural situation promised to inform on characteristics of household expansion and domestic-activity organization intermediate between that suspected of Rooms 309 and 312 and the rooms in Room Block 5.

In addition, Elson's crew completed excavation to the occupation floor of Room 1 at Grasshopper Spring Pueblo, begun in 1978.

In the fall of 1980, Tuggle and Reid attended the First Mogollon Conference, held in Las Cruces, New Mexico. A regional conference that continues to be held every other year, it was begun in 1980 in response to the increased number of researchers working in the Mogollon regions of Arizona and New Mexico and to provide a forum for sharing ideas and research results (see Whittlesey 1999b). At the First Mogollon Conference, the concept of the Mogollon culture was affirmed as though its authenticity had never been questioned (see Olson's [1962b] review of Daifuku [1961]).

The 1981 Season

The Field School was conducted for eight weeks, from June 12 to August 7, with an enrollment of eighteen students. Nine men and nine women, representing five graduate and thirteen undergraduate students, were in residence.

Spring was a busy time for Grasshopper research presentations at the annual meeting of the Society for American Archaeology (SAA) in San Diego. Reid and Whittlesey (1982) presented "Households at Grasshopper Pueblo." We renamed and redefined some of the room categories identified by Ciolek-Torrello's (1978) research and introduced several interpretations—room blocks as distinct residence units, ethnic coresidence of Mogollon and Anasazi, and male sodalities as a crosscutting organizational principle for integration, decision making, and leadership. Tuggle and Reid presented "Fourteenth Century Mogollon Agriculture in the Grasshopper Region of Arizona" (Tuggle, Reid, and Cole 1984), in which they offered the first critique of the Chavez Pass reconstructions of Upham, Lightfoot, and Feinman (1981).

The 1981 field season continued the long-term strategy of expanding regional coverage through survey and excavation. Phase III of the survey and planning grant was revived with funds from Arizona State Parks through the SHPO.

Excavation focused on completing the household analysis in Room Block 5 begun the previous year and on three pueblo sites dated to the late end of the occupation in the Grasshopper region. In Room Block 5, Lowell completed the subfloor excavation of Room 113, and Barbara Klie supervised excavation of Room 112 to floor.

Three sites chosen for testing represented different categories of small

The 1981 Season

Research and Teaching Staff	Support Staff	Apache Crew	Students	Family
Jefferson Reid, Director	Charles Wolchesky, Cook	Forrest Gooday	Susan Albamonte	Erin Reid
Stephanie Whittlesey, Research Archaeologist (volunteer)	Ann Counihan, Assistant Cook	Michael Tessay	Mukunda Aryal	
	Rex Little, Camp Aide	Nathan Tessay	James Baron	
Michael McComas, Assistant Director	Bob Penny, Camp Aide	Orlando Tessay	Nora Besler	
	Steffney Thompson (volunteer)		Harry Bower	
Charles Cole, Senior Dig Foreman			Thomas Cox	
			Margaret Davisson	
Gary Funkhouser, Senior Dig Foreman			Ernest De Los Santos	
			Lisa Eppley	
Christian Downum, Dig Foreman			Thomas McCalla	
			Tracy Nemeth	
Barbara Klie, Dig Foreman			Carolyn Penny	
			Walter Punzmann	
Douglas Craig, Archaeological Assistant			John Stouffer	
			Vicki Thomas	
Elizabeth Pate, Archaeological Assistant			Lisa Valkenier	
			Philip Weiss	
			Ann Williams	

Michael Graves lived in camp while he assisted Keith Basso in his Apache landscape research. Faron Nastacio attended the field school as part of the Zuni training program.

settlements in the region. AZ V:2:12 (ASM) was a small, fourteenth-century pueblo located on a low ridge overlooking Salt River Draw about 9 kilometers south of Grasshopper. It was selected from numerous examples of sites of this type for three reasons: (1) surface ceramics, primarily Fourmile Polychrome, indicated a late occupation; (2) pothunting activity had exposed at least two burials, suggesting activities more substantial than those associated with field-house occupation; and (3) several rooms appeared to be architecturally similar to the low-walled structures of Grasshopper. The work, supervised by Christian Downum, included excavation of three rooms and a controlled surface collection from 10 percent of the site area.

The second small site to be investigated was Spring Ridge Pueblo (AZ P:14:71 [ASM]) located on the southernmost tip of Spring Ridge. Also suspected on the basis of pottery to date in the fourteenth century, it was selected to represent a class of small sites perched on high landforms with an unobstructed view of the countryside. It was located just off the road to Cibecue and far easier to access on a daily schedule than the other sites in this category, which were isolated in the canyon lands on the southern and western edges of the Grasshopper Plateau (Tuggle and Reid 2001). Under Douglas Craig's supervision, one room was tested and a surface collection completed before work ceased at the request of the tribal chairman responding to pressure from the Cibecue community. Although the site was clearly within the permit area approved by the tribal council, there was the expressed sentiment that actual archaeological work was getting too close to Cibecue for the residents' comfort.

The third site we investigated was Hilltop Pueblo, a sixty-room ruin contemporary with Grasshopper Pueblo and located about 4 kilometers to the northwest. One room was chosen for excavation on the basis of its location on the perimeter of the pueblo, indicating its probable construction and occupation late in the site's history. Excavation to floor by Downum and his crew revealed a configuration of artifacts and features conforming to the specialized-habitation room type at Grasshopper (Reid and Whittlesey 1999).

The season was punctuated by the most horrifying experience a field-school director could imagine—the accidental burning of the men's dorm in the darkness of late Saturday night–early Sunday morning. When the occupants appeared, and it was clear that no one was inside the flaming building or hurt, the only concern was to keep the fire from spreading. A bucket brigade was formed, and the roofs of the adjacent buildings were wet down. Fortunately, the night was windless, and the other buildings were saved. The dorm itself and all its contents burned to ashes. A candle placed in a cardboard box on a shelf had been allowed to burn out, causing the fire.

There were other incidents that summer that marked the 1981 season as the worst ever in our own minds. They reinforced the fact that our isolated camp in the wilderness was surrounded by potential dangers and the need for rules and restrictions to ensure everyone's safety.

The 1982 Season

The Field School was in session for eight weeks, from June 11 to August 6, with an enrollment of twelve students—four men and eight women, who were eight graduate students and four undergraduates.

This was one of those signal years in which events and forces converged. By the end of the year, the Cholla Project would conclude with the publication of the last of five volumes. The multidisciplinary volume was published as a UA Anthropological Paper (Longacre, Holbrook, and Graves 1982), and a summary paper by Longacre, Graves, and Holbrook appeared in the *Journal of Field Archaeology*. Last, the

The 1982 Season

Research and Teaching Staff	Support Staff	Apache Crew	Students	Family
Jefferson Reid, Director	Valerie Griffin, Cook	Henrietta Tessay	Janice Cross	Erin Reid
Stephanie Whittlesey, Research	Margaret Davisson Cole	Michael Tessay	Elizabeth Dennis	
Archaeologist (volunteer)	(volunteer)	Orlando Tessay	Joseph Ezzo	
Michael McComas,			Karen Fredman	
Assistant Director			Yasushi Kojo	
Charles Cole, Senior Dig Foreman			Margaret Nelson	
Barbara Klie, Senior Dig Foreman			Hyung Lee Pai	
Douglas Craig, Dig Foreman			Martha Risser	
Chester Shaw,			Barbara Seligman	
Archaeological Assistant			Kathryn St. John	
			Masakazu Tani	
			Andrew Tomlinson	

Michael Graves lived in camp while he assisted Keith Basso in his Apache landscape research.

Grasshopper–Chavez Pass debate was formally initiated at the Mogollon Conference.

The 1982 season also was a turning point for Grasshopper because of unforeseen factors. It was the beginning of tight budgets and a reduced staff. There was no cook's assistant and no camp aides to perform the multitude of chores that kept the camp operating. The dishwashing, water pumping, outhouse scrubbing, trash burning, and general camp cleaning fell to staff-led student crews. There were fewer students beginning in 1982, with only twelve to participate in field projects, although they were assisted by an Apache crew of three. It was necessary to scale down the fieldwork accordingly.

More relevant to field decisions in 1982 was the completion of Crown's (1981) dissertation on painted ceramics from Chodistaas Pueblo. Crown had excavated nine rooms at Chodistaas beginning when Reid was acting director in 1976. Crown's interpretation that the black-on-white pots were made locally came into question, in part because of a Cholla Project compositional analysis that included some Grasshopper ceramics (Tuggle, Kintigh, and Reid 1982). At the time of Crown's writing, there was insufficient evidence to resolve the question. Crown interpreted the nearly two hundred whole or restorable vessels she analyzed as having been originally resting on the roofs of the rooms in which they were found, from which they had fallen intact to the floor when Chodistaas burned. In the context of Grasshopper research, the provenience of the whole pots was critical, as Montgomery (1992a) clearly demonstrated in her analysis of the formation of the ceramic record at Chodistaas Pueblo. Therefore, we returned to Chodistaas in 1982 to gather the hard evidence to determine where the pots had been resting when fire swept the village. Two rooms were excavated at Chodistaas Pueblo—Room 4, supervised by Chester Shaw, and Room 14, supervised by Craig.

Klie concluded the Room Block 5 work at Grasshopper Pueblo with completion of Room 112.

The expanded site-survey project that had been initiated in 1978 had to be curtailed radically with the cessation of funds for survey previously provided through the SHPO. During the 1982 season, survey activity included only the verification of site locations, especially those located on high landforms, and the collection of surface artifacts from a sample of sites contemporary with Chodistaas Pueblo. The objective of these activities was to provide surface-collection data comparable to that of the adjacent Q Ranch region of the Cholla Project.

The fall was marked by the beginning of the Grasshopper–Chavez Pass debate at the second Mogollon Conference, in Las Cruces, New Mexico, where Reid read three papers (Graves and Reid 1984; Reid 1984b; Whittlesey 1984) before an audience containing a number of Chavez Pass researchers. The papers, later published—Graves and Reid (1984), Reid (1984b), and Whittlesey (1984)—addressed our general disbelief in the Chavez Pass interpretations based not on theoretical perspectives but rather on serious methodological inadequacies.

Other presenters criticized ASU archaeology, we think, more devastatingly than in our set of papers. Rosalind Hunter-Anderson (Hunter-Anderson and Zan 1984), in a brilliant and beautifully acerbic presentation—"Proving the Moon Is Made of Cheese: The Structure of Recent Research in the Mogollon Region"—took Lightfoot and Feinman (1982) to task for egregious offenses against reasonable interpretation of the Mogollon pit-house past (also see Schiffer's [1983] critique). Hunter-Anderson and Zan (1984:290) advised that

> scientifically minded archaeologists should be most careful not to accept everything suggested by ethnologists. Yet when we turn to the publications in which the Mogollon big man hypothesis has been offered (Lightfoot and Feinman 1982) and elaborated upon (Upham et al. 1981), we find a reintroduction of pseudo-systematic speculations of a psycho-sociological nature about synchronic processes within a society, using concepts and phrases borrowed uncritically from the ethnological literature.

In a brilliant stroke of defense by attack, this was precisely the misuse of ethnographic data that the Chavez Pass folk would later use to critique Grasshopper interpretations.

The 1983 Season

The Field School ran for eight weeks, from June 10 to August 5, with an enrollment of eleven students. Three men and eight women, who represented eight graduate and three undergraduate students, attended.

The 1983 season was one of those rare summers when the right mix of people and circumstances comes together to form a productive and pleasurable time. When the social history of Grasshopper is written, this season will be held up as an example of what project leaders look for in a near-perfect crew.

The teaching program had temporarily assumed a greater emphasis over research by concentrating activity on one room at one site so that everyone would be exposed to the same wide range of field experiences. It also permitted the staff to test new techniques of instruction. Out of this summer and the feedback we received from the students came a revised teaching program geared more appropriately to the contemporary student. We would employ this program until Grasshopper ended. Its only real drawback was that it required a huge investment of staff time, which, along with camp maintenance, meant that less time could be devoted to actual fieldwork. Fieldwork, then, had to be targeted rather precisely to achieve maximum research returns.

We sought to augment research with an NSF grant proposal that was written and submitted in July, while the Field School was in session. Entitled "The Identification of Settlement Function: Application of Cholla Project Procedures to the Grasshopper Region," the proposed project was to employ Tuggle and graduate assistants in linking the Cholla Project settlement data with that from Grasshopper. It was not funded, and we would apply again in two years.

Room 7 at Chodistaas Pueblo was the only room excavated this season, reflecting the increased staff teaching commitment and overall reduced fieldwork expectations. Room 7 was attached to the previously excavated Room 4 as part of a two-room set that had been identified at Grasshopper Pueblo and other sites. The floor assemblage resembled that of a storage-manufacturing room at Grasshopper Pueblo, although Room 7 was much larger.

The fall was a busy time for the presentation of Grasshopper research and the intensification of the Grasshopper–Chavez Pass debate. In late September, a number of southwestern archaeologists gathered for a week at the School of American Research Advanced Seminar on southwestern prehistory (Cordell and Gumerman 1989). In addition to the editors, participants included Jeffrey Dean, Paul Fish, James Judge, Steven

The 1983 Season

Research and Teaching Staff	Support Staff	Apache Crew	Students	Family
Jefferson Reid, Director	Valerie Griffin Ezzo, Cook	Michael Tessay	Katherine Arnold	Erin Reid
Stephanie Whittlesey, Research Archaeologist (volunteer)		Norton Tessay	Anna Calek	
Julie Lowell, Senior Dig Foreman		Orlando Tessay	Wendy Charko	
Barbara Klie Montgomery, Senior Dig Foreman			Jim Davies	
Vera App, Archaeological Assistant			Kelly Elliott	
Joseph Ezzo, Archaeological Assistant			Laura Levi	
			Joan Lloyd	
			Dale Mayo	
			Diane McNeave	
			Mohammad Kamal Rahman	
			Mary Bane Stevens	

LeBlanc, Fred Plog, Arthur Rohn, Douglas Schwartz, and Gregory Johnson as the outside discussant (see Cordell 1997:184, fig. 6.12). Reid (1989) presented a paper, "A Grasshopper Perspective on the Mogollon of the Arizona Mountains," that contained the conceptual framework underlying Grasshopper research discussed at the beginning of this chapter. Six years later, the seminar was published as *Dynamics of Southwest Prehistory* (Cordell and Gumerman 1989).

The seminar kept the participants comfortably confined for a week of intense and stimulating discussion, including the topic of social complexity. At some point in the discussion, Johnson offered the maxim "If it's complex, it's obvious." Johnson's discussant commentary in its first draft contained favorable comments on the Grasshopper work that were moderated in his published version (G. Johnson 1989), a fact that we attribute to editorial pressures. Looking back, we find it odd that the acrimony soon to appear at the Chacmool Conference was nowhere in evidence in Santa Fe.

The debate reached new heights at the Chacmool Conference, an annual, student-run conference held at the Department of Archaeology at the University of Calgary (Thompson, Garcia, and Kense 1985). The Mogollon Conference of 1982 had inspired Jane Kelley to organize a Southwest session for the 1983 Chacmool Conference and to invite Plog, Steadman Upham, Linda Cordell, and Reid to participate. Plog changed the topic of his original paper, "Chevelon and Chaves: A Tale of Two Regions," to "Status and Death at Grasshopper: The Homogenization of Reality" sometime after the conference program was printed, and also rescheduled his presentation from the opening of the session to after lunch and after Reid's paper. This suggests that his presented paper "Status and Death" (Plog 1985) attacking Whittlesey's (1978) dissertation was a last-minute effort. Certainly the boldly stated but patently false assertions of that paper could not have been the product of a careful reading.

In the presentation and subsequently in the published paper, Plog accused Whittlesey of misrepresenting and distorting data to her own ends. It would be too kind to blame this on a misunderstanding or misreading of the work. We perceive it as a deliberate attempt to falsify, distort, and undermine Grasshopper research by unjustly criticizing a particular study whose author was not even present to defend herself. To say the least, Reid was caught totally off balance by Plog's pointed, personal attack. Even today, it rankles. It also will infuriate us always when others speak sanctimoniously of the "acrimonious" debate, as though both sides contributed vitriolic prose to the literature. We defy anyone to find a published statement more acrimonious than those that held up Whittlesey's dissertation as fraudulent (Plog 1985; Upham and Plog 1986). To our minds, processual archaeology as an explicitly scientific, objective approach to the past died that cold, snowy November day in western Alberta.

The 1984 Season

The Field School lasted for eight weeks, from June 8 to August 3. There were twelve enrolled students—four men and eight women, who were four graduate and eight undergraduate students.

The reduced size of the Field School and further emphasis upon training for the beginning student limited the scope of fieldwork to room excavation at Chodistaas Pueblo. Room 7 was finished with test excavations into the subfloor level. We began excavations in Rooms 13 and 17, located on either side of the previously excavated Room 14.

We selected Room 13, one of the first rooms to be built at Chodistaas Pueblo, for two reasons. First, we were interested in dating more precisely the initial occupation at the site, especially to determine whether the A.D. 1263 beginning date based on dendrochronology could be extended back in time to accord better with the archaeomagnetic dates, which tended to be earlier. This task represented research of crucial importance for refining archaeomagnetic dating that was then ongoing at the UA. Second, we were interested in determining the activity structure of the household that had inhabited Room 13 for comparisons with the

The 1984 Season

Research and Teaching Staff	Support Staff	Apache Crew	Students	Family
Jefferson Reid, Director	Valerie Griffin Ezzo, Cook	Michael Tessay	Rebecca Allen	Erin Reid
Julie Lowell, Assistant Director	Alison Dean, Camp Aide	Norton Tessay	Cristina Angulo	
Barbara Montgomery, Laboratory Supervisor, Senior Dig Foreman	Marcus Griffin, Camp Aide	Orlando Tessay	Halley Eisner	
Joseph Ezzo, Senior Dig Foreman			Alan Fuhrmann	
Laura Levi, Archaeological Assistant			Sandra Hays	
John Welch, Archaeological Assistant			Robin Poague	
			Rupert Ruff	
			Miriam Stark	
			Linda Storm	
			Barbara Strance	
			Javier Tapia	
			Helga Wöcherl	

later-constructed rooms in the southern room block. John Welch supervised the excavations.

Room 17, located between the previously excavated Room 2 and Room 14 and joined to each by a doorway, provided the opportunity to complete the picture of household organization in a set of linked rooms in the northern room block for comparison with those in the southern room block. Ezzo supervised this work.

In the spring of 1984, we undertook an unsuccessful Grasshopper fund-raising campaign. We began with a list of sixty professional archaeologists in Tucson and sent everyone a letter seeking contributions. In return, we received a grand total of one hundred dollars from Michael Jacobs, who had been a student at Grasshopper in 1968.

At the annual meeting of the SAA, in Portland, Donald Graybill read a paper jointly authored by Reid and Graybill, "Paleoclimate and Human Behavior in the Grasshopper Region, Arizona," which combined his reconstruction of precipitation with Reid's pueblo and regional growth model to suggest a rapid response time for the prehistoric farmers to adapt to drought conditions.

The Third Mogollon Conference, again held in Las Cruces, New Mexico, was the occasion to present nonpolemical papers concerning the Mogollon of Grasshopper Pueblo. Reid began the conference with "Historical Perspective on the Concept of Mogollon," followed by Ciolek-Torrello's "Room Function and Domestic Organization at Grasshopper Pueblo" and John Whittaker's "Projectile Points and the Question of Specialization at Grasshopper Pueblo." Tuggle read "Ceramic Trace-Elements and Human Behavior in the Mountains of East-Central Arizona," a condensed version of the Cholla Project study by Tuggle,

Kintigh, and Reid (1982). There was no mention of Chavez Pass at this conference.

The 1985 Season

The Field School was in session from June 7 to July 19, a shift from an eight-week to a six-week season in response to a shrinking budget. Fourteen students participated—four men and ten women, who represented five graduate students and nine undergraduates.

The year began with another attempt to secure long-term funding. Point of Pines and Grasshopper alumni were asked to write a letter in support of the Field School addressed to the provost and the dean. The alumni response was truly gratifying, and helped for a time to ensure a continuation of soft money, especially from the provost's office.

Fieldwork returned to Grasshopper Pueblo and the outliers this year. By this time, ninety-six rooms at Grasshopper Pueblo had been excavated, and about sixty-four of these were considered strong cases for most analytical purposes. The fact that only twelve outlier rooms had been excavated resulted in a small sample of a potentially informative category of structures. Their importance lay in the fact that the outliers were among the last room groups to have been occupied, and they had consistently yielded full arrays of floor artifacts in situations lacking signs of burning or other catastrophe, an abandonment context clearly different from that of Chodistaas Pueblo. In addition, the outliers' occupants organized their domestic activities differently from residents of the main pueblo at Grasshopper and in a manner that was more similar in some ways to the earlier organization of activities found at Chodistaas Pueblo. Because of our long-term research into the household and processes of abandonment, it was necessary to excavate additional outlier rooms before we could regard the work at Grasshopper Pueblo as complete.

Three outlier rooms (353, 355, 356) in Room Block 8 were excavated to the occupational floor under the supervision of Barbara Montgomery and Laura Levi. We selected Rooms 355 and 356 for three reasons: They formed a contiguous architectural pair, no rooms in Room Block 8 had yet been excavated, and the surface vegetation was sparse, reducing the probability of root disturbance to the shallow floors. Room 353, adjacent to Room 355, was excavated when it became apparent that the architectural history of room construction included Room 353 and Room 354, which was excavated in 1986.

The 1985 Season

Research and Teaching Staff	Support Staff	Apache Crew	Students	Family
Jefferson Reid, Director	Neil Nepsky, Cook	Michael Tessay	Kathryn Dixon	Erin Reid
John Welch, Survey Supervisor	Alison Dean, Camp Aide	Travis Tessay	Brooke Fanady	
David Tuggle, Survey Consultant			Nick Foxton	
Barbara Montgomery,			Karen Harry	
Laboratory Supervisor			Andrea Kayser	
Laura Levi, Excavation Supervisor			Janet Langfield	
			Elizabeth Lawlor	
			Jodel Lustyan	
			Paula Molloy	
			Joanne Ryan	
			John Schweikart	
			Teresa Thompson	
			James Vint	
			Douglas Wilson	

The survey direction was determined by preliminary analysis of the three-mile inventory, which had revealed a pattern of clustered settlements during the period of Chodistaas Pueblo's occupation immediately prior to the establishment of the large community at Grasshopper. Two spatial clusters—one that included Chodistaas and another that included Grasshopper Spring Pueblo—were slated for examination during 1985, but only the Chodistaas cluster was investigated.

Prior to the spatial analysis of settlements in the Grasshopper region, we had developed a hypothesis of dispersed settlements functioning loosely as a community prior to the aggregation of settlements at the beginning of the A.D. 1300s. A dispersed community configuration had been proposed for other areas of the mountains, such as the Forestdale Valley, where a great kiva identified the focal settlement (Reid 1989). In the Grasshopper region, the absence of great kivas and the generally lower population density prior to A.D. 1300 led us to hypothesize an alternative form of the dispersed community in which the open plaza settlement was the focus. The isolation of a spatial cluster around Chodistaas Pueblo, which had a plaza, permitted us to tightly bound the domain of investigation. We examined the Chodistaas settlement cluster in three stages: (1) relocation and verification of sites, (2) intensive nonsite recording, and (3) surface collection from selected sites. Tuggle and Welch supervised student crews in these activities.

Relocation and verification of sites were required to ensure that site records were accurate and observations on each site were consistent. In nonsite survey, all artifacts and features within an area are recorded, such that a complete picture of the total distribution of prehistoric remains may be constructed; no sampling is involved.

We were hot on the trail of the Grasshopper settlement system, so it was time again to apply to the NSF for research money to support the analytical work of Tuggle and Whittlesey. The proposal, titled "Function, Variability, and System in Late Prehistoric Settlements of the Central Arizona Mountains," was submitted at the end of July, with Tuggle and Reid as principal investigators, but failed to stir the hearts of the reviewers. Tuggle turned to contract archaeology and consulting. The study of the regional settlement ultimately became a part of Welch's dissertation research (Welch 1996) and eventually his responsibility as Historic Preservation Officer for the White Mountain Apache tribe.

In this year, Plog's paper presented at the 1983 Chacmool Conference was published in the conference proceedings volume (Thompson, Garcia, and Kense 1985). No opportunity was made for Whittlesey to reply, although she had asked the editors of the volume to be allowed to do so.

The 1986 Season

The Field School was in session for six weeks, from June 6 to July 18. There were seventeen enrolled students—six men and eleven women, who were six graduate and eleven undergraduate students.

Reid applied for and received a small research grant of $1,375 from the university's Social and Behavioral Science Research Institute for a project entitled "Defining the Eastern Boundary of the 14th Century Grasshopper Settlement System." The grant helped pay for one four-wheel-drive vehicle from the university garage. The grant also provided funds to pay Apache informants, including Nashley Tessay Sr., to take us to prehistoric sites. This was a particularly efficient way to survey quickly and to understand the landscape from an Apache perspective. One remarkable outcome of this grant-supported work was the discovery of Black Mountain Pueblo, a sixty-room ruin shown to us by Francis Dehose, longtime stockman for the Cibecue Cattle District.

Investigation of late-occupied outlier rooms in Room Block 8 at Grasshopper Pueblo was completed with excavation of Room 354. Its last function was as a habitation room.

The temporary return of Tuggle gave impetus to completing settlement studies in the Grasshopper region. This work, when combined

The 1986 Season

Research and Teaching Staff	Support Staff	Apache Crew	Students	Family
Jefferson Reid, Director	Karen Smith, Cook	Justin Cromwell	Nicole Armstrong-	Erin Reid
David Tuggle,	Kathy Smith, Assistant Cook	Travis Tessay	Best	
Survey Consultant	Alison Dean, Camp Aide		Susan Converse	
Laura Levi,			Alice Gillette	
Excavation Supervisor			Peter Griffiths	
Barbara Montgomery,			Stephen Harvey	
Laboratory Supervisor			Cecilia Haugen	
John Welch,			Catherine Jacobus	
Survey Supervisor			Masashi Kobayashi	
Halley Eisner,			Katherine Lumb	
Archaeological Assistant			Maripat Metcalf	
			Shawn Penman	
			Elizabeth Sandler	
			Sharon Spanogle	
			Daniela Triadan	
			Brian Trostel	
			Jeffrey Walton	
			Edward Wright	

with information from the adjacent Q Ranch region of the Cholla Project, would present a thorough analysis of the dramatic changes in settlement during late prehistoric times within an approximately 450-square-mile area, of which 180 square miles had been surveyed. The survey work was divided between completing data collection on the fourteenth-century settlement system and continuing the investigation of the late-thirteenth-century settlement system, focusing on the Chodistaas and Grasshopper Spring settlement clusters.

Tuggle and Welch investigated the fourteenth-century settlement system. Controlled surface collections were made at Grasshopper Pueblo, Blue House Pueblo, and the newly discovered Black Mountain Pueblo. To estimate settlement function, controlled surface collections were made from five sites on high landforms. Blue House and Black Mountain Pueblos were mapped to complete the analysis of community architectural development.

Tuggle and Welch also investigated the late-thirteenth-century settlement system, anchored in the excavation of Chodistaas Pueblo. Site AZ P:14:197 (ASM), the only site other than Chodistaas Pueblo within the Chodistaas cluster to have a bounded plaza, was tested under Levi's supervision. Controlled surface collections from two additional sites within the Chodistaas cluster were completed. Areal coverage was expanded around the Chodistaas cluster to ensure its spatial integrity and to determine the juncture with the Grasshopper Spring settlement cluster. An intensive survey of the Grasshopper Spring settlement cluster was completed for comparison with the Chodistaas settlement cluster.

In mid-October of 1986, the Fourth Mogollon Conference, organized by Reid, John Ravesloot, and Patricia Spoerl, was held in Tucson. Reid had been coerced at the 1984 conference to host the next one, and in all fairness to the Las Cruces crowd, it was time for Tucson to take on the conference. The year 1986 would commemorate a half century since Emil Haury's publication of *The Mogollon Culture of Southwestern New Mexico* (Haury 1936). To celebrate the theme "Fifty Years of Mogollon: 1936 to 1986," Reid designed an exhibit at the ASM, entitled "Mogollon: Archaeology of the Arizona Mountains," to open the conference. When the exhibit closed the following year, the descriptive panels were donated to the White Mountain Apache Culture Center and were on display in Crook's Cabin at Fort Apache for many years.

Fifty years of Mogollon archaeology also were appraised by a panel comprising Roger Anyon, Jeffrey Dean, Haury, Paul Minnis, John Speth, and David Wilcox and moderated by Reid. The presentations by Dean, Haury, Speth, and Wilcox were published in an issue of *The Kiva* devoted to the conference (vol. 55, no. 2, 1988). The most significant aspect of the conference, however, was the increased tempo and severity of the Grasshopper–Chavez Pass debate, with four totally independent papers—Graves; Longacre, Kenneth Kvamme, and Masashi Kobayashi; Downum; and Alan Sullivan—critical of Upham and his interpretations of Chavez Pass Pueblo. This seemingly planned convergence gave rise to the rumor that Reid had orchestrated a multipronged attack on Chavez Pass. He was bemused and also flattered that anyone would entertain the absurd notion of his orchestrating the strongly dominant personalities of Downum, Graves, and Sullivan, much less Longacre and others. Clearly, such thoughts arise from academic settings where obsequious graduate students abound, which was not then the case for the UA.

By that time, we had become concerned that archaeologists were beginning to take seriously the claim by those working at Chavez Pass that Pueblo III period black-on-white pottery was contemporaneous with Pueblo IV period polychromes. Downum was enmeshed in writing a dissertation on Flagstaff-area archaeology (Downum 1988), a major component of which was discussion of tree-ring-dated black-on-white pottery. He presented a paper demonstrating the well-attested, well-dated temporal separation between black-on-white and polychrome ceramics in the Flagstaff region. Although his objective was simply to marshal the considerable evidence in support of ceramic exclusivity, what he discovered would undermine the Chavez model completely (see chapter 8).

Over the winter, Whittlesey submitted to the *Journal of Field Archaeology* a suite of comments on the Upham and Plog (1986) paper that included the Plog (1985) critique. It was rejected. Rebuttal to Plog would not come until the twenty-first annual Chacmool Conference of 1988.

The 1987 Season

The Field School operated for six weeks, from June 5 to July 17, with eleven students. Four men and seven women, representing six graduate students and five undergraduates, were enrolled.

Fieldwork was conducted under three broad categories: (1) subsistence research, (2) settlement studies, and (3) Apache archaeology. Welch investigated the agricultural base for subsistence as part of his dissertation research. The processual focus of this work was to document the rapid shift in subsistence strategies from hunting-gathering-gardening of the late A.D. 1200s to dependence on maize agriculture in the A.D. 1320s. The methodological issues were the relationship among variables that brought about the rapid shift in subsistence and its organizational consequences. The Grasshopper data provided the unique opportunity to describe and explain the processes involved in the rapid transformation to a full commitment to agriculture some years before contemporary reevaluations of the beginning of food production in the Southwest.

Settlement studies focused on the excavation of three rooms at Grasshopper Spring Pueblo. The rooms produced a set of remains coeval with nearby Chodistaas Pueblo but strikingly different in many critical aspects of material culture, such as thermal facilities, projectile points, architectural layout, and some characteristics of the ceramic assemblage. Rooms 2, 7, and 8 were excavated to floor under the supervision of Triadan and Brian Trostel.

In addition, we tested subfloor deposits in the Room Block 8 rooms of Grasshopper Pueblo that had been taken to floor in the two previous seasons.

Our planned evaluation of the status of Apache archaeology was delayed by the inability of Graves to visit Grasshopper. We did, however, extend our familiarity of Apachean remains through site visitations led by Raymond Palmer of the BIA's Forestry Branch. The Apache sites we

The 1987 Season

Research and Teaching Staff	Support Staff	Apache Crew	Students	Family
Jefferson Reid, Director	Valerie Luedee, Cook	Glenn Cromwell	Wei-Chun Chen	Erin Reid
Barbara Montgomery,	Kim Shea-Tunis,	Nathan Tessay	Jonathan Hearn	
Assistant Director-Excavation	Assistant Cook		Janice Kamrin	
John Welch,			Yuan Liu	
Assistant Director-Survey			Leon Lorentzen	
Daniela Triadan,			Stacie Olson	
Excavation Supervisor			Kathleen Owen	
Brian Trostel,			Andrew Pelcin	
Excavation Supervisor			Heidi Rancin	
Halley Eisner,			Patricia Reitt	
Laboratory Supervisor			Barbara Starnes	
Jeffrey Walton,				
Archaeological Assistant				

visited convinced us of the critical importance of developing a program of research to document and preserve this fragile evidence of the Apache past.

During 1987, Cordell, Upham, and Brock published an article in *American Antiquity* that criticized Grasshopper research.

The 1988 Season

The Field School was in session for six weeks, from June 3 to July 15, with an enrollment of twelve students—four men and eight women, equally divided among graduate students and undergraduates.

Fieldwork focused on the excavation of Rooms 6 and 10 at Chodistaas Pueblo, supervised by Lorentzen and Montgomery. In addition, Montgomery tested extramural areas with eleven 1 × 1 m pits in the plaza and around the perimeter of the pueblo. A 1 × 2 m test pit was excavated outside the door to Room 14 to look for exterior activities associated with the occupation of that room. A quick, two-day test of site GFS 81-133 by Tuggle, Welch, and Triadan sought information on the use of the low-walled pueblos on high landforms found throughout the canyon country around Grasshopper (Tuggle and Reid 2001). Welch continued to investigate the rapid shift from hunting-gathering-gardening to total commitment to agriculture in the Grasshopper region during the early decades of the A.D. 1300s (Welch 1996).

Ken Decker, a doctoral candidate at the University of Minnesota, had analyzed stable-carbon-isotopes on previously excavated skeletal ma-

The 1988 Season

Research and Teaching Staff	Support Staff	Apache Crew	Students	Family
Jefferson Reid, Director	Tiffany Tretschok, Cook	Glenn Cromwell	Joy Lin Eiseman	Erin Reid
Barbara Montgomery, Assistant Director-Excavation	Alison Dean, Assistant Cook		Katherine Evanchuk	
John Welch, Assistant Director-Survey			Kenneth Fordyce	
Leon Lorentzen, Excavation Supervisor			Eve Kappler	
Daniela Triadan, Excavation Supervisor			Cornelia Krauch	
Nieves Zedeño, Laboratory Supervisor			John Lewis	
			Tina Love	
			James McGill	
			Maria O'Donovan	
			Joseph Stumpf	
			Barbara Teso	
			Susan Zodin	

terial from Grasshopper Pueblo. This work had produced valuable information on the character of the diet, especially concerning an evident increase in the contribution of corn over the occupation span of the pueblo. This research was brought to an unfortunate and sad end with Decker's tragic death. It would remain for Ezzo (1991) to complete a similar analysis for his dissertation research at the University of Wisconsin–Madison.

Lorentzen continued his analysis of projectile points from Grasshopper Spring and Chodistaas Pueblos for his master's thesis research (Lorentzen 1993). His study would go well beyond hunting to investigate raiding, warfare, and ethnic identity.

Ceramics had begun to attract a crowd of graduate students bent on attacking contemporary problems with sophisticated analytical techniques. Montgomery, a doctoral student at the UA, had defined her research to focus on ceramic variability and the formation of the ceramic record at Chodistaas Pueblo, from which we would have recovered almost three hundred whole or restorable vessels from room floors by the end of the 1988 season. Fieldwork at Chodistaas in 1988 and 1991 was directed by research questions raised in Montgomery's analysis and reported in her dissertation study (Montgomery 1992a).

Zedeño, at that time one of Crown's doctoral students at SMU, began a compositional study of Chodistaas black-on-white pottery to resolve the question of whether it was made locally and to begin addressing the question of how nonlocally made ceramics came into the Chodistaas community. Zedeño's (1991, 1994) provenance study would complement Montgomery's provenience research concerning the ways in which ceramic vessels and sherds came to be where they were recovered by archaeologists. Together, these two studies demonstrate to the archaeological community the type of in-depth analysis that must be done before ceramics can be used to make reliable inferences about past human behavior.

Triadan, then a graduate student at the Freie Universität–Berlin, began her master's-thesis study of ceramic manufacture in Room 113 of Room Block 5 at Grasshopper (Triadan 1989). This substantial thesis on the floor artifacts from just *one* room at Grasshopper Pueblo gives an idea of the immensity of the ruin's archaeological record. Triadan would go further in her dissertation research to complete a compositional analysis of Fourmile Polychrome ceramics that would revise thinking on trade and migration in late prehistory (Triadan 1994, 1997).

This was also a busy year for attempting to expand Grasshopper research. We joined with Gene Rogge of Dames & Moore, a private environmental consulting firm, to submit a proposal for the Roosevelt Archaeology Project to the U.S. Bureau of Reclamation in mid-April. Part of the archaeological studies carried out for Plan 6 of the Central Arizona Project (CAP), this project would go on to become the largest reclamation-funded CAP study in the Theodore Roosevelt Lake area in budget and number of sites (Whittlesey 2003). The study included a synthesis of all Roosevelt projects undertaken by other consultants. Naively, we assumed that our experience in Salado archaeology—combined, the proposed personnel had several decades of fieldwork experience in the central Arizona transition zone—would make us shoo-ins to be awarded the contract. We were not. What would be named the Roosevelt Platform Mound Study was awarded to the Office of Cultural Resource Management at ASU.

Tuggle and Reid organized a small, informal conference on Grasshopper archaeology funded by the Southwest Center of the UA. The two-day conference was held May 26 and 27 at Grasshopper, prior to the beginning of the Field School but after the camp was operational. In naming it "From Pueblo to Apache: The People of the Arizona Mountains," we had hoped to make it an annual affair, but this was the first and only such conference despite its success. Our conference theme was settlement phenomena of late prehistory in the Grasshopper region, for which Tuggle and Reid prepared a summary paper to be the focus of discussion. The paper was sent in advance to the participants: Roger Anyon and Jackie Rossignol of the Zuni Archaeological Program; Bruce Donaldson of Apache-Sitgreaves National Forest; Keith Kintigh and Brenda Shears of ASU; Stephen Lekson, then at the ASM; James Neely,

University of Texas; Randall Morrison, BIA; and Welch, of the Grass-hopper staff. Invited Apache participants included Ray Palmer, BIA Forestry Branch; Andrew Kane, tribal police chief; and Nashley Tessay Sr., a friend of Grasshopper and later a councilman representing Cibecue, Grasshopper, and Oak Creek. Apache participation in our conference was to signal our growing concern with expanding their involvement in our research program. Invitees unable to attend were Edgar Perry, director of the Apache Cultural Center, Phillip Stago, the tribal councilman who, at that time, had supervisory authority for the Field School, and Scott Wood, archaeologist for the Tonto National Forest.

In late fall of 1988, Whittlesey attended the twenty-first annual Chacmool Conference, where she presented at long last the rebuttal to Plog's earlier attack, on the grounds that a response had been denied in the conference-proceedings volume (Thompson, Garcia, and Kense 1985).

The 1989 Season

The Field School was in session for six weeks, from June 9 to July 21, with eleven students—six men and five women—who represented five graduate and six undergraduate students.

The year began with the knowledge that Reid would succeed Raymond Wood as editor of *American Antiquity*, the journal of the SAA, and that he would begin as editor-elect at the annual meeting in Atlanta. Thus, the next four summers at Grasshopper also would have editorial duties added to the teaching and research activities, replicating Thompson's experience at Point of Pines, where he was book review editor (1956–1958) and editor (1958–1962) of *American Antiquity*.

Excavation concentrated on Grasshopper Spring Pueblo to clarify distinct differences with the nearby and contemporary Chodistaas Pueblo in projectile points, architecture, and hearths. Four rooms (3, 4, 5, 6) were excavated under the direction of Triadan, Lorentzen, and Mark Neupert to facilitate the interpretation of household activities. Rooms 1 and 2 were excavated previously, revealing that Room 1 had been abandoned, the doorway between Rooms 1 and 2 closed, and a new doorway knocked into the wall connecting Rooms 2 and 4, all of which suggested that these rooms housed one domestic unit. Rooms 3, 5, and 6 were excavated to complete the investigation of Room Block 2, a set of contiguous rooms. A test trench was excavated along the exterior of the east wall of Room 2 to measure the amount of wall fall outside of the room, test for postholes, compare artifact densities with interior fill, and

Field School staff and students in 1989. Seated, left to right, are Jefferson Reid, Tiffany Tretschok, Nieves Zedeño, Paula Bader, Regina Chapin, Andrew Friedl, Nathan Tessay; standing, Leon Lorentzen, Edward Baldwin, Daniela Triadan, Charles Riggs, Mark Neupert, Linda Walker, William Saturno, Paula Dorr, Richard Baublitz, Ryan Wheeler, Loa Traxler, Glenn Cromwell, Barbara Montgomery, John Welch.

The 1989 Season

Research and Teaching Staff	Support Staff	Apache Crew	Students	Family
Jefferson Reid, Director	Tiffany Tretschok, Cook	Glenn Cromwell	Paula Bader	Erin Reid
Barbara Montgomery, Assistant Director-Excavation		Nathan Tessay	Edward Baldwin	
John Welch, Assistant Director-Survey			Richard Baublitz	
Leon Lorentzen, Excavation Supervisor			Regina Chapin	
Daniela Triadan, Excavation Supervisor			Paula Dorr	
Nieves Zedeño, Laboratory Supervisor			Andrew Friedl	
Mark Neupert, Archaeological Assistant			Charles Riggs	
			William Saturno	
			Loa Traxler	
			Linda Walker	
			Ryan Wheeler	

investigate how outdoor space was used. Other field activities at Grasshopper Spring Pueblo included the completion of a map of its topography, room blocks, and Apache wickiup circles. The outlining of walls in Room Block 1 revealed it to represent the Pueblo II period occupation that had been evident in some of the surface ceramics.

Montgomery also conducted a small test excavation at Chodistaas Pueblo in the plaza east of Rooms 4 and 10. A rubble mound that looked suspiciously like small, undiscovered rooms was explored, but no rooms were found. Welch's survey fieldwork focused on continuing data collection for his dissertation research, describing Apache sites, and monitoring vandalism to major sites. Glenn Cromwell, Lorentzen, and Welch undertook repair work at Kinishba Ruin. Damage by grazing horses that threatened to undermine the eastern room block and send it crashing into the arroyo was controlled by the repair of the fence around the ruin.

Further evidence that ceramics were rapidly becoming the favored artifact was the paper presented at the fall meeting of the Arizona Archaeological Council entitled "The Birth and Spread of Roosevelt Red Ware: Ceramic Theory beyond Taxonomy," later published (Reid, Montgomery, Zedeño, and Neupert 1992). Montgomery and Reid (1990) published in *American Antiquity* a paper that documented the rapid replacement of Cibola White Ware by Roosevelt Red Ware at Chodistaas Pueblo.

By that time, it had become apparent that a counterattack to the Chavez Pass–ASU critique of Grasshopper research was essential. We began to prepare a reply, which resulted ultimately in the "gang of eight" paper by Reid, Schiffer, Whittlesey, Hinkes, Sullivan, Downum, Long-

The 1990 Season

Research and Teaching Staff	Support Staff	Apache Crew	Students	Family
Jefferson Reid, Director	Kristen Pfaff, Cook	Glenn Cromwell	Susan Beacom	Erin Reid
Julie Lowell, Research Archaeologist (independent)			Randy Dobbs	
Barbara Montgomery, Assistant Director			Sherri Ekers	
Nieves Zedeño, Laboratory Supervisor			Matthew Glendinning	
Leon Lorentzen, Excavation Supervisor			Deborah Harvey	
Mark Neupert, Excavation Supervisor			Robert Heckman	
Daniela Triadan, Excavation Supervisor			Clare Leader	
			Yung-ti Li	
			Jennifer Ross	
			Richard Treadway	
			Josef Wegner	
			Steve West	

acre, and Tuggle that was published in *American Antiquity*. It is unclear whether the paper slowed the publication of misperceptions and attacks on Grasshopper research, or the opposition got involved in other pursuits. Clearly, the compulsion to uncover social and economic complexity in late pueblo prehistory had run its course by the 1990s, and fashionable research had turned again to investigate migration and ethnic identity, topics with a long history in Grasshopper research.

Also in 1989, Whittlesey's Chacmool paper was published in the conference-proceedings volume. Whittlesey pointed out the serious errors and distortions that littered the Plog attack and that indicated "at best gross misunderstanding and at worst misrepresentation" of the dissertation (Whittlesey 1989:229).

The 1990 Season

The Field School was in session for six weeks, from June 8 to July 20. Twelve students—seven men and five women, seven graduate students and five undergraduates—were enrolled.

Lowell, a Field School alumna and former staff member and currently on the faculty at the University of Northern Iowa, contributed to the teaching and research program through an independent research project. Work concentrated once more at Grasshopper Spring Pueblo, this time in the Pueblo II period Room Block 1. Triadan supervised the excavation of Rooms 10, 11, and 12, and Lorentzen managed the excavation of Room 14 and several trenches in extramural areas to the east of the room block. Lowell's independently funded pursuit of research questions concerning thermal features, such as fire pits and hearths, and the differences between Chodistaas and Grasshopper Spring Pueblos in these features, led her to excavate extensively in the eastern extramural areas outside Room Block 2. The results of this work were later published (Lowell 1995, 1999).

The 1991 Season

The Field School was in session for six weeks, from June 1 to July 12, with an enrollment of eleven students—five men and six women, representing seven graduate and four undergraduate students.

Fieldwork targeted Grasshopper and Chodistaas Pueblos. At Grasshopper, we excavated Rooms 414 and 420 in Room Block 10, an outlier located on a low hill 150 meters northwest of the main ruin. At Chodistaas, we excavated Room 18, the last unexcavated room in the southern room block. It proved to be the ritual room (protokiva) we had always believed it to be (Reid and Montgomery 1999).

Excavation of outlier rooms was designed to obtain chronological, ceramic, and other information on the last occupation at Grasshopper Pueblo. Previous excavations of outlier rooms had indicated differences in household structure as well as in the frequency of certain types of painted ceramics relative to the early occupation. Room Block 10 was chosen for investigation because only one room had been excavated previously. Room 198 had been excavated in 1968 and yielded a noncutting tree-ring date of A.D. 1318vv and an estimated date range of 1318 to 1337, which suggested that the room block may have been built late in the occupation at Grasshopper. Room 414 was chosen for excavation because it was adjacent to the south wall of Room 198 and thus had a reasonable probability of containing dateable roof beams. We chose Room 420, by contrast, because it was built late in the construction sequence of the room block.

As part of Triadan's dissertation research on ceramic production in the Grasshopper region, specifically the local production of painted wares, she conducted a systematic survey for sources of clays and tempering materials. The survey covered an area of approximately ten kilometers around Grasshopper Pueblo and included deposits outside this range. In addition, fourteen Pueblo IV period sites were revisited to check the accuracy of sketch maps and survey records and collect qualitative samples of painted sherds for chemical analysis.

The 1991 Season

Research and Teaching Staff	Support Staff	Apache Crew	Students	Family
Jefferson Reid, Director	Kristen Pfaff, Cook	Glenn Cromwell	Lisa Armstrong	Erin Reid
Barbara Montgomery, Assistant Director			Candice Doan	
Nieves Zedeño, Laboratory and Excavation Supervisor			Kathryn Keith	
			Angela Keller	
			James Miller	
			Scott Pletka	
Leon Lorentzen, Excavation Supervisor			Michael Scafuri	
Daniela Triadan, Excavation Supervisor			Sabina Shahrokhizadeh	
Charles Riggs Archaeological Assistant			Bruce Smithhammer	
			Geraldine Toste	
			David Williamson	

The year was also a busy one for public and professional presentations of Grasshopper research. We organized a symposium on episodic change for the Southwestern Anthropological Association annual meeting, a poster symposium on the same topic at the SAA annual meeting, and a highly condensed version of these presentations for the Anthropology Department colloquium at the UA. Two dissertations were completed. Zedeño's research (Zedeño 1991, 1994) was funded partially by an NSF Dissertation Improvement Grant to SMU, and Ezzo's study (Ezzo 1991, 1993) also was finished with a similar NSF grant to the University of Wisconsin-Madison.

Late in the fall of 1991, Ezzo and Reid submitted an unsuccessful grant proposal to the NSF for "The Grasshopper Burial Assemblage: A Catalog and Synthesis of Skeletal Research." We would conclude the last decade and a half of Grasshopper fieldwork without assistance from the NSF.

The 1992 Season

The thirtieth and final season of the UA Archaeological Field School at Grasshopper ran for six weeks, from June 1 to July 10. There were seven students, four men and three women, who were two graduate students and five undergraduates.

In the absence of a cook, cooking duties were distributed among the staff. Reid and Riggs cooked breakfast, everyone fixed their own lunch, and the staff supervised dinner preparations. Students washed dishes

The 1992 Season

Research and Teaching Staff	Support Staff	Apache Crew	Students	Family
Jefferson Reid, Director	None	Glenn Cromwell	Michael Diehl	Erin Reid
Barbara Montgomery, Assistant Director		Glenn Cromwell Jr.	Jerry Forstadt	
Charles Riggs, Excavation Supervisor			Jennifer MacCormack	
Daniela Triadan, Excavation Supervisor			James Pepe	
			Mary Ann Pouls	
			Ellen Ruble	
			Jonathan Walz	

and cleaned the kitchen. Other maintenance duties were shared by staff and students, as they had been since 1982.

In April, the Second Salado Conference was held in Globe, Arizona. Four papers were presented on Grasshopper research in relation to the Salado. In 1963, Thompson listed the question of Salado origins as one of the reasons for moving the UA field school to Grasshopper. Montgomery discussed the ritual abandonment of Chodistaas Pueblo. Zedeño reevaluated Roosevelt black-on-white pottery in relation to dramatic changes in ceramic assemblages at the end of the Pueblo III period. With Montgomery, Zedeño, and Neupert, Reid discussed the chronology and behavioral implications of the first Salado ceramics, Pinto Black-on-red and Pinto Polychrome, using data from Chodistaas Pueblo. Whittlesey and Reid argued for a revised chronology of Gila Polychrome based on recent analysis of ceramics from Grasshopper Pueblo. This work on Salado ceramics influenced our excavation decisions for the 1992 field season.

Fieldwork concentrated on the excavation of three rooms at the southern end of Room Block 1 at Grasshopper. Rooms 104, supervised by Riggs, and 107, by Triadan, were chosen because of the relatively large numbers of Gila Polychrome ceramics recovered from surrounding rooms that had been excavated in 1963 and 1964. Rooms 104 and 107 also were part of a construction unit of six rooms (2, 7, 10, 15, 104, 107), of which four (2, 7, 10, 15) had been excavated previously. Finishing Rooms 104 and 107 would yield a completely excavated construction unit that also would provide an inventory of the rooms originally built as an isolated group.

After two weeks of excavation in Rooms 104 and 107, we decided that there was time enough to allow Montgomery to supervise excavation of Room 97, a room constructed late in the Room Block 1 sequence and adjacent to Room 11. The latter had also been excavated previously and had yielded a full array of floor artifacts. Room 97 met the expectations that it would produce a similar assemblage.

Closing camp was anticlimactic. Three of the staff cabins were dismantled and taken away one weekend to the new field-school location at Pinedale, thirteen miles west of Show Low. The weekend after the students left, Barbara Mills, the new field-school director, joined her crew with ours to complete the move of the last two staff cabins, screens, drying racks, shovels, and miscellaneous equipment. The 1992 season and thirty years of research at Grasshopper were over.

8

Archaeological Lessons from a Mogollon Pueblo

I have, for some time, held the view (Renfrew 1982a) that for valid insights into the theoretical positions of archaeologists we would do better to look at their working papers, that is to say to the application of their thinking to specific cases, than to their more programmatic statements or to their attempts to write philosophy.
—**Colin Renfrew** (1994:4-5)

We have borrowed the title of this chapter from the early ethnoarchaeological study by Longacre and Ayres (1968), "Archaeological Lessons from an Apache Wickiup." In so doing, we extend the Grasshopper heuristic metaphor as we reconnect with a major theme of this narrative—Grasshopper research as a proving ground for method and theory, a thirty-year study that reveals some important features of American archaeology's recent history.

In this chapter, we evaluate the questions, concepts, and procedures of three archaeologies—culture history, processual archaeology, and behavioral archaeology—as they were expressed at Grasshopper and as they permitted access to the past behavior reflected in that specific archaeological record. We do not attempt a global examination of these archaeologies or a thorough historical treatment of the full range of questions, concepts, and procedures embraced by each. Such an admittedly worthwhile analysis will remain for future students of archaeological historiography with larger purpose. We qualify our subject matter further by labeling the archaeologies after the traditional type-variety system. We refer to the culture history we examine as the Point of Pines

174

variety, processual archaeology as the Hay Hollow variety, and behavioral archaeology as the Grasshopper variety. These represent distinctly southwestern expressions of research programs that may have been presented differently in other domains.

Our purpose, then, is straightforward. Three directors went to Grasshopper, each with a different approach to acquiring knowledge of a large, prehistoric pueblo community. We consider the basic question—how did these three approaches fare in addressing the prehistory of this place and its interesting questions of past behavior? In our evaluation, we seek to determine which questions, concepts, and procedures worked to produce knowledge of the past and which did not. We approach our appraisal by looking broadly at research issues, theory, and methods, recognizing that there is not complete symmetry among the three archaeologies in these arenas. After considering each archaeological approach in turn, we present the Grasshopper–Chavez Pass debate as an illustration of the differences between processual and behavioral archaeology.

Culture History at Grasshopper

The first three years of fieldwork at Grasshopper—the 1965 season already influenced by William Longacre's presence as field director—are not fully representative of culture history in the Pueblo Southwest and certainly not in American archaeology. The initial field examination of a five-hundred-room neolithic village would have been much the same, regardless of the conceptual frame of reference. Apart from the immense task of setting up a camp and providing essential services to twenty students and ten staff in the midst of the central Arizona mountains, there were three essential objectives—map the site, determine the archaeological and geological context, and assess the qualitative and quantitative characteristics of the cultural remains.

Research Issues and Concepts

Culture history has taken a beating over the past forty or so years, especially at the hands of aggressive, young, processual archaeologists seeking a place within a highly structured, academic network (see Gibbon 1989:64–66). A less jaundiced perspective reveals that culture history in the Southwest and at Grasshopper was neither atheoretical nor lacking research problems, as some have suggested (e.g., Binford 1972).

Moreover, many of the research questions tackled by Raymond Thompson and crew have returned to popularity in the 1990s, indicating their perennial importance.

The criteria for selecting Grasshopper for investigation—it was a relatively unknown place dating to a relatively unknown time—were justifiable within the framework of cultural history. Culture history tackled the research questions set forth by A. V. Kidder, which we discussed in chapter 3. The archaeologist chose an unknown region or period for investigation by selectively excavating sites that would fill the gaps in knowledge. In the most general sense, "knowledge" meant the punctuations in the time-space matrix that are labeled phases. The phase is the conceptual workhorse of culture history, representing "the smallest unit into which a culture history could be divided" (Haury 1988:18).

Thompson had no need to create a local phase sequence for Grasshopper. Emil Haury (1985:377; Haury and Sayles 1947) already had established phase sequences for the Forestdale Valley, only twenty miles to the northeast of Grasshopper, and for Point of Pines (see Haury 1989: 115), sixty miles to the southeast. In addition, Haury (Haury and Hargrave 1931) had defined the Pinedale phase (A.D. 1275–1325) for an area just above the Mogollon Rim to the north and the Canyon Creek phase (A.D. 1325–1400), well dated by tree rings, at the Canyon Creek cliff dwelling on the western edge of the Grasshopper Plateau (Haury 1934).

It is difficult to ascertain to what extent Thompson's and Longacre's acceptance of the existing phase sequence and Longacre's lack of interest in developing a new one influenced later approaches. Regardless, the phase concept simply was not used in Grasshopper research or in our reconstruction of Grasshopper prehistory in any meaningful way (see Reid 1989; Reid and Whittlesey 1999). Because the phase remains a prominent conceptual tool in the Southwest (e.g., E. Adams 1999; Ciolek-Torrello 1998; Elson 1996; Mills and Herr 1999), our reasons for abandoning the concept deserve elaboration.

Willey and Phillips (1958:22) define the phase as "an archaeological unit possessing traits sufficiently characteristic to distinguish it from all other units similarly conceived, whether of the same or other cultures or civilizations, spatially limited to the order of magnitude of a locality or region and chronologically limited to a relatively brief interval of time." The phase represents an archaeological culture, which, like any historical culture, has a defined range in time and a position in space. Also, as with any other historical culture, a phase has characteristics or traits that distinguish it from other phases. The traits of an archaeological phase almost always include pottery, but also may include architecture, stone tools, textiles, and features of settlement and subsistence. The phase and phase description are similar conceptually in archaeological expression and application to the pottery type and type description. As in pottery identification, usually only one or two criteria are sufficient for a phase assignment, and these are commonly a pottery type or set of types.

Appropriate culture-history method calls for the development of a chart or matrix of phases sequenced in time and space, or "phase stacking," in the Berrys' terminology (Berry and Berry 1986; see Willey and Phillips 1958:22–24). We also suspect that, like pottery classification masquerading as analysis, the assignment of a particular set of archaeological remains to a phase is viewed as a research end in itself and not simply a matter of classification. Phase stacking more obviously substitutes for research when the definition of new phases parades as a significant research outcome, particularly when phases are used as bridges linking periods of significant change in the archaeological record, thus creating a spurious sense of cultural continuity (e.g., Doyel 1976, 1977, 1978).

One of two chronic difficulties with the phase concept is the confusion of culture content and time, both of which may be loaded into a specific phase label. But as information accumulates, especially as new dates appear, the temporal referent may shift, often dramatically, without any change in cultural content. The confusion that results when the same phase label is given multiple date ranges obfuscates comparisons. Even if we were to understand how other archaeologists applied the Pinedale phase, for example, it would have no significance at Grasshopper other than to mark a block of time. When considering time, we have tried to be consistent in using standard temporal labels—e.g., A.D. 1276–1299, A.D. 1300s, fourteenth century, Pueblo IV period—to avoid the confusion inherent in mixing time and culture.

The second major problem with the phase concept is that it assumes cultural homogeneity, in that a specific phase name designates a specific archaeological culture. Because two phases cannot comfortably occupy the same space at the same time in a phase chart, it is difficult for the phase concept to distinguish instances of ethnic coresidence. The phase only does so with some awkwardness, as in the contemporaneous Maverick Mountain and Pinedale phases at Point of Pines Pueblo (see Haury 1989:115).

The phase may be a useful conceptual device for initially organizing cultural material over long stretches of time, over large areas, or in structuring large blocks of time when instances of rapid change are invisible, as during the southwestern Archaic period. At Grasshopper, and we suspect in other contexts as well, the phase concept may not only fail to enhance but also may hinder attempts to understand the past by obscuring significant patterns in the record. Given that it did so little to clarify archaeological discourse at Grasshopper, we suspect that the phase may be equally useless in other contexts, and urge that archaeologists scrutinize their motives closely when the compulsion to employ phases, or even more important, the urge to define a new phase, arises. (For a history of the phase concept in the Southwest, see Olson 1959:399–458, 1962a.)

By contrast, the concepts of horizon, horizon style, and tradition (Willey and Phillips 1958:29–43)—as subsumed within closely related notions of ceramic cross dating, decorative styles, and manufacturing technologies—have proven their utility at Grasshopper and in broader research arenas.

The Use of Theory

Culture history was criticized routinely by processual archaeologists (e.g., Binford 1972) for its lack of attention to theory, particularly social theory, or "principles for explaining behavioral variability and change" (Schiffer 1988:464). An alternative appraisal held that theory existed but was neither explicit nor bundled into a neat conceptual package (Schiffer 1988:466). Lewis Binford's (1972:3) comment on James Griffin demonstrates how many culture historians approached theory—it was viewed as isomorphic with speculation: "Of all the anthropologists I met during my student years Griffin was the least self-conscious about being antitheoretical. To Griffin, theory was to be equated with speculation, and one only did that when there were no data."

Haury's point of view, by contrast, was neither atheoretical nor inexplicit, but an empirically driven perspective that influenced how he approached problem solving. Haury, who was trained by A. E. Douglass, the astronomer who discovered dendrochronology and dendroclimatology, certainly understood theory and how it could be useful in handling facts. Haury believed strongly that the past is knowable, and knowledge is based in empirical evidence. His questions about the past, and we think our questions as well, largely were answerable within the boundaries of archaeological context and evidence without having to invoke social theory.

The Thompson and Longacre (1966) article assists in sorting out the conceptual differences between culture history and processual archaeology. That Thompson, a theoretical culture historian, and Longacre, one of the earliest Binfordians, could meld their two approaches in a coauthored summary article merits mention again. On the surface, the two approaches appear compatible—Thompson's culture-history questions led directly into the dual processual themes of ecology and sociology enumerated by Longacre. Although sociology—features of social action and organization—never dominated the research agenda of Point of Pines archaeologists, southwestern culture historians built no insurmountable conceptual barriers to the study of social phenomena. In fact, Martin and Rinaldo (1950) raised these types of questions within a context that was clearly culture historical.

Thompson and Longacre (1966), therefore, leave us with the impression that processual archaeology, at least in the American Southwest, was less a radical departure from established archaeological thinking than it was an expansion of the range of questions that one can ask about the past and a heightened confidence that enhanced methods would provide accurate answers to these questions. In other words, the distinction was more one of jargon and expression than thought and practice. This may be a particular fact of southwestern culture history, which was problem oriented from its inception (see Fowler 2000).

Methods

At Grasshopper, there were significant differences in data-recovery techniques and recording procedures as well as language to differentiate culture history from processual archaeology. Today, these methods may appear to be quaint, but a canon of sound fieldwork supported culture-history methods, despite the lack of contemporary technological flash.

Fieldwork Procedures. Scanning the fieldwork accomplished during the first three years at Grasshopper, we can speculate how it might have been done by archaeologists of different theoretical persuasions. Defining the rubble-and-brush-covered surface of a five-hundred-room pueblo ruin and mapping its topographic and cultural characteristics with plane table and alidade would be essential first tasks for any archaeologist. These tasks largely were incomplete by the end of the 1965 season. In fact, an accurate map of the site defied the processual-archaeology era and was not completed until the early 1980s. We can blame the failure of culture history to achieve the fundamental mapping objective on technological factors. Yesterday's long hours in the bright sun bent over a plane table, squinting at minute markings and inverted numbers on a distant

Stephanie Whittlesey and Tim O'Meara show students how to map with alidade and plane table.

stadia rod while fighting a mind-numbing headache, are unnecessary in the age of laser optics and computer-assisted drafting.

Moreover, we think it unlikely that either processual archaeology or behavioral archaeology would have developed an excavation strategy much different from the one Thompson devised to ascertain the nature of cultural and geological deposits. The twenty-two rooms excavated during the first three years, which were scattered throughout the southern portion of Room Blocks 1 and 2, provided soundings of the full range of two-story, single story, and low-walled rooms. In addition, the rooms ranged in time from early to late construction and from early to late abandonment, probably as random a collection as the rooms that were selected when sampling was pursued self-consciously. Extensive hand-excavated and backhoe trenches were dug into the alluvial clays in and around the main ruin to determine subsurface characteristics. Thus, we conclude that the establishment of baseline data through similar procedures would be requisite to any investigation of a five-hundred-room pueblo.

The most obvious point where Grasshopper research diverged from the culture-history field program outlined by Kidder and followed by Haury at Point of Pines was the absence of a systematic survey of the Grasshopper region to chart the range of variability in site types. From the onset of fieldwork, research emphasized the large pueblo ruin of Grasshopper, because Thompson's design for Grasshopper research was driven by a desire to provide a well-documented case for comparison with Point of Pines Pueblo.

Processing and Analysis. Culture history at Grasshopper approached the material record as Haury and Thompson had at Point of Pines. Artifacts were processed and recorded by the laboratory staff on catalog and stone-list cards according to Arizona State Museum specifications. We imagine it was expected that graduate students preparing master's theses or dissertations would write up the ceramics, ground stone, and other artifacts along with their other research, much as had been done at Point of Pines. In addition, in the early years of exploratory excavation, mapping, and backhoe trenching, and when screening was not employed routinely, the total material collection remained comparatively small.

Whereas it might have been reasonably successful at Point of Pines, this strategy was not effective with the astonishing material record of Grasshopper and Chodistaas Pueblos. Processual archaeology also failed to come to grips with processing and analysis. The problem of a unique and voluminous material record stumped us all, regardless of conceptual framework. Culture history at Grasshopper was over before excavation had created the material monster that later archaeologies would be forced to tackle.

Research Products and Interpretations of the Past

The brief span of culture history at Grasshopper was insufficient to produce any dissertations. Thus, there is no research record with which to evaluate the efficacy of the research and training program. The years did, however, introduce a number of individuals to the field and to the discipline, and their training in culture history must be seen as an important factor in molding the research that is attributed to the school.

Processual Archaeology at Grasshopper

Iconoclastic and contentious as the statement may appear, the simple truth is that processual archaeology had design flaws that could not address a complicated context like Grasshopper, and these inadequacies prompted the development of behavioral archaeology's methodology package. Whereas processual concepts and procedures may have worked well on small and simple contexts, such as those found in the lithic scatters of hunter-gatherers or at small village-farmer sites, they did not function to provide a coherent, behavior-reconstruction strategy for a large pueblo community such as Grasshopper. The most prominent failures are discussed elsewhere (Gibbon 1989) and are summarized here as they apply to Grasshopper.

As Thompson and Longacre (1966:270) expressed it, processual archaeologists believed that to attain their research goals it was "necessary to make another primary assumption. This is that all of the material remains in an archaeological site are highly patterned or structured directly as a result of the ways in which the extinct society was organized and the patterned ways in which the people behaved. Thus, our first task is to define the archaeological structure of the site and then from that infer the organization of the society and aspects of behavior."

Schiffer (1972, 1976, 1983, 1987) provides ample discussion of the discontinuity between the archaeological context of the present and the systemic context of the past. This disjunction, which may qualify as the core tenet of behavioral archaeology, nullifies the simple assumption of a site as a fossilized, past social system and promotes the study of site-formation processes as essential to any reconstruction or explanation of past human behavior. Recognition of this context distinction at Grasshopper was marked by a shift from theory-down studies characterizing the early, processual-inspired dissertation research (Griffin 1969; Reid 1973; Tuggle 1970) to studies that sought refinements in methods and middle-range theory (Trigger 1995) — the label applied to the investigation of principles of formation processes and material correlates of behavior (Ciolek-Torrello 1978; Montgomery 1992b; Whittaker 1984; Whittlesey 1978).

Research Issues

Processual research questions served to guide studies through the transitional and behavioral archaeology years, proving their long-term usefulness. Terminological differences notwithstanding, response to environmental change; sociological and demographic processes of population movement, aggregation, and organizational responses; economy and agricultural dependence; and interaction and exchange were issues posed by Thompson and Longacre (1966:257) that were addressed in numerous dissertations and theses. The perennial importance of these research themes demonstrates that processual archaeologists were asking the right questions. The problem was simply that the methods they used to answer those questions could not stand up against the obstacles posed by Grasshopper Pueblo's complicated archaeological record.

Methods

Fieldwork Procedures. Processual archaeology, Hay Hollow variety, was incredibly wordy and little concerned with fieldwork precision. According to Hill (1972:88–89), "there is really no such thing as the 'good field man' who can gather data in expert fashion without understanding how the data are to be analyzed" (cf. Taylor 1954). It was always our impression that processualists sought to remedy inadequate fieldwork through sophisticated analyses and statistical tests, and at times we have thought, less kindly, that the heavy emphasis on theory was as much camouflage for poor field skills as it was a sincere effort to invigorate the conceptual basis of archaeology.

Regardless, the field techniques of processual archaeology were inadequate for coping with the requirements of excavating a large mountain pueblo, especially one under investigation as part of a field-school teaching program. The difference between the archaeological context of Grasshopper and that of the Hay Hollow sites has been discussed in chapter 2, but a quick comparison serves as a reminder. Excavation of seventeen low-walled rooms at Chodistaas Pueblo produced almost as many potsherds as all of the pueblo rooms excavated by Paul Martin's crews in the Hay Hollow Valley and surrounding areas. The Grasshopper ceramic yield, which can be taken as an index of total artifacts, is several orders of magnitude greater than that of Chodistaas Pueblo. No one has ever had the necessary time, equipment, personnel, or budget to summarize the ceramic collection, but we suspect that it numbers in the millions.

A cavalier regard for fieldwork is incompatible with the need for control of formation processes responsible for deposits and artifact associations. In point of fact, formation-process research requires the application of field skills far surpassing the general level of field competence. We speculate that basic inattention to and generalized disregard for fieldwork are among the reasons that formation-process research has been rather sluggish over the past quarter century.

Laboratory Processing and Recording. The initial years of processual archaeology at Grasshopper can be perceived as an extension of the field, laboratory, and recording strategy that had been successful at Point of Pines and the culture-history years of Grasshopper. The 1966 season's revolution in recording did much to increase standardization of observations but could not ameliorate the fact that it was students who were responsible for the bulk of laboratory processing and reporting. Just as fieldwork is highly variable from student to student, so is the ability to take good field notes, make sound observations, and write a coherent and descriptive synthesis of fieldwork results.

Students were responsible for ceramic classification and simple sorting of bulk flaked stone artifacts, recording these data on sherd count and lithic forms, and filling out stone-list cards for other artifacts (individual stone, bone, and ceramic artifacts) from noncritical proveniences. Laboratory personnel acted as supervisors in this and other laboratory work, but their primary responsibility was cataloguing the endless streams of artifacts from critical proveniences (floors, roofs, features, and so on). This meant that much of the laboratory work carried out by students was by necessity essentially unsupervised.

Although recording forms (e.g., level and feature) were standardized, no such format was developed for room reports. Each excavation team and supervisor discussed the content of the room report. For this reason, the quality of room reports is variable in the extreme. Some are excellent, even publishable; others are dismal. In room reporting, as in the procedures for laboratory processing and many aspects of fieldwork—filling out forms, taking field notes, and the provenience designation system—vital information was typically conveyed to students in the form of daytime lectures in the first week and evening lectures thereafter. This persisted until 1970, when Reid instituted a laboratory-processing flow chart and, in the following year, required procedural manuals to be developed. As a student who was required to acquire information in the verbal-lecture format, Whittlesey can attest to its mind-numbing inefficiency.

Such laid-back approaches to processing and recording may have worked reasonably well at Vernon, where the material record was more or less manageable. At Grasshopper, with its millions of potsherds and flaked stone artifacts in room fill, rich de facto refuse assemblages, and burials with numerous accompaniments, the results were far less successful.

Arguably, the most far-reaching effect of processual data recording was to democratize observations, whereby student notes on the archaeological record were accorded the status of basic data. The critical and essential teaching exercise of note taking formed an unfiltered database. The net effect was to convert objective relationships of the archaeological record to a highly subjective language that would require subsequent translation to make the data useful for inferences about the past. As a learning experience for students, it may have been a reasonable approach; as a means of creating the primary data record, it was not.

This is one reason why we have always considered it unwise to con-

Painted pottery vessels from Grasshopper Pueblo: back row, left to right, Tonto Polychrome jar, Fourmile Polychrome bowl, Pinedale black-on-white jar; middle row, left to right, Pinto Polychrome bowl, Cedar Creek Polychrome bowl; front, Cibicue Polychrome jar.

template publishing student room reports as the descriptive monograph of Grasshopper Pueblo, a product that Haury (1964) envisioned as "the final scientific record of the research" (see chapter 1). Student room reports would fall short as an accurate description of the archaeological record.

Sampling Procedures and Concepts. Sampling was a recurring methodological issue and an overriding concern of Longacre's processual archaeology. We took seriously the dictum that a representative sample was absolutely essential for any statement about a past behavioral parameter. Earlier sampling techniques based on the room-size categories used at Broken K Pueblo and modified by Bion Griffin and David Tuggle turned out to be unsuitable for the long-term, multilayered research program into which Grasshopper developed.

The practical solution was to target specific data populations and justify their representativeness for a particular interpretation, so that independent investigators could evaluate the evidentiary basis for an inference (Reid, Schiffer, and Neff 1975). This approach to sampling recognized that a slavish adherence to up-front, statistical sampling procedures was inappropriate to a large pueblo and to complicated, long-term research questions.

We disagree on root causes for the processualists' apparent retreat from sampling and arguments of representativeness. Reid lays the blame at the feet of contract archaeology. Its mandated necessity to concentrate on rights-of-way and fractions of sites makes determinations of representativeness difficult and unnecessary. In the late 1970s, the Cholla Project (Reid 1982) had argued that an adverse impact to a site forming part of a settlement system was an impact to the whole system, and thus it was necessary that the whole be the target of mitigation efforts. Conceptualizing the whole is not a commonplace phenomenon in contract archaeology.

Whittlesey, by contrast, does not see contract archaeology as the culpable force behind this inattention to sampling adequacy. Rather, she insists it is academic careerism and pressures to publish, regardless of data quality or quantity. There is probably some truth in both positions. Regardless of cause, the inherent irony was the diminution of a concern with sampling and representativeness throughout southwestern archaeology, when this was one of the few procedural contributions of processual archaeology.

Hypothesis Testing Procedures and Concepts. A major contribution of processual archaeology was to raise awareness of useful and appropriate scientific procedures of inquiry, the most important of which was explicitly designed hypothesis testing and its concomitant concern with specifying variables and measurements. Some muddle did accompany early discussions of induction versus deduction and covering-law models of explanation versus hypothetico-deductive models of confirmation, and we believe that too much emphasis was placed on grand social theory and not enough on the operationalization and measurement of variables in the archaeological record. Despite these issues, the crusade for increased rigor and explicitness was a significant achievement. The ideal procedure for hypothesis testing was not well adapted to the peculiarities of archaeological data in a large-pueblo context. Like other procedures of Hay Hollow processualism, hypothesis testing worked best on tightly bounded questions applied to uncomplicated contexts.

Ethnography and Analogy in Concept and Procedure. In his comment in *Man the Hunter*, Binford (reprinted in Binford 1972:59–61) summed the role of ethnographic analogy and the use of ethnographic information for model building:

> It is frequently stated that one of the main tasks of the archaeologist is the interpretation of the past and that the primary means available is reconstruction based on analogies to living peoples. Such a view presupposes that our knowledge of the past is only as good as our knowledge of the

present and that our reconstructions are valid only insofar as we are justified in projecting knowledge of living peoples into the past. . . . Archaeologists are not limited to analogies to ethnographic data as the sole basis for offering explanatory postulates; models can be formulated in a theoretical calculus some of which may deal with forms without ethnographic analogs. Archaeologists are certainly indebted to ethnographers for providing sources which can be used as inspirations for model building. The crucial point, however, is that our understanding of the past is not simply a matter of interpreting the archaeological record by analogy to living societies, as has been commonly asserted (cf. Thompson, 1956, p. 329). Our knowledge is sound to the degree that we can verify our postulates scientifically, regardless of the source of their inspiration. Scientific verification for archaeologists is the same as for other scientists; it involves testing hypotheses systematically.

Although processual archaeologists borrowed heavily from ethnographic information to develop models, curiously enough, information was drawn from a worldwide ethnographic database that excluded the Western Apache. This can be explained in part by Keith Basso's prohibition on ethnography, but it seems extraordinarily odd that Griffin (1969) could derive test implications from Pacific Northwest ethnographies but neglect the Cibecue Apache. Behavioral archaeology would remedy this defect in interpretations of Grasshopper prehistory.

The Use of Theory

The inadequacies of processual archaeology's fieldwork, processing, and analysis may be labeled mechanical deficiencies that are quickly remedied and can be adjusted for context. The infatuation with social theory, by contrast, has had a pervasive and, in not a few cases, a deleterious effect on archaeological epistemology.

Social theory consists of bodies of general knowledge about sociocultural phenomena expressed in postulates, premises, assumptions, principles, and models. Often having rich empirical implications, social theories ostensibly answer *how* and *why* questions about human behavior and societies. Under this definition virtually all theories that archaeologists use to explain behavioral and/or societal variability and change, including theories of Darwinian evolution and behavioral ecology, qualify as social theory. (Schiffer 2000a:1)

Processual archaeology raised the issue of grand social theory of human culture and behavior as the ultimate goal toward which a scientific archaeology should aspire. It was believed that, like the physical sciences from which they freely borrowed, archaeologists could generate general, lawlike principles and contribute to building theory. This goal has been transformed into the mantra of contemporary archaeology, and in some instances, it has obscured the actual happenings of prehistory. Old processualists and neoprocessualists alike assign greater intellectual value to discussing social theory than trying to interpret the past. Admittedly, this is a harsh indictment, and it does not apply to those contemporary archaeologists who have moved away from prehistory to focus attention on the development of social theory within a framework of archaeology as the science of technology (Leone 1973; Schiffer 1995a, 1999, 2000a). This criticism does pertain, however, to those pretending to illuminate the past through the simplistic mapping of social theory onto the archaeological record.

The theory-down methodology of processual archaeology made it acceptable to explain a certain configuration of archaeological data as an instance of a particular theory. This procedure for explaining the record became widespread among academics for a number of reasons. First, the time, money, and personnel needed for an exhaustive examination of almost any sizeable archaeological record simply were unavailable. Second, tenure was best achieved with short-term, small-scale projects, regardless of the size of the record under investigation. Third, the vast funds being poured into contract archaeology greatly altered our expectations. It was assumed that archaeological research would involve specialists and physical-chemical techniques that drove up costs and mandated multivolume reports. Ample time to analyze and ruminate was no longer available. These new expectations and the contrast between academic and contract archaeology became manifest during the Cholla Project, where the six-year budget was probably twice the amount available for the past two decades of Grasshopper research.

Despite the concern with theory among processual archaeologists, no overarching theoretical framework ever developed at Grasshopper. Elsewhere, regional archaeology is dominated by singular paradigms and explanatory models. We can point to Great Basin archaeology, where evolutionary ecology and optimal-foraging theory have long dominated research agendas (see Beck 1999). The seemingly atheoretical nature of Grasshopper research may be in part a product of the unique pueblo context of well-dated behavioral spaces, such as room floors, being amply provisioned with a wide range of domestic implements and facilities. Other archaeological contexts characterized by low-resolution data may be interpretable only through appropriate application of social theory. A deemphasis of theory also was a component of our strategy in the Grasshopper–Chavez Pass debate.

Research Products and Interpretations of the Past

Looking back over what, in 2003, was forty years of Grasshopper research, we think we can see that social theory did not contribute much to our understanding of the past and even contained hazards that could obscure or falsify knowledge of the past. The dissertations of Griffin (1969), Tuggle (1970), and Reid (1973), along with Clark's (1967) dissertation-quality thesis, represent the deficiencies of narrow hypothesis-testing procedures in a complicated archaeological context. Generally speaking, other than Reid's growth model for Grasshopper Pueblo, there is little systemic-context knowledge—true statements about the past—contained in these studies, despite large numbers of analytical cases. Clark studied 197 burials, Griffin had data from thirty-seven pueblo rooms, and Tuggle's database included seventy-nine sites, the majority from a stratified random sample of the Grasshopper Plateau.

One of the unsettling features of these studies is that we now know so much more about Grasshopper Pueblo and the region after thirty years of work that we can evaluate earlier knowledge claims. Had we ceased work in 1973 after only a decade—an eternity for many projects—we might well have accepted and perpetuated false claims. It is the latent fear of many archaeologists that someone will return to reinvestigate their site, at best only adding new interpretations and at worst nullifying previous work. This reinvestigation nightmare rarely occurs in the academic world but is chronic in contract work, where different companies routinely perform the survey, testing, and data-recovery phases.

The scariest feature of these early studies is the unquestioned coexistence of two contradictory explanations of the past—Clark's (1967) interpretation of social stratification at Grasshopper and Griffin's (1969) inference that egalitarian principles prevailed. These countervailing notions persisted unchallenged until Whittlesey's (1978) dissertation analysis directly addressed the methodological problems in the hypothesis-testing program that permitted this paradox. (A more cynical commentary would speculate that no one noticed because no one actually read these works). Processual archaeology had poorly developed methods for avoiding "false positives" and for evaluating contradictory knowledge claims. In its rigidly simplistic expression, hypothesis testing was then and remains now a fragile method for producing systemic-context knowledge.

We can use Reid's dissertation (1973) to illustrate the analytical problems that prompted development of behavioral archaeology. The deductive component—the hypothesis test of the diversity-stability rule (Margalef 1968; Odum 1971) within an examination of responses to stress—has not survived the test of time and was even suspect at the time it was written (Reid 1973:155–64, 167; 1978). The outstanding archaeological record of Grasshopper was insufficient for a convincing test of that ecological principle, and there was no explanatory compulsion to summarily map it onto the Grasshopper case merely to account for a particular pattern of data.

By contrast, the inductive components of Reid's (1973) study—the pueblo growth model and measurement techniques—have withstood the test of time (Graves 1991; Riggs 1999a, 2001) and continue to provide the temporal framework for understanding what happened at Grasshopper Pueblo (Reid 1989; Reid and Whittlesey 1997, 1999).

These rather sketchy assertions concerning the deficiencies of processual archaeology as they were revealed at Grasshopper acquire further meaning in our discussion of behavioral archaeology. Unlike processual archaeology, it assisted us in acquiring systemic-context knowledge of the past.

Behavioral Archaeology at Grasshopper

The Grasshopper variety of behavioral archaeology places greater emphasis on prehistory than the other strategies (Reid, Schiffer, and Rathje 1975), and toward this research objective, it concentrates first on developing methods and middle-range theory for accurate reconstructions of past behavior. We accorded little prominence to the development and application of social theory for the practical reason that social theory repeatedly failed to provide authentic solutions to complicated problems of interpretation. We believe strongly that control of formation processes must precede reconstructions of past human behavior, which in turn must be verified before moving on to explanations of that behavior (Reid 1995:18). Integral to this focus are procedures of inference generation and verification, operationalization of variables, and development of measurement techniques. These methodological procedures and concepts lie at the heart of Grasshopper research.

Research Issues

The conceptual basis for the Grasshopper research program of the 1980s continued to be guided by questions and concerns within three major realms. First, we remained interested in traditional culture-historical questions of population movement and interaction, settlement and subsistence, ethnic identity and coresidence, and the economics of trade and exchange. Second, we sought answers to processual questions of social structure and organization and environmental adjustment expressed in contemporary ecological language. Third and most distinct, behavioral archaeology emphasized methodology, measurement, operationalization of variables, formation of the archaeological record, and middle-range theory.

The immediate goals of our research were the principles and measurements for identifying past behavior from material remains, which we retrospectively label middle-range research. The archaeological literature of the 1980s supplied a number of conceptions of middle-range theory (Binford 1977; Raab and Goodyear 1984; Schiffer 1988), but what we were doing at Grasshopper is articulated best by Trigger (1995: 450):

> As defined by Binford (1977, 1981), this approach postulates that if a strong correlation can be established between specific aspects of behaviour and special aspects of material culture in the modern (actual) world, the presence of such material culture in the archaeological record allows the archaeologist to assume that the associated behaviors also were present in the past. The bridging or warranting argument, which establishes the relevance of the modern generalization for inferring past behavior, is that of uniformitarianism. It is assumed that the correlation applies to all situations in which human cognitive and behavioral capacities were the same as those of modern human beings. The goal of middle-range theory is not to explain human behavior but to infer it from material remains recovered from archaeological contexts.

The inordinate attention paid to developing secure, accurate reconstructions of Grasshopper behavior contributed significantly to misunderstandings among our colleagues, many of whom thought that our seeming retreat from explanation was antitheoretical. Although it is true that we embraced social theory reluctantly, if at all, our position has always been that a particular behavior first must be demonstrated to exist before we legitimately have anything to explain. Because the archaeological context of Grasshopper was so complicated, it has taken us far longer than we ever anticipated to reach a period of analysis oriented toward the application of social theory to the explanation of past human behavior on the Grasshopper Plateau.

The Use of Theory

If any school of scientific philosophy guided Grasshopper research after 1979, it derived from American pragmatism. Pragmatism stems from the works of William James, Oliver Wendell Holmes, John Dewey, and more recently, Richard Rorty. Five themes characterize the pragmatic ethos: antifoundationalism, fallibilism, critical communities, pluralism, and contingency (Bernstein 1997) (see Reid and Whittlesey [1998] for a summary).

Briefly, pragmatism is a workable and honest approach to scientific inquiry that begins with the notion that inquiry is grounded in a humanistic and commonsense understanding of how people address problem solving in daily life. Pragmatism is capable of producing interesting new discoveries about the past while at the same time guarding against the perpetuation of false interpretations. New ideas and models can be adopted if the data demand it. Pragmatism is sufficiently versatile to permit the incorporation of ethnographic information that may include supernatural components well beyond the explanatory requirements of a stridently empirical science. Free of ecodeterministic taint, ideological features of the past can be examined for what they may reveal about past human behavior. Sometimes the pragmatist must accept that there is no logical explanation for events.

For archaeology, a major principle of pragmatism, adopted from Dewey's philosophy of learning by doing and adapting, is that of "knowledge through performance." Ethnoarchaeology, replication, and experimental archaeology all testify to the vast significance of knowledge gained from and solidly grounded in personal experience. For this reason, and recognizing the importance of fallibility, the pragmatist must never be afraid to change his or her mind.

Another important intellectual influence on Grasshopper research might be labeled for convenience a form of postprocessualism, as long as we clearly distinguish the unique source. Our inquiry into ideology and the ritual character of Grasshopper life owes nothing to the writings of Foucault, Derrida, or Lacan and everything to the words and deeds of Tessays, Cromwells, and Quays—Cibecue Apache people who lived and worked with us at Grasshopper. Throughout most of the 1970s, the Apache were integrated into fieldwork, dining hall, and volleyball court, but they remained culturally isolated because of Keith Basso's admonitions that we archaeologists were not to pretend to do ethnography with the Apache who lived and worked among us. This separatism and cultural specialization had the effect of isolating archaeological research from an important source of information about native lifeways and particularly Apache use of the Grasshopper Plateau and environs.

When Reid took over as director in 1979, the Field School's relationship with the Cibecue Apache changed markedly. In addition to establishing a working relationship with members of the Cibecue community and the tribal council and ceasing burial excavation, we began to hire Apaches to show us prehistoric sites known to them, a more cost-effective survey technique than our traditional pedestrian methods.

Perhaps the most significant result of our newfound association with the Cibecue Apache was to realize the overwhelming importance of spiritual elements to everyday activities, as well as to public ceremonial occasions, such as the girl's puberty ceremony (Basso 1970). For the Apache, concepts of supernatural power and being, which are standard introductory anthropology topics, play an integral role in everyday decisions for social action—not in every social decision or action, of course, but ever-present in thought and ordinary behavior. Thus, it was Tessay, Cromwell, and Quay, to mention a few of the most important families, who directed our attention to the ideological realm of past life at Grasshopper. It is a coincidence that the expansion of Grasshopper research into areas of ideology occurred as the postprocessual critique was gaining in popularity, and it is an irony of disciplinary compartmentalization that this research expansion did not happen at Grasshopper at least a decade earlier.

The lessons learned from this newly forged relationship with the Cibecue Apache served us well. Armed with cultural-landscape concepts and a notion of the importance of ideology, ritual, and spirituality to everyday life, Grasshopper researchers would go on to reconstruct ancient secular and sacred landscapes in other places (e.g., Whittlesey 1998a, 1998b, 2003; Whittlesey, Ciolek-Torrello, and Altschul 1998).

Methods

Behavioral archaeology at Grasshopper was preoccupied with methods, measurement, and middle-range theory. Unfortunately, field and laboratory methods of observation and data recording presented continuous challenges to the research-teaching staff, many of which we have discussed in chapter 7.

Data Collection. We recognized early on that the observations made by students on the archaeological record, especially ceramic classification, were so fraught with errors that they could not be relied upon as basic data for interpretation. We made a sharp distinction between pedagogical exercises and basic record keeping. Furthermore, in contrast to the early days of a single staff member overseeing all or a number of excavation units, each excavation unit was supervised by an experienced staff member who was in turn responsible for the room or excavation-unit report. Students took daily field notes and kept a notebook, which was collected and evaluated regularly, and contributed to interpretations of the archaeological record, but they were no longer the primary or only source of information about an excavation unit.

After 1979, far more attention was given to student-training exercises than previously, and far less was required of them as primary-data collectors. This placed an additional responsibility upon the staff, of course, and reinforced the need to retain experienced staff members.

A Model of Archaeological Inference. A Grasshopper model of archaeological inference grew out of the turgid discourses of the 1960s and 1970s on the nature of hypothesis testing and explanation. Rather than exhume this literature, we can conceptualize archaeological inference within the framework of an inferential model known to every prehistorian—using chronometric data to date events of the prehistoric past. Dendrochronology provides the best set of concepts and principles for this construction. Definitions are found in Dean (1978).

A tree-ring date is a fact that we can treat, for the sake of example, as an inference. It is an absolute date in that the last ring on the wood specimen is expressed as a calendar year with no standard deviation. The inside, or pith ring, also may be present and provide an absolute date for the birth of the tree, most generally an event that is related less frequently to an archaeological question than the death of a tree (see Reid 1998a for an example of the significance of a pith date as a terminus ante quem). The problem with the great majority of tree-ring dates is that the wood sample does not contain the final growth ring, and therefore, the absolute date is not a cutting date.

Noncutting dates also may vary in the quality of the temporal signal, in that the last ring on the sample may be estimated to be near the final growth ring or to be an unknown distance from it. In the latter case, an absolute date for the last ring on a single specimen is not very useful, because it floats in time antecedent to any past human behavior to which a cutting date might apply. To estimate the final growth ring—

a cutting date—on a specimen producing a noncutting date, Michael Graves (1991) developed mathematical equations to estimate construction events at Grasshopper Pueblo (see Riggs 1994, 1999a, 2001).

A single tree-ring date, therefore, may be treated as an inference, even though it is an absolute date. It varies in strength depending on whether it is a cutting date (a strong inference) or a noncutting date (a weak inference). The strength of the chronometric inference is weighted further by dendrochronologists using standard symbols (Bannister and Robinson 1971:4–5).

A weak inference may be strengthened by application of the cluster principle. In the case of noncutting dates, a single, dated specimen provides only a weak chronometric inference, whereas a cluster of noncutting dates can approach the inferential strength of cutting dates. In this context, the cluster of noncutting dates assumes a probability character similar to a group of radiocarbon dates—the larger the number of individual dates that cluster, the greater the probability of their estimating the true date.

The Laboratory of Tree-Ring Research at the University of Arizona provides a weighted date for a wood sample without consideration of the specimen's provenience or associations in the archaeological record. Inferring the occurrence of a behavioral event requires additional work. The next step, therefore, is to associate the dated specimen with a behavioral event of interest, a task only the archaeologist can perform, and it is accomplished most securely in the field at the time of collection. It must be argued from field observations that the dated event—the death of a tree—corresponds to a behavioral event of interest, such as the construction of a pit structure or a pueblo room (see Dean 1978).

In the rare and special case of a cliff dwelling, for example, the archaeologist may look for patterns in the cutting dates from primary beams, secondary beams, lintels, and the shingles above the secondary beams. Decades of analysis have shown that primary beams are more reliable indicators of initial room construction than lintels or shingles (see Dean 1969). In fact, shingles are usually "old wood" that may date several hundred years prior to room construction. Thus, even in the tree-ring-dated, prehistoric pueblo world, there are many factors that must be considered in deriving and evaluating a chronometric inference about a past behavioral event.

Behavioral inferences also are strengthened through the convergence principle. The convergence principle incorporates two characteristics of inference independence—the independence of data categories and procedures and the independence of investigators. When, for example, tree-ring dates, wood-use behavior, and architectural information converge, they give a particular inference greater strength than could any single data category. Furthermore, the convergence of independent analytical techniques and independent investigators on a particular interpretation of the past provides additional strength to the inference.

Dating provides a convenient summary of the factors involved in generating and evaluating an archaeological inference. Tree-ring dates, radiocarbon dates, and archaeomagnetic dates are absolute in providing a calendar date, and they are independent in that the dating technique is independent of human behavior. In partial contrast, ceramic cross dating is an absolute, intrinsic technique, because the human behavior involved in making, using, and discarding pottery is intrinsic to the chronometric property being measured. All archaeologists understand that these four dating techniques and the dates they produce are not equivalent chronometric inferences and may be ranked according to inferential strength. From strongest to weakest, these are a tree-ring date, a ceramic cross date based on dendrochronology, and radiocarbon and archaeomagnetic dates.

A simple model of archaeological inference, therefore, has critical properties and characteristics. A single inference, like a chronometric estimate, may be weighted according to standard criteria consistent with the analytic technique. More critical to the evaluation of these associations is the cluster principle, whereby distinct and recurrent patterns are stronger than a single instance. The archaeological associations and representativeness of the data used to construct the inference may be evaluated and weighted. As inferences become more complicated and distant from easily verifiable observations of the archaeological record, the convergence principle—analytical agreement in multiple data categories, techniques or investigators—assumes critical importance in determining the strength of an inference. The strength of an archaeological inference should not be based on the popularity of the paradigm, the current explanatory fashion, or solely on the subjective evaluation of an investigator's schooling and experience.

Behavioral versus Processual Archaeology: The Grasshopper–Chavez Pass Debate

The Grasshopper–Chavez Pass debate provides an excellent forum for demonstrating the differences between processual archaeology and behavioral archaeology. Because the archaeological contexts on which the debate centered were so similar—two large, fourteenth-century Mogollon pueblos in similar mountain environments—the debate offers a venue for examining the successes and failures of each, much like Grasshopper provided a single window into three different archaeologies. Although promoted by some as a conflict of theory (Upham and Plog 1986), the debate actually centered on methodological concerns. Questions about the equivalence of archaeological data sets, inference justification, data quantity, and data quality were among the issues that Grasshopper researchers raised and that went unanswered.

The debate also was a politicized and protracted struggle for professional dominance, control of archaeological resources, and a fight for personal success. We are poorly prepared to analyze this indisputably personal and sociological element, and in dissecting the debate we may stray from complete objectivity.

The Grasshopper–Chavez Pass debate pitted two groups of archaeologists who maintained diametrically opposed interpretations of the past. One group was led by Fred Plog of ASU, who, with students Steadman Upham, Kent Lightfoot, and others, was investigating the heavily vandalized Chavez Pass Ruin, also called Nuvakwewtaqa. Beginning in 1977, ASU archaeologists began working at the site, which is located above the Mogollon Rim on the Coconino National Forest (CNF) east of Flagstaff. Two years of National Science Foundation funding, dissertation improvement grants, and USDA Forest Service support enabled fieldwork to continue through 1982. The ASU researchers inferred a high degree of social complexity at Chavez Pass Pueblo, including a managerial elite with centralized decision-making authority, control of regional exchange, and restricted access to labor-intensive commodities and agricultural surpluses.

The second group represented UA researchers and Grasshopper alumni, whose nineteen seasons of fieldwork at Grasshopper at the time of the debate's inception in 1982 have been detailed previously. Although we concluded that Grasshopper social and religious organization was not unlike that of historically recorded Pueblo peoples, our research went far beyond this to examine issues of demography and population movement, ethnic coresidence, conflict-management strategies, migration, agricultural dependence, and more (Reid and Whittlesey 1999).

This bare outline does not capture the atmosphere of the debate. Friend and colleague Steve Lekson (1999:18) provides an introduction that does:

Archaeologists of a certain age will remember the Grasshopper–Chavez Pass "debates," which rivaled Ali-Frazier and Hatfield-McCoy for endless bloodletting. (Archaeologists of uncertain age might want to review that "debate"; see Cordell; 1984:346–351 and 1997:421–423). At issue: Was there or was there not "complexity" at two 14th-century pueblos in central Arizona? A simple question with dire and dreadful results. Single combat pitted professor against professor; platoons of students rushed in; surrounding regions were engulfed; battle became general. Journals filled with invective essays. Meetings crackled with jabs and insults. Those of us not caught in the mangle looked on, appalled. We hoped the combatants would wear themselves out before something awful happened. "Can't we all just get along?" more-or-less summed it up.

In presenting the essential elements of the debate, we follow the format used throughout this chapter, looking at research issues, methods and data, theoretical framework, and research products.

Research Issues

As far as we can tell, both sides of the debate began with similar research questions. According to Upham and Plog (1986:226–27), the Chavez Pass research was oriented toward identifying processes that might be involved in the formation of an aggregated pueblo settlement such as Chavez Pass. In the 1978 NSF proposal, researchers identified agricultural intensification and regional exchange as causal processes in settlement growth and development (Upham and Plog 1986:227). Because CNF had requested that ASU investigate Chavez Pass to ameliorate the effects of pothunting, particularly to vandalized human burials (Upham and Plog 1986:226), it is unclear precisely how the NSF proposal goals were to articulate with the project's purpose. Regardless, as Upham and Plog (1986:226) stress, the research goals of the Grasshopper and Chavez Pass projects seemingly were similar. If their appraisal is accurate, this would seem to discount Upham and Plog's (1986:235) claim that theoretical differences were at the heart of the debate.

Methods and Data

Although the research issues at Grasshopper and Chavez Pass may have been similar, the data brought to bear on them and the methods of attack were not. From the beginning, the Grasshopper critique of the Chavez Pass work was framed around issues of data adequacy, especially sample representativeness; operationalization of variables and their measurement in the archaeological record; and the structure of behavioral inferences—methodological issues with little if any connection to social theory. Similar inattention to data pervaded processual archaeology in general and its application at Grasshopper (Whittlesey 1978).

Our basic point was that the Chavez Pass data simply were inadequate to support the inferences that Plog, Upham, and others made. The Chavez Pass database was not comparable to Grasshopper in length of research history, sample size, sample representativeness, or data quality. Whereas research at Grasshopper went on for thirty years (1963–1992), only six years of fieldwork were undertaken at Chavez Pass (1977–1982) (G. Brown 1990:5). Grasshopper Pueblo was in pristine condition, barely touched by amateurs or turn-of-the-twentieth-century archaeological explorers, such as Walter Hough. Chavez Pass Ruin had been so severely vandalized that salvaging what information remained was the rationale for fieldwork.

The initial fieldwork at Chavez Pass was largely "custodial," therefore, focusing on recovery of human skeletal material from potholes (Upham 1978:42). The Chavez Pass researchers (Upham and Plog 1986:230–31) refer to one hundred "burial loci" resulting from extensive vandalism, of which forty-four were used in their burial analysis. In fact, the mortuary collection was so inadequate that other researchers excluded the Chavez Pass burials. Hohmann (1983:36), for example, eliminated them from his study of Sinagua mortuary practices because they did not meet his criteria of data quality (Whittlesey 1984:279). At Grasshopper, nearly seven hundred individuals were excavated, of which about 410 were articulated and undisturbed. Even the disarticulated burials had considerable research potential, because they were disturbed prehistorically by successive interment practices and not by pothunters (Whittlesey 1978).

A testing program at Chavez Pass Ruin was initiated during the first season. Stratigraphic tests involved primarily 1 × 1 m units, although a few larger units were excavated (Upham 1978:10). Thus, Chavez Pass was excavated by means of "telephone booth" units inside architectural features that were dug in arbitrary 10-cm levels, rather than natural or cultural stratigraphic units. At Grasshopper Pueblo, 103 rooms were excavated in natural or cultural strata (Riggs 1999a, 2001), whereas for Chavez Pass Pueblo there is no record of any *one* room having been completely excavated.

The extraordinary weaknesses of the Chavez Pass data are revealed in a short paper Christian Downum presented at the 1986 Mogollon Conference, in Tucson, that effectively destroyed the "empirical basis" of the

Chavez Pass model. The critical excavation unit was a 2 × 2 m test pit at locus 33.8 S–295.0 E; Upham and Bockley (1989:467, fig. 15.2) published its profile. The ceramics from the unit were central to Upham's chronology for Chavez Pass, which was based on South's (1972) mean-ceramic-date formula. Importantly, the unit supposedly documented the co-occurrence of black-on-white ceramic types (early) and bichrome and polychrome types (late). Upham (1982:193) described the test unit as a "deep, unmixed stratigraphic sequence." It was nothing of the kind, but rather "a relatively shallow, pothunted, rodent-churned pueblo room, marked by at least one intrusive pit of unknown age, a 25 cm layer of slopewash, several highly uneven and questionable stratigraphic contacts, and a complicated basal deposit described variously by Upham [as] 'uninterpretable' (1978:15) and 'collapsed roofing material' (Upham 1978:16)" (Downum 1986:6–7).

Downum (1986:8) also discovered that sample-size deficiencies in the materials collected from the unit had been masked by use of percentages, a common strategy among processualists who tended to obscure poor data with statistical manipulations. "If Upham's '28.6 percent of the stratigraphic levels' at 33.8S–295.0E is in fact the four out of fourteen 10 cm levels it appears to be, the *maximum* number of Sosi-style potsherds that could have occurred mixed in the same level with Jeddito Black-on-yellow is *one*" (Downum 1986:8, emphasis in original).

The Chavez Pass data-recovery strategy produced artifact collections whose representativeness was not demonstrated (Upham 1978) and chronological information of dubious quality. Because tree-ring dating yielded few dates, ASU researchers relied on mean ceramic dates (Batcho 1977), a pollen chronology (Schoenwetter 1986), and relative ceramic frequencies (Upham and Bockley 1989). The latter ultimately were rejected. Upham and Bockley (1989:488–89) claim that, because "substantial nonage, nonsex-based status systems developed at Nuvakwewtaqa, one cannot use material assemblages for strictly chronological analyses, unless one first controls for the biases created by status-determined restrictions of access." Dating methods with links to tree-ring-dated pottery were considered "inappropriate." Faced with mixed ceramic collections and inadequate chronometric dates, Chavez Pass researchers compressed the construction sequence and explained the different ceramic distributions as the product of different exchange systems and access to material goods, rather than temporal differences in pueblo room blocks. Graves (1987:246) points out that this procedure "harkens back to Harold Gladwin's . . . failed attempts to make tree-ring dates congruent with his temporal expectations."

By contrast, Grasshopper researchers relied on tree-ring dates and reliably cross-dated ceramics, and we considered the establishment of an accurate intrasite chronology a prerequisite to further investigations. As discussed in previous chapters, we viewed chronological data as an essential framework for developing a model of site growth, resulting in the cornering project, the growth project, and much of the excavation sampling strategy.

The Chavez Pass researchers also made an assumption of equivalence between the archaeological and systemic contexts, as McGuire and Saitta (1996:207) point out. "The Chavez Pass researchers tend to view material culture as a direct reflection of culture and social organization. Thus, when confronted with a positively skewed distribution of goods, they conclude that a hierarchical social organization existed." This flawed equivalence assumption permeated processual methods and was one of the prime movers in spurring development of behavioral archaeology.

In light of these vastly different research databases, it is unfathomable that some archaeologists (e.g., Cordell 1984:346–51) believe that the information collected from Grasshopper and Chavez Pass represents equivalent bodies of evidence. This sentiment is one of the major flaws of McGuire and Saitta's (1996:207) discussion of the debate, and it raises serious questions about the scientific aspirations of archaeologists.

The inadequacy of the Chavez Pass data did not stop the Chavez Pass researchers from making elaborate inferential constructions. A similar "house of cards" effect tainted much well-intentioned processual archaeology. Other errors in Chavez Pass interpretations were born of inexperience, opportunism, and inadequate fieldwork, none of which were then uncommon in southwestern archaeology—sadly, another legacy of the new archaeology.

Issues of data quantity, quality, and representativeness were paramount in the first papers we presented at the 1982 Mogollon Conference, which unwittingly initiated the debate and ensuing debacle. We urged our colleagues to be cautious and circumspect in their interpretations, rather than enthusiastically leaping to unsupportable conclusions. In "Implications of Mogollon Settlement Variability in Grasshopper and Adjacent Regions," Reid (1984a) addressed problems with inferences made on the basis of settlement-size hierarchies. It opened with the statement that "reliable inferences of settlement function and chronology must precede the reconstruction of settlement systems, which often form the basis for higher level analysis of organizational systems. Occasionally, in a rush to fashion models of political and social organization, investigators neglect the task of inferring function in favor of making simple equivalence assumptions" (Reid 1984a:59).

In "Uses and Abuses of Mogollon Mortuary Data," Whittlesey (1984) took up the thread by observing the inadequacy of the Chavez Pass mortuary collection. She stated (Whittlesey 1984:284): "Complex research questions cannot be answered with poor quality data. This means that archaeologists who have only small or nonrepresentative burial samples must adjust their research questions, even if this requires remaining content with less elaborate or exciting reconstructions of human behavior. Sweeping, but unsupported, claims about the past litter prehistory with unsubstantiated and often erroneous reconstructions."

Last, in "Social Complexity in the American Southwest: A View From East-Central Arizona," Graves and Reid (1984) examined methodological problems affecting the conclusions of Chavez Pass researchers (Graves and Reid 1984:275):

> We believe that the nature of social and political complexity in the American Southwest is a substantive research topic with theoretical implications for all anthropologists; but assumption, assertion, and hypothetical embroidery are not demonstration. We recommend Romer's Rule—that the simplest explanation requiring the fewest assumptions is to be preferred over the less elegant hypothesis. To substantiate claims of social complexity archaeologists must devote considerably more time and attention to eliminating simpler alternative hypotheses with higher prior probabilities. This procedure would ensure fewer just-so stories as it assists in developing credible reconstructions of human behavior that could face the test of time and future fieldwork.

The tony, academic language we used in our Mogollon Conference papers camouflaged the real criticism—the Chavez Pass work was simply sloppy fieldwork and bad archaeology (see Longacre 2000). Our critique had nothing to do with theory, accusations to the contrary notwithstanding. That the Chavez Pass archaeologists could happily eschew the processual requirement of data representativeness is one of the unfortunate revelations of the Grasshopper–Chavez Pass debate (see Reid 1999).

To answer Downum's critique and the skepticism with which Grasshopper researchers had greeted the Chavez Pass interpretations, the Chavez Pass folk neatly turned the debate to theoretical issues unaffected by concern with data adequacy. The new archaeology's infatuation with social theory meant that the rules of engagement would be on theoretical grounds, well above the mundane level of empirical evidence. Upham and Plog (1986:235) claimed that "most basic of these disagreements are not ones related to analysis, but to the appropriate theoretical models that should structure interpretation."

By contrast, behavioral archaeology was focused intently on data adequacy and operationalization of variables. Reid's (1985b:168) Chacmool Conference paper, "Measuring Social Complexity in the American Southwest," states this problem focus explicitly:

> More immediately at issue, however, is the methodological problem of how we operationalize and measure variables. Units of analysis—the household, agricultural intensification, or social inequality—are not directly observable in the archaeological record. Units of analysis must be operationalized through what I call identification transformations (Reid 1978:203–204) to units of observation that are the bits of space and pieces of material remains recognizable in the record from their formal, spatial, quantitative, and relational attributes (see Schiffer 1976:55–57).

Reid and others (1989:803) make the important point that the Chavez Pass interpretations were flawed because the researchers did not control for formation processes of the archaeological record (Schiffer 1987) and other sources of variability unrelated to the problems under investigation. Although several natural and cultural formation processes could have mixed black-on-white, bichrome, and polychrome pottery in archaeological context at Chavez Pass, Upham (1982) did not rule out this highly probable cause of association. The interpretation that the three wares were contemporaneous was, therefore, flawed. Behavioral archaeologists believe that evidence to support inferences can be identified only after alternative sources of variation have been evaluated, controlled, and if necessary, eliminated (Reid et al. 1989:803).

These concerns also meant that behavioral archaeology sought to answer criticisms with fieldwork and additional data, whereas processual archaeology tended to respond by elaborating verbal arguments and seeking theoretical support. We were not playing on a level field. Behavioral archaeology assumed that the spoils would go to the side with the strongest body of data, and we put our research energy into strengthening evidence with more fieldwork. Because social theory had been established by the Chavez Pass crowd as the central element of the debate, we downplayed its role deliberately. Like Haury at Snaketown, we argued with shovel and trowel. Also like Haury at Point of Pines, with the Mogollon controversy swirling around him, we would broaden dissertation research to build a corpus of data and analysis. This was the contemporary expression of Haury's often-cited response to criticism—

"Don't get mad, get new data." The Haury approach, which had worked so well in the culture-history years of the discipline, had become obsolete in the academic environment of the eighties.

It is an intriguing and disturbing fact of the Grasshopper–Chavez Pass debate that our colleagues held the two sides to different standards of evidence. For example, Cordell's (1985) summary paper for the published volume of the 1983 Chacmool Conference papers questions the Grasshopper inference that a cluster of arrowheads at the shoulder of a deceased male could represent a quiver of arrows. She writes, "I would further caution that statements such as 'the fourth group is represented by clusters of arrows carried in quivers worn at the left shoulder' . . . suggests that quivers and arrows were found intact. A more careful and accurate description would, I think, simply mention clusters of projectile points at the left shoulder" (Cordell 1985:193).

By contrast, Chavez Pass researchers made far bolder inferential leaps, positing alliances, managerial elites, and pronounced social inequality, as well as estimates of one-, two-, and three-story rooms and frequency of storage rooms based on nothing more than test pits. Such conclusions were allowed to stand unquestioned (see Cordell 1984:349). Inferences made by Grasshopper researchers, no matter how simple and straightforward, were held to a much higher gauge. This double standard confirmed what we had suspected of processual archaeology—an objective archaeology had died a quiet death. If the Grasshopper–Chavez Pass debate did anything constructive, it was to clarify the subjective nature of most archaeological inference and raise again the need to revisit procedures for verifying statements about the past (see Reid 1998b).

The Grasshopper–Chavez Pass debate revealed one of processual archaeology's worst methodological defects—its inability to exclude weak hypotheses. As Whittlesey (1978) demonstrated in her dissertation—not a reconstruction of Grasshopper social organization, as has been claimed (e.g., Upham and Plog 1986:231), but a methodological experiment—archaeologists using similar data to investigate similar problems can come to contradictory conclusions when their inferential structure is weak. Whittlesey demonstrated this point by using two different correlate models applied to the same data, which happened to be the burials and associated funerary objects from Grasshopper.

The study was inspired by the contradictory conclusions of Clark (1967) and Griffin (1969) concerning Grasshopper social organization. How could it be explained that one study (Clark) found evidence for social stratification and the other (Griffin) found support only for an egalitarian model of organization? Using standard processual techniques and deriving test implications following the procedures of the era, Whittlesey showed that it was possible to discover evidence for social stratification. With a different approach and test implications, the opposite interpretation was achieved. The reason for this paradox, Whittlesey argued, lay largely in the nature of the database. The deductive model hypothesizing social stratification did not eliminate weak cases; the alternative model did.

Reid and others (1989:803-4) underscore that such typical processual procedures ultimately are unscientific, because they do not seek to eliminate specious reconstructions. Processualists (e.g., Cordell et al. 1987) are satisfied if a plausible fit exists between their interpretive models and some characteristics of the archaeological record. This "matching" method is highly problematical. Simpler and more parsimonious hypotheses were rarely tested at Chavez Pass, often because the necessary data were either unavailable or had not been collected (Graves 1987:247). Graves's (1987:247) succinct summation characterizes much processual archaeology, not only the Chavez Pass work: "A complex archaeological manifestation has thus been simplified and a series of naive bivariate analyses implemented to test a very complicated sociocultural model." It is unfortunate that the Chavez Pass contingent not only failed to learn from Whittlesey's experimental demonstration of this problem, but also failed to see that the problem existed.

The Use of Theory

In 1985, Reid (1985b:167) wrote a brief of the Grasshopper–Chavez Pass debate that stated: "The Chavez Pass workers . . . interpret social and political organization at that prehistoric pueblo community to be more complex than that which is recorded for modern Pueblo communities. In contrast, I interpret the organization of Grasshopper Pueblo to be broadly similar to a generalized ethnographic account of the historic Pueblos." These differing interpretations would be expanded to form the core of the debate, neatly sidestepping behavioral archaeology's real concerns.

The differences between Grasshopper and Chavez Pass, the Chavez Pass researchers claimed, were not ones of data or inference but of theory and terminology (Upham, Lightfoot, and Jewett 1989; Upham and Plog 1986). To a certain extent, this was true. Upham and Plog (1986:234), for example, litter their writing with au courant jargon and mysterious terms: "The results of shortfalls in agricultural production coupled with centralization of the banking system may have had the effect of transforming the character of leadership at the site from a system based on consensus to one in which cooptation, the coercive manipulation of the population by a newly emerging, decision-making elite, became the social and political basis of leadership." It is unclear precisely how "banking," "cooptation," "coercive manipulation," and the like could be observed in the archaeological record, and this inability to operationalize complicated organizational concepts was one of processual archaeology's most prominent failures (Reid 1998b; Whittlesey 1978).

Cordell (1985:194) has suggested that the Grasshopper–Chavez Pass debate ultimately rested on whether the models used to interpret archaeological variability were appropriate. A central piece in the debate, therefore, was the proper use of ethnographic analogy. Because behaviors such as "productive specialization," "agricultural intensification," and "restricted access to certain labor-intensive, exotic non-local commodities" (Upham and Plog 1986:227) could not readily be discerned among ethnographically described Pueblo peoples, the Chavez Pass researchers denigrated the usefulness of Puebloan ethnographic analogy. Upham and Plog (1986:237) claimed that the magnitude of changes induced by contact with Europeans affected all aspects of Pueblo life. Behavioral archaeologists were inclined to think that the depth of contact-induced changes in Pueblo social organization were not sufficient to transform societies characterized prehistorically by social stratification, hierarchical rank, and managerial elites controlling resources. We were cautious in our use of analogy, however, and remained open to alternative interpretations.

Even the broad use of ethnographic analogues was misinterpreted. Reid (1985b:167) interprets "the organization of *Grasshopper Pueblo* to be broadly similar to a generalized ethnographic account of the historic Pueblos" (emphasis added). Lightfoot and Upham (1989a:14) either misinterpreted or misquoted the paper, writing:

> Historically, archaeologists have employed ethnographic studies of the Pueblos as models for interpreting the past. And many archaeologists today still feel that the prehistoric Pueblo were "broadly similar to a generalized ethnographic account of the historic Pueblos" (Reid 1985[b]:167). While Reid and others emphasize that they do not use ethnographic information to interpret the archaeological record directly, they nonetheless are skeptical of interpretations that deviate from ethnographic accounts of egalitarian Pueblos.

Contrary to the misquote, we have no firm knowledge of what the social organization of other prehistoric pueblos may have been, and we do not think that the Chavez Pass researchers have better access to such knowledge. Our skepticism derived from the processualists' inability to confirm from a limited and nonrepresentative database that social stratification, managerial elites, and coercive decision making characterized social organization at Chavez Pass.

The Chavez Pass processualists went further still to argue that there was something fundamentally antiquated in the behavioral archaeologists' rejection of these interpretations. Because our interpretations of the Grasshopper past were not too dissimilar from ethnographic accounts of the Western Pueblos, we were considered to be unimaginative, stuck in Benedict's traditional and misleading Apollonian view of Pueblo societies, and clinging to a view of Pueblo egalitarianism that was outmoded and worse (Upham and Plog 1986:237). As Upham (1989: 83) writes, "Such attitudes [Pueblo egalitarianism] are at best simplistic and at worst racist and ethnocentric." Unsuccessfully, we mentioned that the southwestern anthropologist most often cited for an egalitarian interpretation of the Pueblo past was Edward Dozier, a native of Santa Clara Pueblo, New Mexico.

Last, we consider how inferences were evaluated. The Chavez Pass workers, like processual archaeologists in general, evaluated knowledge claims using subjective criteria, although they would protest this fact. Graves (1987:247) sums it up nicely: "Their collective work [Upham and Plog] suggests that archaeological reporting is largely a persuasive activity in which a particular point of view is bolstered by vague generalizations, simplistic analyses, under-reporting of data and contextual information, and selective use of evidence." We consider the criteria by which inferences are evaluated by behavioral archaeologists in chapter 7. Suffice it to say that the primary criteria were evidentiary. During the 1980s, we were blinded by the notion that knowledge of the past lay in data adequacy, representative samples of materials, and inferential rigor. We believe this still, but it was not a good strategy for winning a debate in southwestern archaeology.

Research Products and Interpretations of the Past

A common misperception by outsiders to the debate is that neither Chavez Pass nor Grasshopper had published sufficiently to permit independent observers to evaluate the different interpretations. Moreover, many of our colleagues accept the conclusions of both sides as equally valid.

In Cordell's *Prehistory of the Southwest*, for example, she took a rather neutral stance in concluding that the Grasshopper and Chavez Pass interpretations were alternative accounts of the past (Cordell 1984:346–51). As with the nature of the databases, there is no comparison between the research products of the two projects.

To consider the published and readily available information for Grasshopper, we note that the publication record is substantial (see Reid 1999) and continues to grow. It includes two books (Reid and Whittlesey 1997, 1999), two edited volumes (Longacre et al. 1982; Reid 1974), five additional volumes when the closely related Cholla Project (Reid 1982) is included, and six research monographs (Ezzo 1993; J. Olsen 1990; Riggs 2001; Triadan 1997; Van Keuren 1999; Zedeño 1994). More than one hundred book chapters or articles have been published. The most startling publication statistic is that, by the fall of 2003, twenty-four dissertations and nine master's theses had been completed, with more in progress. Grasshopper research, therefore, continues long after fieldwork ceased.

By contrast, the Chavez Pass research is published poorly, mostly available only as unpublished reports on file with the CNF (see Upham and Plog 1986 for a bibliography). In light of the prodigious output for a recently concluded and hopelessly underfunded academic project such as Grasshopper, how could mature archaeologists (Cordell 2000:596; McGuire and Saitta 1996:206; Spielmann 1998:13–14; Wilcox 1991: 128) lament the unavailability of information relevant to interpretations of the Grasshopper past? Yet so it is; Cordell (2000:596) perpetuates the blind misconception and misinformation in writing that "one of the most contentious recent disputes, the Grasshopper–Chavez Pass debate . . . ended without resolution for many reasons; certainly salient among them that neither side published their data so that independent evaluation was precluded." There may be truth in the assumption that we have often made that no one must read anymore; misconception after misconception is handed down in the literature because no one checks the primary sources for himself or herself.

The Debate and Grasshopper Research

The Grasshopper–Chavez Pass debate was not simply an academic exercise on an abstract plane. The debate affected the last decade of Grasshopper research in concrete ways. Its most immediate effect was to influence fieldwork. We had determined that more and better data, bigger samples, and multiple researchers working on the same problems would give such enormous weight to our interpretations that the other side would be forced to cry uncle before being crushed. As it turned out, of course, this was a strategic error, but it was the principal reason we continued to strengthen our database through fieldwork. Moreover, while we were busily increasing the size and quality of our samples, the discipline had begun to forget that sampling was ever much of an issue in southwestern archaeology. The trend toward publishing articles and reports based on scanty and nonrepresentative samples that continues today had begun. The role of contract archaeology in setting standards of fieldwork intensity and data quality is partly to blame. It provided a rationale for using small, nonrepresentative pieces of sites, generally along a limited, often linear, right-of-way, as a basis for inferences of the whole. Processual archaeologists' infatuation with probabilistic sampling faded as they took up the lucrative business of excavating pipeline corridors and highway rights-of-way.

Less immediate was the debate's influence on our ability to obtain funding for Grasshopper research and to conduct research outside of Grasshopper. We described in chapter 7 our unsuccessful attempts to persuade the NSF to fund Grasshopper fieldwork and analysis. We do not know to what extent these attempts were doomed by the debate, particularly by the common misperception that we had not published, but reviewers must have been influenced. As we discussed in chapter 7, our bid with Dames & Moore to conduct archaeological studies in the Theodore Roosevelt Lake area for the Central Arizona Project also was unsuccessful. It does not seem coincidental that the contract was awarded to the Office of Cultural Resource Management in the Department of Anthropology at ASU, although Plog was no longer there. The Roosevelt Platform Mound Study, as it came to be known, would go on to posit some complicated interpretations of Salado prehistory that seem eerily like Upham and Plog's (1986) reconstructions at Chavez Pass, involving managerial elites, craft specialization, long-distance exchange, and vertical status differentiation—although these would ultimately be disproved (Rice 1998). Did the debate cause us to lose this project? *Quien sabé*, but it certainly could not have helped us win it.

Grasshopper research became a victim of changing times in other ways as well. Large projects were not being undertaken by universities but under contract auspices, where sufficient funds mandated multidisciplinary research and time constraints demanded rapid reporting. The expectations for the archaeology of big things far exceeded the capabilities of old-time field schools like Grasshopper, which, as at Point of Pines, had survived on graduate student research spread over many years. Haury's (1985) publication on the work at Tla Kii Pueblo as part of the field school in the Forestdale Valley appeared forty-four years after fieldwork was completed—a publication schedule no client on earth would tolerate.

The third and most insidious effect of the debate was to alter, perhaps permanently, outsiders' view of Grasshopper research and researchers. We have alluded to this previously, and we believe the effects linger today. The persistent myth that the debate was equally acrimonious on both sides (Varien 1999:12; see Feinman, Lightfoot and Upham 2000 and Cordell 2000 for the most recent and unapologetic versions of this misconception) is one example. Acrimonious it certainly was, although it was unilaterally so on the Chavez Pass side. Probably also affecting collegial perceptions were the widespread perceptions that the data from the two pueblo sites were equivalent in quantity and quality, and that the debate was about theoretical issues.

The reader may be wondering at this point why we would care, given Grasshopper's stunning success in producing research of enduring quality and archaeologists of tremendous talent. The answer is simple—the accurate reconstruction of prehistory is important. As Graves (1987: 247) phrases it: "Until we observe somewhat more rigorous standards for analyzing and reporting our research results this problem [subjective arguments] will persist and valuable space in our journals will be devoted to debating specious issues, while the general problem concerning the evolution of social complexity in the American Southwest will remain unresolved." As Binford (1972:59–61) makes clear, only when we are able to verify our hypotheses scientifically is our knowledge about the past sound.

Most frightening to those of us who lived through the debate is its revival in the new millennium. Feinman, Lightfoot, and Upham (2000) resuscitate in the pages of *American Antiquity* the debate we thought long dead, without ever mentioning the principals involved or that there even was another side. In this revisionist history, they reinforce the erroneous view that the debate was mutually acrimonious and further solidify the misconception that it was about theory rather than methodological adequacy. The most recent contribution (Feinman, Lightfoot, and Upham 2000:450) makes apologies for youthful indiscretion and zeal in the name of pseudoscience:

> With the clarity of nearly perfect hindsight, we now see that we drew explicitly and sometimes uncritically on neoevolutionary models that had defined a set of test implications for hierarchical political formation. . . . Al-

though our thinking remains partly rooted in these models, our application of them may have been too rigid as we tended to expect that hierarchical societies would be characterized by one set of features, and egalitarian societies by another. Moreover, we employed measurement techniques from other disciplines that sometimes led us to characterize prehistoric Pueblo cultural systems in the language of market systems and capitalist economies. Although these measurement techniques helped us define developmental process and changing configurations of settlement systems and artifact distributions, they almost may have exaggerated interpretations about the centralized, hierarchical nature of prehistoric Pueblo political systems.

As an apology, this is simply insufficient.

According to Feinman, Lightfoot, and Upham (2000:450), the 1979 Cordell and Plog article on "Escaping the Confines of Normative Thought"

> began a major period of revision in Southwestern archaeology. During the subsequent 10 years, we published contributions that considered archaeological evidence for complex Pueblo sociopolitical structures and economics. . . . The dialogue over the points we raised quickly turned into a debate regarding the character and complexity of prehistoric Southwestern political systems. This debate regrettably became adversarial and was characterized by arguments that presumed a polar dichotomy between hierarchical and nonhierarchical political formations.

A full reply to this stunning, revisionist tour de force will require careful consideration and demands a more public venue than this history.

Research in Review

Questions of chronology, migration, cultural affiliation and contact, and the explanation of historical events—questions that occupied culture historians and were roundly criticized as old-fashioned by processualists—have returned to dominate pueblo archaeology in the 1990s. These questions always were part of the Grasshopper research agenda, although they fluctuated in popularity, depending on prevailing fashion and personality. It is intriguing that, other than in the early years of unrestrained processualism, the research questions we explored at Grasshopper have tended to be unfashionable. This asynchronous relation to the academic community was in part a product of the complicated archaeological context and the methodological requirements of developing middle-range theory. Early in the behavioral-archaeology years, we were alerted to the inadequacies of the processual paradigm, its rather narrow range of questions, and the inability of social theory to provide help in unraveling the mysteries of the past. Behavioral archaeology at Grasshopper could not be done quickly enough to satisfy the requirement of fashionable research—that it be published widely and rapidly.

Contributing to the unfashionable character of Grasshopper research was an adherence to Haury's interpretations of the past. These could not be summarily dismissed simply because he was a traditional culture historian with old-fashioned ways. Haury had personally traversed, investigated, and defined an incredible range of archaeological variability throughout all of the environmental provinces of the Southwest and parts of northern Mexico. Anthropology—a discipline nurtured and sustained on the exotica of distant lands and peoples—justly accords a special authority to "those who have been there," and we were not about to dismiss Haury's judgments or speculations.

A retrospective appraisal reveals Grasshopper research to be an amalgam of archaeologies, an eclectic mix of culture history, processual archaeology, and behavioral archaeology, along with an inescapable resemblance to features of postprocessual archaeology, though we have never claimed influence from the latter's critical literature or advocates. We are tempted to offer behavioral archaeology, Grasshopper variety, as the expression of this eclectic mix that retained some questions, concepts, and procedures characteristic of all three archaeologies while rejecting those elements that proved unworkable in the Grasshopper context. It is also possible, as colleague Steven Kuhn has pointed out, that behavioral archaeology, with its broad range of questions and emphasis on site formation, is actually contemporary archaeology in the same manner that once upon a time culture history was everybody's archaeology. We are not convinced that southwestern archaeologists share a common set of questions, concepts, and procedures, and we are not wedded to any particular label or allegiance. We are convinced, however, that systemic knowledge of the past is obtainable, and we have sketched in this chapter and throughout this book how we and others did it for Grasshopper Pueblo (Reid and Whittlesey 1999). We offer the following list of principles, procedures, and points to ponder as a summary of behavioral archaeology eclecticism at Grasshopper.

From Culture History
1. The archaeologist must know the environment firsthand, and not only the environmental context of the site, locality, or region, but also the larger geographic areas and physiographic provinces (see Willey and

Phillips 1958:18–21). Environmental knowledge is a profitable source of hypotheses as well as a reservoir of fundamental information on behavioral possibilities. One factor in Haury's success in interpreting the past was knowledge of the Southwest gained through field trips as a student with Byron Cummings and the extensive regional surveys he conducted for Gila Pueblo Archaeological Foundation.

2. Knowledge of the prehistoric past is gained solely through fieldwork—survey and excavation. Thus, fieldwork as the data-recovery phase of archaeological research must be conducted by experienced personnel according to rigorous procedures for observing and recording.

3. Culture and ethnic group are useful concepts for conceptualizing social groupings of the past, as well as accounting for dimensions of variability in the archaeological record.

4. Processes of diffusion, innovation, acculturation, assimilation, and migration are evident in the prehistoric record and may be rephrased as the transfer and acceptance of matter, energy, and information.

From Processual Archaeology

1. Multiple working hypotheses are essential to long-term research into the prehistoric past. They insulate the researcher from becoming overly attached to particular hypotheses and from falling victim to the whims of explanatory fashion.

2. Where feasible, statistical sampling, and always arguments of data adequacy and representativeness, are essential to the support of any inference or knowledge claim about the past.

3. General ethnography is an indispensable source of behavioral hypotheses and behavioral possibilities. Our identification of ceremonial societies at Grasshopper (Reid and Whittlesey 1982, 1999) derived from general anthropological studies of sodalities and not from specific ethnographic analogies.

4. Direct application of an ethnographic analogue to a prehistoric case is an inappropriate use of ethnographic and contemporary Native American information.

From Behavioral Archaeology:

1. It is essential to maintain in language and practice the distinction between the archaeological context of the present and the systemic context of past human behavior (Schiffer 1972, 1976:28; also Montgomery 1992b:17–21; Reid 1995:19–20). This distinction is most critical in separating units of observation and units of analysis (Binford 1972:98).

2. Variability in the archaeological record has multiple possible

causes, including those that may be time dependent, space dependent, and a result of functional differences or different effects of natural and cultural formation processes, as well as the human behaviors that are the target of archaeological investigation.

3. Of three research domains, the first is determining the formation of the archaeological context under investigation—answering the question "How?" (Reid 1995:17; Schiffer 1987; Wood and Johnson 1978).

4. The second research domain is to reconstruct and describe human behavior and to answer confidently the questions "Where?," "When?," and "What?" (Reid 1995:18). Site formation and behavioral reconstruction are subsumed under middle-range theory (see Trigger 1995).

5. The third research domain is the explanation of human behavior, grappling with the ultimate question—"Why?" It is our firm belief that explanatory research can only proceed after the relevant behaviors have been demonstrated to exist. To assert that a particular behavior may have occurred in the past is the point where research begins, not where it ends (Reid 1995:18).

6. An inference or knowledge claim about the past is only as strong as the supporting evidence and arguments. Archaeological inferences increase in strength with arguments of representativeness, independent lines of evidence, and independent investigators (Reid 1998a).

7. Two considerations are essential to developing accurate measurement techniques. One, the measure actually must monitor the characteristic it is supposed to measure. (A thermometer measures temperature, not velocity.) Second, the item or items measured actually must reflect the characteristic to be measured.

8. Operationalization of analytical variables is a two-step process. The first step is to connect systemic context variables to specific units of analysis. This generates relational statements similar in structure and content to test implications (see Hill 1970, 1972). The second step is to operationalize units of analysis within the systemic context to units of observation in the archaeological context (Reid 1978, 1995:20; Schiffer 1976:55–57; cf. Binford 1977).

From the Cibecue Apache

1. There is a critical distinction between a scientifically objectified environment and the cognized landscape within which human beings act.

2. Successfully "adapting" to an environment depends to a great degree upon the personal skills and abilities of individuals who extract a livelihood from the land and its areally dispersed and highly restricted

resources. There also is a large amount of chance involved in any interaction with the natural environment.

3. Supernatural power (mana) and beings (animism) are deeply significant in cultural beliefs and social actions.

4. Expediency and multifunctionality dominate in almost every activity involving tool use to a previously unimagined extent.

5. Among those who interact closely with the landscape, cognitive skills involved in image processing—mental storage and recall—are developed highly.

From American Pragmatism

1. Antifoundationalism labels "arguments directed against the idea that knowledge rests upon fixed foundations, and that we possess a special faculty of insight or intuition by which we can know these foundations" (Bernstein 1997:385).

2. Fallibilism recognizes "that although we must begin any inquiry with prejudgments and can never call everything into question at once, nevertheless there is no belief or thesis—no matter how fundamental —that is not open to further interpretation and criticism" (Bernstein 1997:387).

3. Pluralism embraces a plurality of traditions, perspectives, and philosophic orientations (Bernstein 1997:397).

4. Nurturing a critical community of inquirers is essential, for "it is only by submitting our hypothesis to public critical discussion that we become aware of what is valid in our claims and what fails to withstand critical scrutiny" (Bernstein 1997:388).

5. A theme running throughout the pragmatic tradition, one opposite the doctrine of mechanical necessity, is "the awareness and sensitivity to radical contingency and chance that mark the universe, our inquiries, our lives" (Bernstein 1997:388).

We could surely provide a longer list of principles and procedures gleaned from thirty years of fieldwork and another ten years of research and reconstruction, but that handbook must wait for a future time. The present list covers the major points we think most useful to other archaeologists and to their understanding of ongoing Grasshopper research— the analysis and explanation of past human behavior.

9

Retrospect and Prospect

What is claimed as knowledge [must] be both testable and attainable by everyone. This rules out the claims of mystics, intuitionists, and faddists to transcendental knowledge based on special experiences, capacities, or faith. —**Richard Watson** (1991:276)

The thirty-year research and training experience that was the Field School at Grasshopper ended after the summer of 1992. The camp was closed down, its buildings moved, and the surrounding area was cleared and returned to the exclusive use of the Cibecue Apache. For thirty years, Grasshopper's students and staff had labored to uncover from its red dirt and stones the information that would help us reconstruct the lives of the Mogollon people who once had lived there. We had struggled to keep the camp from falling into complete disrepair and to support the fieldwork. We had worked just as hard to analyze the raw data, and we had assisted others in writing about Grasshopper's past.

At the end of fieldwork, we were jubilant that our samples were now complete and we could finalize our tables at last. We had excavated seventeen rooms at Chodistaas Pueblo and 103 numbered rooms at Grasshopper Pueblo, and that was it. We would dig no more forever. These moments of euphoria and fragments of nostalgia for the lost pleasures of the field were tempered with a sober realization. Although the archaeological fieldwork had ended, the hardest work had just begun. The task facing us was as difficult as hefting wall stones out of a deep two-story room or backfilling by hand—to synthesize thirty years of research and explain what happened in prehistory at the place we call Grasshopper.

In this final chapter, we conclude our historical overview by looking at the Field School's accomplishments and outlining its prospects for the future. Now that the fieldwork is finished, we can see with some clarity that more remains to be done.

Advanced Training through Research Participation

The catalog of eminent archaeologists who trained at Grasshopper is unmatched by any other field school, except perhaps Point of Pines. As the yearly rosters of staff members and students demonstrate, an extraordinary percentage of Field School alumni have gone on to distinguished careers in the discipline. The catalog of important scholars in southwestern archaeology who graduated from Grasshopper is too long to include here, but the Field School also trained students who would emerge as scholars in other fields.

With apologies to the respected researchers and teachers omitted, we can list Latin Americanists such as Mark Aldenderfer, Wendy Ashmore, Arlen Chase, William Fash, William Saturno, Izumi Shimada, Barbara Stark, and Rebecca Storey; historical archaeologists including James Ayres, Mark Leone, James Rock, and Robert Schuyler; and others who work in diverse areas, such as T.J. Ferguson, Margaret Hardin, Kathy Kamp, Susan Kus, William Rathje, Kenneth Sassaman, Polly Wiessner, and Alison Wylie. Students who have gone on to serve the discipline in cultural resource management, federal archaeology, and the USDA National Forest include Judith Connor, Nancy Curriden, John Hanson, Terry Klein, Linda Mayro, Shela McFarlin, James McDonald, Glen Rice, Gene Rogge, and Cherie Scheick. Field School alumni also have distinguished themselves as state archaeologists in several foreign countries. When we consider the second-generation archaeologists who trained under these well-known archaeologists and the many we have not mentioned in this brief catalog, Grasshopper's direct and indirect contributions to teaching and training are enormous indeed.

We think that the success of the Field School program can be traced to the notion set forth in Haury and Thompson's first National Science Foundation proposal (Haury 1964) and later elaborated by Longacre and Reid (1974). The Field School emphasized graduate student involvement in a long-term, multidisciplinary research program. Teaching and research were inseparable, strengthening both. Teaching was enhanced by involving students in ongoing research, and research was augmented by encouraging students to formulate new questions, problems, and hypotheses. This important positive-feedback situation existed throughout Grasshopper's history and was vital regardless of the theoretical and methodological paradigm that was dominant. As Longacre and Reid (1974) observed, only within the context of professional research can students acquire the theoretical and technical skills necessary to meet the demands of contemporary archaeology.

As we have seen, the dedication of graduate students pursuing their research interests through master's theses, dissertations, and conference papers provided the primary outlet for publication of Grasshopper research results. This important body of work represents the second major contribution of the Field School, to which we turn next.

Research Contributions

By the fall of 2003, when the manuscript of this book was finished, twenty-four dissertations and nine master's theses, two books (Reid and Whittlesey 1997, 1999), two edited volumes (Longacre et al. 1982; Reid 1974), five additional volumes including the closely related Cholla Project (Reid 1982), six research monographs (Ezzo 1993; J. Olsen 1990; Riggs 2001; Triadan 1997; Van Keuren 1999; Zedeño 1994), and more than one hundred book chapters or articles were completed and published. More are currently in progress. Beyond demonstrating without doubt that the accusation Grasshopper has not published is false, these research contributions form a reservoir of information on a level of specificity that likely will not be repeated within our lifetimes.

Anyone with a specific question about what happened in a prehistoric village-farming community should go first to this database for answers. The thirty-year research experience has created a sort of longitudinal research compendium, a classic case study in the ethnography of a neolithic village. Among the topics of enduring interest and wide application that were investigated at Grasshopper, we can list population movement and migration, ethnogenesis, ethnic coresidence, responses to population growth, agricultural intensification, agricultural dependence, technological change, ceramic production and distribution, mortuary variability, infant and maternal health and mortality, religious organization, development of the *katsina* cult, domestic-group development and household organization, architectural variability, exchange, diet and nutrition, settlement mobility, and many more.

Many of these studies also supply a body of useful information concerning methodological and analytical procedures. Strontium isotope analysis, inductively coupled plasma spectroscopy, and instrumental neutron activation analysis are among the analytic techniques considered in Grasshopper studies. Through Grasshopper research, we know a great deal about what happens when different groups of people come together in an often difficult mountain environment and about the technical analyses that can yield such information—lessons that can be applied in numerous contexts.

We attribute this research success in part to Grasshopper's enviable material record. One of the great lessons of the Field School is one that archaeologists tend to forget in their enthusiasm—that not all research questions are answerable within certain archaeological contexts. Because of the unparalleled archaeological contexts and the contributions of so many dedicated scholars over thirty years, research, analysis, and synthesis of Grasshopper prehistory will continue.

Synthesis and Explanation

Now that the fieldwork is over, Grasshopper research can turn at last to theory and explanation. Although specific research interests consume us still, and graduate students will continue to pursue specific research topics, the tide of research energy has turned. We see our current and future obligations to synthesize and explain what happened at Grasshopper, Chodistaas, and Grasshopper Spring Pueblos and elsewhere on the Grasshopper Plateau. We also see different constituencies and audiences for our explanatory efforts. General audiences—the public and the Cibecue Apache to whom we owe so much—must come first. It is extremely curious that the professional community does not equate archaeological books written for a general audience with those prepared for the professional community. Much as contract archaeology typically has been viewed as a sort of second-class archaeological citizen, so popular archaeology always has been faintly disreputable. We see it differently. Writing good books grounded in facts for general audiences not only is more difficult than writing the often incomprehensible material that passes for scholarly publications but also is more important. We will continue to seek outlets that present Grasshopper's history in readable, interesting formats that entertain as well as inform.

Past publications have targeted these audiences. *The Archaeology of Ancient Arizona*, which placed Grasshopper in the larger context of southwestern and Arizona archaeology and prehistory, was available in the early part of 1997. Next, we turned to a summary of all that we knew, thought we knew, and speculated upon concerning the establishment, growth, and ultimate abandonment of Grasshopper Pueblo and the Grasshopper region. This book also talked a bit about archaeology, archaeologists, and the arrival of the Western Apache in the mountains of Arizona. This no-nonsense, jargon-free summary of prehistoric life at Grasshopper was crafted to serve three purposes. First, it fulfilled our obligation to provide the White Mountain Apache, especially those of Cibecue, with a readable account of what we did during all those summers at Grasshopper. Second, it met any lingering need on the part of colleagues for a document to justify our 1977 NSF grant to synthesize the three areas of Grasshopper research already available in the dissertations of Reid (1973), Whittlesey (1978), and Ciolek-Torrello (1978). Third, it served as a guide and corpus of hypotheses for future researchers by presenting a coherent picture of the prehistoric behavior at Grasshopper as we saw it. The book—*Grasshopper Pueblo: A Story of Archaeology and Ancient Life*—was published by the University of Arizona Press in 1999, and all royalties from this book are assigned to benefit the Cibecue Apache.

The current book also is directed largely to a general audience. Although a scholarly approach, our tack here has been to summarize and seek generalities, referring the reader to the references for most of the technical details.

We cannot predict what shape future syntheses will take, but our experience with the existing work allows us to be sure what form such syntheses will not take. With the close of fieldwork, we came smack against some of archaeology's harshest realities. The general public, funding agencies, and not a few professional archaeologists view excavation and fieldwork as the only legitimate activity of the "real" archaeologist. Many of us cling to romantic notions about digging in remote, exotic locales; it is no coincidence that Spielberg did not portray Indiana Jones in his office behind a mound of field notes and records. Money can be more readily obtained for fieldwork than for analysis, synthesis, and writing. By contrast, archaeologists know, although they may not admit it, that the real work of archaeology takes place behind closed doors, in dusty basements full of artifacts, and in front of glaring computer screens.

Moreover, we ran headlong into the brick wall of the great archaeological research paradox. Once fieldwork ceased, it was extremely difficult to attract students and research funds. At the same time, our colleagues have come to expect that publication of results will follow closely on the heels of the fieldwork. Lack of funds meant that we were left with the hardscrabble strategy of do-it-yourself analysis, which required that we be more expedient and flexible than in an ideal situation. The postfieldwork phase of Grasshopper research, therefore, depends by necessity upon volunteer effort, such as that of the junior author in this and previous books, and on graduate students completing degree requirements, especially the doctoral dissertation. In the early 1990s, there were enough advanced students working on Grasshopper projects and a scattering of postdoctoral folks doing research that we did not perceive the full impact of the postfieldwork financial paradox on our ability to recruit new student researchers.

Contract and academic archaeologists alike know well that fieldwork is accomplished easily compared to the tasks of analyzing and writing up the data. When data collection and analysis extend over a thirty-year span, the task of synthesizing the information and explaining what happened in prehistory truly is intimidating. Charles Riggs's research gives a taste of the task's monumental aspect. His research history at Grasshopper began when he was a student in 1989, expanded into a 1994 thesis on Grasshopper architecture and growth, and developed into his dissertation (Riggs 1999a), which was published by the University of Utah Press (Riggs 2001). Riggs's research record illustrates with great clarity that secure knowledge of the past is not achieved quickly. If we mark the start of collecting architectural information with the cornering project of 1967; add the subsequent fieldwork and analyses of David Wilcox (1982), Michael Collins, Izumi Shimada (Scarborough and Shimada 1974), William Reynolds (1981), David Tuggle, Michael Graves (1991), and Reid (Reid 1973; Reid and Shimada 1982); and include the time and effort put into collecting and analyzing tree-ring samples (Dean and Robinson 1982)—then Riggs's architectural analysis and synthesis of Grasshopper Pueblo took thirty-three years and many experienced research assistants.

Five years in the making of *The Archaeology of Ancient Arizona* also alerted us to another factor in presenting the synthesis of Grasshopper research—the glacial pace at which publication proceeds when writing and rewriting and editing and proofing and indexing and making and remaking illustrations must be done in the evening and on weekends. This book also taught us the difference between an authored, book-length publication and a loosely edited collection of student papers or a compendium of site and feature descriptions. The clothbound, eight-volume set on Grasshopper Pueblo mimicking Charles Di Peso's Casas Grandes tour de force will not appear in our lifetime, given our current employment status with full-time responsibilities in areas unrelated to Grasshopper research.

It was clear that not only would we have to compartmentalize publication and dissemination efforts, but we also would have to prioritize them. We have organized our synthetic and explanatory studies into three areas of presentation—readable yet scholarly books, dissertations and theses, and conference papers. We will continue to use these avenues to present the results of Grasshopper research, our synthetic presentations, and our attempts at explanation.

The conference-presentation strategy has been particularly effective in signaling our platform of issues, provoking discussion, and allowing students a forum for testing ideas. For example, the 1996 Mogollon Conference was an opportunity to present five papers that were subsequently published in the volume edited by Whittlesey (1999c)—Ezzo 1999; Reid and Montgomery 1999; Riggs 1999b; Whittlesey 1999a, plus Reid's (1999) discussions of the Grasshopper–Chavez Pass debate.

At the 2000 Mogollon Conference, we organized a session titled "Last of the Mogollon: Central Arizona in the Fourteenth Century." Reporting thesis and dissertation research and soon-to-be-published papers were Charles Riggs on "Architecture," Joseph Ezzo on "Complexity," Scott Van Keuren on "Potters," Sarah Dahlen on "Gender," David Tuggle on "Warfare," John Welch on "Tactical Sites," Reid on "Ethnic Coresidence," and Whittlesey on "Mortuary Ritual." Of these, only Van Keuren's research was assisted financially by an NSF Dissertation Improvement Grant and a small award from the Wenner-Gren Foundation.

The Prospect

What lies ahead for Grasshopper? It is clear that the Field School's success in training archaeologists will not be repeated, but the education of new generations of archaeologists by Grasshopper-trained researchers will continue, as will Grasshopper's established record of excellent research and intensive publication. Grasshopper's productivity is unparalleled. Publication and analysis have been more active during the 1990s than during the previous thirty years of fieldwork. Both books (Reid and Whittlesey 1997, 1999) and all research monographs (Ezzo 1993; J. Olsen 1990; Riggs 2001; Triadan 1997; Van Keuren 1999; Zedeño 1994) were published during this decade or later. Eight Grasshopper dissertations were completed in the 1990s. There is no reason to believe that Grasshopper research and publication will take another course.

We have emphasized throughout this volume the character, size, and representativeness of the Grasshopper database. Although variable in quality of recording and observations, this information remains extraordinarily well documented compared to many large projects. We see few limitations to the ability of this database to answer our questions about Grasshopper's past and assist in constructing valid explanations for the phenomena of prehistory. This is perhaps the most singular aspect of the unique place that was Grasshopper and the greatest achievement of the Field School—its ability to carry us into new decades of research with the same excitement that we experienced when we first set foot upon its red clay and smelled its piney air.

Grasshopper was a unique place that generated prodigious data, trained critical thinkers and outstanding teachers, inspired creative ideas, and yielded important information about the past and how best to access it through the archaeological record. Over its thirty-year history, Grasshopper shifted paradigms along with the larger discipline and was in no small way responsible for shaping these changes. We have tried to give our readers a sense of this extraordinary place and its singular window on our discipline. Grasshopper was the scene of petty dramas and some fairly traumatic experiences. It also was a place of small pleasures and everyday joys, an environment where one could grow and learn. The debates it inspired were personal as well as academic, as were the solutions. For every question Grasshopper raised, we eventually found an answer. We miss it still.

Bibliography

Adams, E. Charles

1999   Late Prehistory in the Middle Little Colorado River Area: A Regional Perspective. In *Migration and Reorganization: The Pueblo IV Period in the American Southwest*, edited by K. A. Spielmann, 53–63. Anthropological Research Papers 51. Tempe: Arizona State University.

2002   *Homol'ovi: An Ancient Hopi Settlement Cluster.* Tucson: University of Arizona Press.

Adams, E. Charles, and Kelley Ann Hays

1991   *Homol'ovi II: Archaeology of an Ancestral Hopi Village, Arizona.* Anthropological Papers 55. Tucson: University of Arizona Press.

Adams, Robert McC.

1968   Archaeological Research Strategies: Past and Present. *Science* 160: 1187–92.

Agenbroad, Larry D.

1982   Geology and Lithic Resources of the Grasshopper Area. In *Multidisciplinary Research at Grasshopper Pueblo, Arizona*, edited by W. A. Longacre, S. J. Holbrook, and M. W. Graves, 42–45. Anthropological Papers 40. Tucson: University of Arizona Press.

Allen, Wilma H., Charles F. Merbs, and Walter H. Birkby

1985   Evidence for Prehistoric Scalping at Nuvakwewtaqa (Chavez Pass) and Grasshopper Ruin, Arizona. In *Health and Disease in the Prehistoric Southwest*, edited by C. Merbs and R. Miller, 23–42. Anthropological Research Papers 34. Tempe: Arizona State University.

Bannister, Bryant, and William J. Robinson

1971   *Tree-Ring Dates from Arizona U-W, Gila-Salt Rivers Area.* Laboratory of Tree-Ring Research. Tucson: University of Arizona Press.

Barnes, Will C.

1935   *Arizona Place Names.* Tucson: University of Arizona Press (reprinted 1988).

Basso, Keith H.

1970   *The Cibecue Apache.* New York: Holt, Rinehart, and Winston.

1979   *Portraits of "The Whiteman": Linguistic Play and Cultural Symbols Among the Western Apache.* Cambridge: Cambridge University Press.

1990   *Western Apache Language and Culture: Essays in Linguistic Anthropology.* Tucson: University of Arizona Press.

1996   *Wisdom Sits in Places: Landscape and Language Among the Western Apache.* Albuquerque: University of New Mexico Press.

Batcho, David G.

1977   Report of Investigations at Chavez Pass Ruin, Coconino National Forest, Arizona. Report on file, Coconino National Forest, USDA Forest Service, Flagstaff, Arizona.

Baxter, Sylvester

1996   Archaeological Camping in Arizona, Parts 1–4. In *The Southwest in the American Imagination: The Writings of Sylvester Baxter, 1881–1889*, edited by C. M. Hinsley and D. R. Wilcox, 145–77. Tucson: University of Arizona Press.

Beck, Charlotte (editor)

1999   *Models for the Millennium: Great Basin Archaeology Today.* Salt Lake City: University of Utah Press.

Bennett, Kenneth A.

1973   *The Indians of Point of Pines, Arizona: A Comparative Study of Their Physical Characteristics.* Anthropological Papers 23. Tucson: University of Arizona Press.

Bernstein, Richard J.

1997   Pragmatism, Pluralism, and the Healing of Wounds. In *Pragmatism: A Reader*, edited by L. Menand, 382–401. New York: Vintage.

Berry, Claudia F., and Michael S. Berry

1986   Chronological and Conceptual Models of the Southwestern Archaic. In *Anthropology of the Desert West: Essays in Honor of Jesse D. Jennings*, edited by C. J. Condie and D. D. Fowler, 255–327. Anthropological Papers 110. Salt Lake City: University of Utah Press.

Berry, David R.

1983   "Disease and Climatological Relationships among Pueblo III–Pueblo IV Anasazi of the Colorado Plateau." Ph.D. dissertation, Department of Anthropology, University of California, Los Angeles.

1985a   Aspects of Paleodemography at Grasshopper Pueblo, Arizona. In *Health and Disease in the Prehistoric Southwest*, edited by C. Merbs and R. Miller, 43–64. Anthropological Research Papers 34. Tempe: Arizona State University.

1985b   Dental Paleopathology of Grasshopper Pueblo, Arizona. In *Health*

and Disease in the Prehistoric Southwest, edited by C. Merbs and
R. Miller, 253–74. Anthropological Research Papers 34. Tempe: Arizona State University.

Berry, Michael S.

1982   *Time, Space, and Transition in Anasazi Prehistory*. Salt Lake City: University of Utah Press.

Binford, Lewis R.

1962   Archaeology as Anthropology. *American Antiquity* 28:217–25.

1965   Archaeological Systematics and the Study of Culture Process. *American Antiquity* 31:203–10.

1972   *An Archaeological Perspective*. New York: Seminar Press.

1977   General Introduction. In *For Theory Building in Archaeology*, edited by L. R. Binford, 1–10. New York: Academic Press.

1981a   Behavioral Archaeology and the "Pompeii Premise." *Journal of Anthropological Research* 37:195–208.

1981b   *Bones: Ancient Men and Modern Myths*. New York: Academic Press.

1999   Forces That Shaped the Past: Origins of the New Archaeology. *Archaeology* January/February:54.

Binford, Sally R., and Lewis R. Binford

1968   *New Perspectives in Archeology*. Chicago: Aldine.

Birkby, Walter H.

1973   "Discontinuous Morphological Traits of the Skull as Population Markers in the Prehistoric Southwest." Ph.D. dissertation, Department of Anthropology, University of Arizona, Tucson.

1982   Biosocial Interpretations from Cranial Nonmetric Traits of the Grasshopper Pueblo Skeletal Remains. In *Multidisciplinary Research at Grasshopper Pueblo, Arizona*, edited by W. A. Longacre, S. J. Holbrook, and M. W. Graves, 36–41. Anthropological Papers 40. Tucson: University of Arizona Press.

Blinman, Eric

2000   The Foundations, Practice, and Limitations of Ceramic Dating in the American Southwest. In *It's About Time*, edited by S. E. Nash, 41–59. Salt Lake City: University of Utah Press.

Bohrer, Vorsila L.

1973   Ethnobotany of Point of Pines Ruin, Arizona W:10:50. *Economic Botany* 27:423–37.

Boserup, Ester

1965   *The Conditions of Agricultural Growth*. Chicago: Aldine.

Brace, Martha A.

1986   On the Road and in the Field in 1919: The University of Arizona Summer Archaeological Field Season. *The Kiva* 51:189–200.

Bradley, Ronna J.

1996   "The Role of Casas Grandes in Prehistoric Shell Exchange Networks within the Southwest." Ph.D. dissertation, Department of Anthropology, Arizona Sate University, Tempe.

Braun, David

1983   Pots as Tools. In *Archaeological Hammers and Theories*, edited by A. Keene and J. Moore, 107–34. New York: Academic Press.

Breternitz, David A.

1956   "The Archaeology of Nantack Village, Point of Pines, Arizona." Master's thesis, Department of Anthropology, University of Arizona, Tucson.

1959   *Excavations at Nantack Village, Point of Pines, Arizona*. Anthropological Papers 1. Tucson: University of Arizona Press.

1966   *An Appraisal of Tree-Ring Dated Pottery in the Southwest*. Anthropological Papers 10. Tucson: University of Arizona Press.

Breternitz, David A., James C. Gifford, and Alan P. Olson

1957   Point of Pines Phase Sequence and Utility Pottery Type Revisions. *American Antiquity* 22:412–16.

Brown, Gary M.

1990   *Technological Change in the Chavez Pass Region, North-Central Arizona*. Anthropological Research Papers 41. Tempe: Arizona State University.

Brown, Jeffrey L.

1969   A Supplement to "High Status Burial from Grasshopper Ruin, Arizona." *The Kiva* 35:87–90.

Carlson, Roy L.

1970   *White Mountain Redware: A Pottery Tradition of East-Central Arizona and Western New Mexico*. Anthropological Papers 19. Tucson: University of Arizona Press.

Cassels, E. Steve

1972   A Test Concerning Artificial Cranial Deformation and Status from the Grasshopper Site, East-Central Arizona. *The Kiva* 37:84–92.

Ciolek-Torrello, Richard S.

1978   "A Statistical Analysis of Activity Organization: Grasshopper Pueblo, Arizona." Ph.D. dissertation, Department of Anthropology, University of Arizona, Tucson.

1984   An Alternative Model of Room Function from Grasshopper Pueblo, Arizona. In *Intersite Spatial Analysis in Archaeology*, edited by H. J. Hietala, 127–53. New York: Cambridge University Press.

1985   A Typology of Room Function at Grasshopper Pueblo, Arizona. *Journal of Field Archaeology* 12:41–63.

1986   Room Function and Households at Grasshopper Pueblo. In *Mogollon Variability*, edited by C. Benson and S. Upham, 107–19. Occasional Papers 15. Las Cruces: New Mexico State University.

1989   Households, Floor Assemblages, and the "Pompeii Premise" at Grasshopper Pueblo. In *Households and Communities*, edited by

S. MacEachern, D. Archer, and R. Garvin, 201–8. Calgary: University of Calgary.

1998   Chronology. In *Vanishing River: Landscapes and Lives of the Lower Verde Valley; The Lower Verde Archaeological Project*, edited by S. M. Whittlesey, R. S. Ciolek-Torrello, and J. H. Altschul, 662–72. Tucson: SRI Press.

Ciolek-Torrello, Richard S., and J. Jefferson Reid

1974   Change in Household Size at Grasshopper. *The Kiva* 40:39–47.

Claiborne, Robert, and the editors of Time-Life Books

1973   *The First Americans*. New York: Time-Life Books.

Clark, Geoffrey A.

1967   "A Preliminary Analysis of Burial Clusters at the Grasshopper Site, East-Central Arizona." Master's thesis, Department of Anthropology, University of Arizona, Tucson.

1969   A Preliminary Analysis of Burial Clusters at the Grasshopper Site, East-Central Arizona. *The Kiva* 35:57–86.

Cordell, Linda S.

1984   *Prehistory of the Southwest*. Orlando: Academic Press.

1985   Status Differentiation and Social Complexity in the Prehistoric Southwest: A Discussion. In *Status, Structure, and Stratification: Current Archaeological Reconstructions*, edited by M. Thompson, M. T. Garcia, and F. J. Kense, 191–95. Calgary: University of Calgary.

1997   *Archaeology of the Southwest*. San Diego: Academic Press.

2000   Review of *Migration and Reorganization: The Pueblo IV Period in the American Southwest*, edited by K. A. Spielmann. *American Antiquity* 65:596–97.

Cordell, Linda S., and George J. Gumerman

1989   *Dynamics of Southwest Prehistory*. Washington, D.C.: Smithsonian Institution Press.

Cordell, Linda S., Steadman Upham, and Sharon L. Brock

1987   Obscuring Cultural Patterns in the Archaeological Record: A Discussion from Southwestern Archaeology. *American Antiquity* 52:565–77.

Croissant, Jennifer L.

2000   Narrating Archaeology: A Historiography and Notes Toward a Sociology of Archaeological Knowledge. In *It's About Time*, edited by S. E. Nash, 186–206. Salt Lake City: University of Utah Press.

Crown, Patricia L.

1981   "Variability in Ceramic Manufacture at the Chodistaas Site, East-Central Arizona." Ph.D. dissertation, Department of Anthropology, University of Arizona, Tucson.

Cummings, Byron

1940   *Kinishba: A Prehistoric Pueblo of the Great Pueblo Period*. Tucson: Hohokam Museums Association and the University of Arizona.

1952   *Indians I Have Known.* Tucson: Arizona Silhouettes.

1953   *First Inhabitants of Arizona and the Southwest.* Tucson: Cummings Publication Council.

Daifuku, Hiroshi

1961   *Jeddito 264.* Peabody Museum Papers 33. Cambridge: Harvard Peabody Museum.

Dean, Jeffrey S.

1969   *Chronological Analysis of Tsegi Phase Sites in North-Eastern Arizona.* Papers of the Laboratory of Tree-Ring Research 3. Tucson: University of Arizona Press.

1978   Independent Dating in Archaeological Analysis. In *Advances in Archaeological Method and Theory*, vol. 1, edited by M. B. Schiffer, 223–55. New York: Academic Press.

1988   The View from the North: An Anasazi Perspective on the Mogollon. *The Kiva* 53:197–99.

Dean, Jeffrey S., and William J. Robinson

1982   Dendrochronology of Grasshopper Pueblo. In *Multidisciplinary Research at Grasshopper Pueblo, Arizona*, edited by W. A. Longacre, S. J. Holbrook, and M. W. Graves, 46–60. Anthropological Papers 40. Tucson: University of Arizona Press.

Donaldson, Bruce R., and John R. Welch

1991   Western Apache Dwellings and Their Archaeological Correlates. In *Mogollon V*, edited by P. H. Beckett, 93–105. Las Cruces, New Mexico: COAS Publishing Co.

Douglass, Andrew E.

1950   Our Friend, Byron Cummings. In *For the Dean*, edited by E. K. Reed and D. S. King, 1–3. Santa Fe: Southwestern Monuments Association.

Downum, Christian E.

1986   "Potsherds, Provenience, and Ports of Trade: A Review of the Evidence from Chavez Pass." Paper presented at the Fourth Mogollon Conference, Tucson.

1988   "'One Grand History': A Critical Review of Flagstaff Archaeology, 1851 to 1988." Ph.D. dissertation, Department of Anthropology, University of Arizona, Tucson.

Doyel, David E.

1974   *Excavations in the Escalante Ruin Group Southern Arizona.* Archaeological Series 37. Tucson: Arizona State Museum.

1976   Revised Phase System for the Globe-Miami and Tonto Basin Areas, Central Arizona. *The Kiva* 41:5–16.

1977   "Classic Period Hohokam in the Escalante Ruin Group." Ph.D. dissertation, Department of Anthropology, University of Arizona, Tucson.

1978   The Miami Wash Project: Hohokam and Salado in the Globe-Miami

Areas, Central Arizona. Highway Salvage Archaeology in Arizona 52. Tucson: Arizona State Museum.

1994 Charles Corradino Di Peso: Expanding the Frontiers of New World Prehistory. *American Antiquity* 59:9–20.

Duff, Andrew I.

2002 *Western Pueblo Identities*. Tucson: University of Arizona Press.

Elson, Mark D.

1996 A Revised Chronology and Phase Sequence for the Lower Tonto Basin of Central Arizona. *Kiva* 62:117–47.

Ezzo, Joseph A.

1991 "Dietary Change at Grasshopper Pueblo, Arizona: The Evidence from Bone Chemistry Analysis." Ph.D. dissertation, Department of Anthropology, University of Wisconsin, Madison.

1992a Dietary Change and Variability at Grasshopper Pueblo, Arizona. *Journal of Anthropological Archaeology* 11:219–89.

1992b A Refinement of the Adult Burial Chronology of Grasshopper Pueblo, Arizona. *Journal of Archaeological Science* 19:445–57.

1993 *Human Adaptation at Grasshopper Pueblo, Arizona: Social and Ecological Perspectives*. Archaeological Series 4. Ann Arbor: International Monographs in Prehistory.

1994 Paleonutrition at Grasshopper Pueblo, Arizona. In *Diet and Health of Prehistoric Americans*, edited by K. D. Sobolik, 265–79. Center for Archaeological Investigations Occasional Paper 22. Carbondale: Southern Illinois University Press.

1999 A Heterarchical Perspective on Aggregated Pueblo Social Organization. In *Sixty Years of Mogollon Archaeology: Papers from the Ninth Mogollon Conference, Silver City, New Mexico, 1996*, edited by S. M. Whittlesey, 31–37. Tucson: SRI Press.

Ezzo, Joseph A., Clark M. Johnson, and T. Douglas Price

1997 Analytical Perspectives on Prehistoric Migration: A Case Study from East-Central Arizona. *Journal of Archaeological Science* 24:447–66.

Ezzo, Joseph A., and T. Douglas Price

2002 Migration, Regional Reorganization, and Spatial Group Composition at Grasshopper Pueblo, Arizona. *Journal of Archaeological Science* 29: 499–520.

Feinman, Gary M., Kent G. Lightfoot, and Steadman Upham

2000 Political Hierarchies and Organizational Strategies in the Puebloan Southwest. *American Antiquity* 65:449–70.

Feltskog, E. N.

1995 The Range of Vision: Landscape and the Far West, 1803 to 1850. In *Landscape in America*, edited by G. F. Thompson, 75–92. Austin: University of Texas Press.

Fenton, Todd W.

1998 "Dental Conditions at Grasshopper Pueblo: Evidence for Dietary

Change and Increased Stress." Ph.D. dissertation, Department of Anthropology, University of Arizona, Tucson.

Ferguson, Leland

1992   *Uncommon Ground: Archaeology and Early African America 1650–1800*. Washington, D.C.: Smithsonian Institution Press.

Fewkes, Jesse W.

1904   *Two Summers' Work in Pueblo Ruins*. Bureau of American Ethnology Twenty-Second Annual Report 1900–1901. Washington, D.C.: Smithsonian Institution Press.

Fowler, Don D.

2000   *A Laboratory for Anthropology*. Albuquerque: University of New Mexico Press.

Fritz, John M., and Fred T. Plog

1970   The Nature of Archaeological Explanation. *American Antiquity* 35: 405–12.

Fulginiti, Laura C.

1993   "Discontinuous Morphological Variation at Grasshopper Pueblo, Arizona." Ph.D. dissertation, Department of Anthropology, University of Arizona, Tucson.

Gerald, M. Virginia

1958   "The Great Kivas at Point of Pines." Master's thesis, Department of Anthropology, University of Arizona, Tucson.

Gibbon, Guy

1989   *Explanation in Archaeology*. Oxford: Basil Blackwell.

Gifford, Carol A., and Elizabeth A. Morris

1985   Digging for Credit: Early Archaeological Field Schools in the American Southwest. *American Antiquity* 50:395–411.

Gifford, James C.

1957   "Archaeological Explorations in the Caves of the Point of Pines Region." Master's thesis, Department of Anthropology, University of Arizona, Tucson.

1980   *Archaeological Explorations in Caves of the Point of Pines Region, Arizona*. Anthropological Papers 36. Tucson: University of Arizona Press.

Graves, Michael W.

1982a   Anomalous Tree-Ring Dates and the Sequence of Room Construction at Canyon Creek Ruin, East-Central Arizona. *The Kiva* 47:107–31.

1982b   Breaking Down Ceramic Variation: Testing Models of White Mountain Redware Design Style Development. *Journal of Anthropological Archaeology* 1:305–54.

1983   Growth and Aggregation at Canyon Creek Ruin: Implications for Evolutionary Change in East-Central Arizona. *American Antiquity* 48:290–315.

1984   Temporal Variation among White Mountain Redware Design Styles. *The Kiva* 50:3–24.

1987   Rending Reality in Archaeological Analysis: A Reply to Upham and Plog. *Journal of Field Archaeology* 14:243–49.

1991   Estimating Ring Loss on Tree-Ring Specimens from East-Central Arizona: Implications for Prehistoric Pueblo Growth at Grasshopper Ruin. *Journal of Quantitative Anthropology* 3:83–115.

Graves, Michael W., Sally J. Holbrook, and William A. Longacre

1982   Aggregation and Abandonment at Grasshopper Pueblo: Evolutionary Trends in the Late Prehistory of East-Central Arizona. In *Multidisciplinary Research at Grasshopper Pueblo, Arizona*, edited by W. A. Longacre, S. J. Holbrook, and M. W. Graves, 110–21. Anthropological Papers 40. Tucson: University of Arizona Press.

Graves, Michael W., William A. Longacre, and Sally J. Holbrook

1982   Aggregation and Abandonment at Grasshopper Pueblo, Arizona. *Journal of Field Archaeology* 9:193–206.

Graves, Michael W., and J. Jefferson Reid

1984   Social Complexity in the American Southwest: A View from East-Central Arizona. In *Recent Research in Mogollon Archaeology*, edited by S. Upham, F. Plog, D. G. Batcho, and B. E. Kauffman, 266–75. Occasional Papers 10. Las Cruces: New Mexico State University.

Graybill, Donald A., and J. Jefferson Reid

1982   A Cluster Analysis of Chipped Stone Tools. In *Cholla Project Archaeology*, vol. 1: *Introduction and Special Studies*, edited by J. J. Reid, 47–50. Archaeological Series 161. Tucson: Arizona State Museum.

Griffin, P. Bion

1967   A High Status Burial from Grasshopper Ruin, Arizona. *The Kiva* 33:37–53.

1969   "Late Mogollon Readaptation in East-Central Arizona." Ph.D. dissertation, Department of Anthropology, University of Arizona, Tucson.

Griffin, P. Bion, Mark P. Leone, and Keith H. Basso

1971   Western Apache Ecology: From Horticulture to Agriculture. In *Apachean Culture History and Ethnology*, edited by K. H. Basso and M. E. Opler, 69–73. Anthropological Papers 21. Tucson: University of Arizona Press.

Gumerman, George J., and R. Roy Johnson

1971   Prehistoric Human Population Distribution in a Biological Transition Zone. In *The Distribution of Prehistoric Population Aggregates*, edited by G. J. Gumerman, 83–102. Anthropological Reports 1. Prescott, Arizona: Prescott College.

Hagenbuckle, Kristin A.

2000   "Ritual and the Individual: An Analysis of Cibicue Painted Corrugated Pottery from Grasshopper Pueblo, Arizona." Master's thesis, Department of Anthropology, University of Arizona, Tucson.

Haury, Emil W.

1934   *The Canyon Creek Ruin and the Cliff Dwellings of the Sierra Ancha.*
        Medallion Papers 14. Globe, Arizona: Gila Pueblo.

1936   *The Mogollon Culture of Southwestern New Mexico.* Medallion Papers
        20. Globe, Arizona: Gila Pueblo.

1940   *Excavations in the Forestdale Valley, East-Central Arizona.* University
        of Arizona Bulletin 11(4), Social Science Bulletin 12. Tucson: Univer-
        sity of Arizona.

1950   *The Stratigraphy and Archaeology of Ventana Cave, Arizona.* Albu-
        querque: University of New Mexico Press. Reprint, Tucson: Univer-
        sity of Arizona Press, 1975.

1957   An Alluvial Site on the San Carlos Indian Reservation, Arizona.
        American Antiquity 23:2–27.

1958   Evidence at Point of Pines for a Prehistoric Migration from North-
        ern Arizona. In *Migrations in New World Culture History*, edited by
        R. H. Thompson, 1–6. Social Science Bulletin 27. Tucson: University
        of Arizona Press.

1964   "Advanced Field Training through Research Participation in Archae-
        ology." Proposal to Advanced Science Seminar Program, National
        Science Foundation, Washington, D.C.

1985   *Mogollon Culture in the Forestdale Valley, East-Central Arizona.*
        Tucson: University of Arizona Press.

1988   Gila Pueblo Archaeological Foundation: A History and Some Per-
        sonal Notes. *Kiva* 54:1.

1989   *Point of Pines, Arizona: A History of the University of Arizona Archaeo-
        logical Field School.* Anthropological Papers 50. Tucson: University of
        Arizona Press.

1995   Wherefore a Harvard Ph.D.? *Journal of the Southwest* 37:710–33.

Haury, Emil W., and Lyndon L. Hargrave

1931   *Recently Dated Pueblo Ruins in Arizona.* Miscellaneous Collections
        82(11). Washington, D.C.: Smithsonian Institution Press.

Haury, Emil W., and E. B. Sayles

1947   *An Early Pit House Village of the Mogollon Culture, Forestdale Valley,
        Arizona.* University of Arizona Bulletin 18(4), Social Science Bulletin
        16. Tucson: University of Arizona.

Heindl, Leo A.

1955   "Clean Fill" at Point of Pines, Arizona. *The Kiva* 20:1–8.

Hill, James N.

1970   Prehistoric Social Organization in the American Southwest: Theory
        and Method. In *Reconstructing Prehistoric Pueblo Societies*, edited by
        W. A. Longacre, 11–58. Albuquerque: University of New Mexico
        Press.

1972   The Methodological Debate in Contemporary Archaeology: A

Model. In *Models in Archaeology*, edited by D. L. Clarke, 61–107.
London: Methuen.

Hinkes, Madeleine J.

1983 "Skeletal Evidence of Stress in Subadults: Trying to Come of Age at
Grasshopper Pueblo." Ph.D. dissertation, Department of Anthropology, University of Arizona, Tucson.

Hinsley, Curtis M.

1996 The Promise of the Southwest: A Humanized Landscape. In *The
Southwest in the American Imagination: The Writings of Sylvester Bax-
ter, 1881–1889*, edited by C. M. Hinsley and D. R. Wilcox, 181–206.
Tucson: University of Arizona Press.

Hinsley, Curtis M., and David R. Wilcox (editors)

1996 *The Southwest in the American Imagination: The Writings of Sylvester
Baxter, 1881–1889*. Tucson: University of Arizona Press.

Hohmann, John W.

1983 *Sinagua Social Differentiation: Inferences Based on Prehistoric Mortuary
Practices*. The Arizona Archaeologist 17. Phoenix: Arizona Archaeological Society.

Holbrook, Sally J.

1982a Prehistoric Environmental Reconstruction by Mammalian Microfaunal Analysis, Grasshopper Pueblo. In *Multidisciplinary Research
at Grasshopper Pueblo, Arizona*, edited by W. A. Longacre, S. J.
Holbrook, and M. W. Graves, 73–86. Anthropological Papers 40.
Tucson: University of Arizona Press.

1982b The Prehistoric Local Environment of Grasshopper Pueblo. *Journal of
Field Archaeology* 9:207–15.

1983 *Paleoecology of Grasshopper Pueblo, Arizona*. National Geographic
Research Reports, 1974 Projects. Washington, D.C.: National Geographic Society.

Holbrook, Sally J., and Michael W. Graves

1982 Modern Environment of the Grasshopper Region. In *Multidisci-
plinary Research at Grasshopper Pueblo, Arizona*, edited by W. A.
Longacre, S. J. Holbrook, and M. W. Graves, 5–11. Anthropological
Papers 40. Tucson: University of Arizona Press.

Hough, Walter

1920 *Archaeological Excavations in Arizona*. Smithsonian Miscellaneous
Collections 72:64–66. Washington, D.C.: Smithsonian Institution
Press.

1935 Exploration of Ruins in the White Mountain Apache Indian Reservation, Arizona. *U.S. National Museum Proceedings* 78(2856):1–21.
Washington, D.C.: U.S. National Museum.

Hunter-Anderson, Rosalind L., and Yigal Zan

1984 Proving the Moon Is Made of Cheese: The Structure of Recent Research in the Mogollon Region. In *Recent Research in Mogollon Archaeology*, edited by S. Upham, F. Plog, D. G. Batcho, and B. E. Kauffman, 285–93. Occasional Papers 10. Las Cruces: New Mexico State University.

Jennings, Jesse D.
1994   *Accidental Archaeologist: Memoirs of Jesse D. Jennings*. Salt Lake City: University of Utah Press.

Johnson, Alfred E.
1961   A Ball Court at Point of Pines, Arizona. *American Antiquity* 26:563–67.

Johnson, Alfred E., and Raymond H. Thompson
1963   The Ringo Site, Southeastern Arizona. *American Antiquity* 28:465–81.

Johnson, Gregory A.
1989   Dynamics of Southwestern Prehistory: Far Outside—Looking In. In *Dynamics of Southwest Prehistory*, edited by L. S. Cordell and G. J. Gumerman, 371–89. Washington D.C.: Smithsonian Institution Press.

Joiner, Carol
1992   The Boys and Girls of Summer: The University of New Mexico Archaeological Field School in Chaco Canyon. *Journal of Anthropological Research* 48:49–66.

Judd, Neil M.
1950   Pioneering in Southwestern Archaeology. In *For the Dean*, edited by E. K. Reed and D. S. King, 11–27. Santa Fe: Southwestern Monuments Association.
1954   Byron Cummings: 1860–1954. *American Antiquity* 20:154–57.

Kelley, James E.
1974   Bighorn Sheep at Grasshopper Ruin: Precautions in Analysis. *The Kiva* 40:71–80.

Kelso, Gerald K.
1982   Two Pollen Profiles from Grasshopper Pueblo. In *Multidisciplinary Research at Grasshopper Pueblo, Arizona*, edited by W. A. Longacre, S. J. Holbrook, and M. W. Graves, 106–9. Anthropological Papers 40. Tucson: University of Arizona Press.

Kidder, Alfred V.
1931   *The Pottery of Pecos*. New Haven: Phillips Academy.
1939   Review of *Starkweather Ruin*, by Paul H. Nesbitt. *American Anthropologist* 41:314–16.
1960   Reminiscences in Southwest Archaeology: 1. *The Kiva* 25:1–32.

Kobayashi, Masashi
1996   "An Ethnoarchaeological Study of the Relationships between Vessel Form and Function." Ph.D. dissertation, Department of Anthropology, University of Arizona, Tucson.

Kus, Susan

2000   Ideas Are Like Burgeoning Grains on a Young Rice Stalk: Some Ideas
        on Theory in Anthropological Archaeology. In *Social Theory in Ar-
        chaeology*, edited by M. B. Schiffer, 156–72. Salt Lake City: Univer-
        sity of Utah Press.

Lekson, Stephen H.

1999   *The Chaco Meridian*. Walnut Creek, Calif.: Altamira Press.

Leone, Mark P.

1973   Archeology as the Science of Technology: Mormon Town Plans and
        Fences. In *Research and Theory in Current Archeology*, edited by C. L.
        Redman, 125–50. New York: Wiley.

Lightfoot, Kent G.

1984   *Prehistoric Political Dynamics: A Case Study from the American South-
        west*. DeKalb: Northern Illinois University Press.

Lightfoot, Kent G., and Gary M. Feinman

1982   Social Differentiation and Leadership Development in Early Pithouse
        Villages in the Mogollon Region of the American Southwest. *Ameri-
        can Antiquity* 47:64–86.

Lightfoot, Kent G., and Steadman Upham

1989a   Complex Societies in the Prehistoric American Southwest: A Con-
        sideration of the Controversy. In *The Sociopolitical Structure of Prehis-
        toric Southwestern Societies*, edited by S. Upham, K. G. Lightfoot, and
        R. A. Jewett, 3–30. Boulder: Westview Press.

1989b   The Sociopolitical Structure of Prehistoric Southwestern Societies:
        Concluding Thoughts. In *The Sociopolitical Structure of Prehistoric
        Southwestern Societies*, edited by S. Upham, K. G. Lightfoot, and
        R. A. Jewett, 583–93. Boulder: Westview Press.

Lindsay, Alexander J.

1987   Explaining an Anasazi Migration to East Central Arizona. *American
        Archeology* 6:190–98.

Longacre, William A.

1969   "Archaeological Research at the Grasshopper Ruin, Arizona." Re-
        search Proposal to the National Science Foundation, Washington,
        D.C.

1970   *Archaeology as Anthropology: A Case Study*. Anthropological Papers
        17. Tucson: University of Arizona Press.

1975   Population Dynamics at the Grasshopper Pueblo, Arizona. *American
        Antiquity* 40:71–74.

1976   Population Dynamics at the Grasshopper Pueblo, Arizona. In *Demo-
        graphic Anthropology: Quantitative Approaches*, edited by E. B. W.
        Zubrow, 169–84. Albuquerque: University of New Mexico Press.

1977   Field Training in Archaeology for the Graduate Student. *University
        Museum Studies* 10:136–43. Carbondale: Southern Illinois University
        Press.

2000   Exploring Prehistoric Social and Political Organization in the American Southwest. *Journal of Anthropological Research* 56:287–300.

Longacre, William A., and James E. Ayres
1968   Archaeological Lessons from an Apache Wickiup. In *New Perspectives in Archeology*, edited by S. R. Binford and L. R. Binford, 151–59. Chicago: Aldine.

Longacre, William A., and Michael W. Graves
1982   Multidisciplinary Studies at Grasshopper. In *Multidisciplinary Research at Grasshopper Pueblo, Arizona*, edited by W. A. Longacre, S. J. Holbrook, and M. W. Graves, 1–4. Anthropological Papers 40. Tucson: University of Arizona Press.

Longacre, William A., Sally J. Holbrook, and Michael W. Graves (editors)
1982   *Multidisciplinary Research at Grasshopper Pueblo, Arizona*. Anthropological Papers 40. Tucson: University of Arizona Press.

Longacre, William A., Kenneth L. Kvamme, and Masashi Kobayashi
1988   Southwestern Pottery Standardization: An Ethnoarchaeological View from the Philippines. *The Kiva* 53:101–12.

Longacre, William A., and J. Jefferson Reid
1971   Research Strategy for Locational Analysis: An Outline. In *The Distribution of Prehistoric Population Aggregates*, edited by G. J. Gumerman, 103–10. Anthropological Reports 1. Prescott, Arizona: Prescott College.
1974   The University of Arizona Archaeological Field School at Grasshopper: Eleven Years of Multidisciplinary Research and Teaching. *The Kiva* 40:3–38.

Longacre, William A., and Raymond H. Thompson
1971   "Archaeological Investigations at the Grasshopper Ruin, Arizona." Proposal to the National Science Foundation, Washington, D.C.

Lorentzen, Leon H.
1993   "From Atlatl to Bow: The Impact of Improved Weapons on Wildlife in the Grasshopper Region." Master's thesis, Department of Anthropology, University of Arizona, Tucson.

Lowell, Julie C.
1991   *Prehistoric Households at Turkey Creek Pueblo, Arizona*. Anthropological Papers 54. Tucson: University of Arizona Press.
1995   Illuminating Fire-Feature Variability in the Grasshopper Region of Arizona. *Kiva* 60:351–69.
1999   The Fires of Grasshopper: Enlightening Transformations in Subsistence Practices through Fire-Feature Analysis. *Journal of Anthropological Archaeology* 18:441–70.

Lowenthal, David
1985   *The Past Is a Foreign Country*. Cambridge: Cambridge University Press.

Lyman, R. Lee, Michael J. O'Brien, and Robert C. Dunnell

1997   *The Rise and Fall of Culture History*. New York: Plenum.

Madsen, David B., and David Rhode

1994   *Across the West: Human Population Movement and the Expansion of the Numa*. Salt Lake City: University of Utah Press.

Mangum, Richard K., and Sherry G. Mangum

1997   *One Woman's West: The Life of Mary-Russell Ferrell Colton*. Flagstaff, Arizona: Northland Publishing.

Margalef, Ramon

1968   *Perspectives in Ecological Theory*. Chicago: University of Chicago Press.

Martin, Paul Schultz, and James Schoenwetter

1960   Arizona's Oldest Cornfield. *Science* 132(3418):33–34.

Martin, Paul Sidney, and John B. Rinaldo

1950   Sites of the Reserve Phase, Pine Lawn Valley, Western New Mexico. *Fieldiana: Anthropology* 38:3.

Mauer, Michael D.

1970   "Cibecue Polychrome: A Fourteenth Century Ceramic Type from East-Central Arizona." Master's thesis, Department of Anthropology, University of Arizona, Tucson.

Mayro, Linda L., Stephanie M. Whittlesey, and J. Jefferson Reid

1976   Observations on the Salado Presence at Grasshopper Pueblo. *The Kiva* 42:85–94.

McClelland, John A.

2003   "Refining the Resolution of Biological Distance Studies Based On the Analysis of Dental Morphology: Detecting Subpopulations at Grasshopper Pueblo." Ph.D. dissertation, Department of Anthropology, University of Arizona, Tucson.

McGuire, Randall H., and Dean J. Saitta

1996   Although They Have Petty Captains, They Obey Them Badly: The Dialectics of Prehispanic Western Pueblo Social Organization. *American Antiquity* 61:197–217.

McKusick, Charmion R.

1982   Avifauna from Grasshopper Pueblo. In *Multidisciplinary Research at Grasshopper Pueblo, Arizona*, edited by W. A. Longacre, S. J. Holbrook, and M. W. Graves, 87–96. Anthropological Papers 40. Tucson: University of Arizona Press.

Menand, Louis

1997   An Introduction to Pragmatism. In *Pragmatism: A Reader*, edited by L. Menand, xi–xxiv. New York: Vintage.

Merbs, Charles F.

1967   Cremated Human Remains from Point of Pines, Arizona: A New Approach. *American Antiquity* 32:498–506.

Mills, Barbara J.

2005   Curricular Matters: The Impact of Field Schools on Southwest Ar-
        chaeology. In *One Hundred Years of Southwestern Archaeology*, edited
        by D. D. Fowler and L. S. Cordell. University of Utah Press: Salt Lake
        City. In press.

Mills, Barbara J., and Sarah Herr

1999   Chronology of the Mogollon Rim Region. In *Living on the Edge of
        the Rim: Excavations and Analysis of the Silver Creek Archaeological
        Research Project 1993-1998*, edited by B. J. Mills, S. Herr, and S. Van
        Keuren, 269-93. Archaeological Series 192 (2 vols.). Tucson: Arizona
        State Museum.

Mills, Barbara J., Sarah Herr, and Scott Van Keuren (editors)

1999   *Living on the Edge of the Rim: Excavations and Analysis of the Silver
        Creek Archaeological Research Project 1993-1998*. Archaeological
        Series 192 (2 vols). Tucson: Arizona State Museum.

Montgomery, Barbara K.

1992a   Pueblo Room Fill and Prehistoric Ritual. In *Proceedings of the Sec-
        ond Salado Conference, Globe, AZ, 1992*, edited by R. C. Lange and
        S. Germick, 125-30. Phoenix: Arizona Archaeological Society.

1992b   "Understanding the Formation of the Archaeological Record: Ce-
        ramic Variability at Chodistaas Pueblo, Arizona." Ph.D. dissertation,
        Department of Anthropology, University of Arizona, Tucson.

1993   Ceramic Analysis as a Tool for Discovering Processes of Pueblo
        Abandonment. In *Abandonment of Settlements and Regions: Ethno-
        archaeological and Archaeological Approaches*, edited by C. Cameron
        and S. Tomka, 157-64. Cambridge: Cambridge University Press.

Montgomery, Barbara K., and J. Jefferson Reid

1990   An Instance of Rapid Ceramic Change in the American Southwest.
        American Antiquity 55:88-97.

Morris, Elizabeth A.

1957   "Stratigraphic Evidence for a Cultural Continuum at the Point of
        Pines Ruin." Master's thesis, Department of Anthropology, University
        of Arizona, Tucson.

Neely, James A.

1974   "The Prehistoric Lunt and Stove Canyon Sites, Point of Pines, Ari-
        zona." Ph.D. dissertation, Department of Anthropology, University of
        Arizona, Tucson.

Nelson, Ben A., and Roger Anyon

1996   Fallow Valleys: Asynchronous Occupations in Southwestern New
        Mexico. *Kiva* 61:275-94.

Nelson, Ben A., and Steven A. LeBlanc

1986   *Short-Term Sedentism in the American Southwest: The Mimbres Valley
        Salado*. Albuquerque: University of New Mexico Press.

Nesbitt, Paul H.

1938   Starkweather Ruin. *Anthropology* 6. Beloit, Wisconsin: Logan Museum.

Netting, Robert McC.

1971   *The Ecological Approach in Cultural Study*. Reading, Mass.: Addison-Wesley Modular Publications.

Odum, Eugene P.

1971   *Fundamentals of Ecology*. Philadelphia: W. B. Saunders.

Olsen, John W.

1980   "A Zooarchaeological Analysis of Vertebrate Faunal Remains from the Grasshopper Pueblo, Arizona." Ph.D. dissertation, Department of Anthropology, University of California, Berkeley.

1982   Prehistoric Environmental Reconstruction by Vertebrate Faunal Analysis, Grasshopper Pueblo. In *Multidisciplinary Research at Grasshopper Pueblo, Arizona*, edited by W. A. Longacre, S. J. Holbrook, and M. W. Graves, 63–72. Anthropological Papers 40. Tucson: University of Arizona Press.

1990   *Vertebrate Faunal Remains from Grasshopper Pueblo, Arizona*. Anthropological Papers 83. Ann Arbor: University of Michigan.

Olsen, Sandra L.

1979   A Study of Bone Artifacts from Grasshopper Pueblo. *The Kiva* 44: 341–93.

Olsen, Stanley J.

1968   Canid Remains from Grasshopper Ruin. *The Kiva* 34:33–40.

1982   Water Resources and Aquatic Fauna at Grasshopper Pueblo. In *Multidisciplinary Research at Grasshopper Pueblo, Arizona*, edited by W. A. Longacre, S. J. Holbrook, and M. W. Graves, 61–62. Anthropological Papers 40. Tucson: University of Arizona Press.

Olsen, Stanley J., and John W. Olsen

1970   A Preliminary Report on the Fish and Herpetofauna of Grasshopper Ruin. *The Kiva* 36:40–43.

1974   The Macaws of Grasshopper Pueblo. *The Kiva* 40:67–70.

Olson, Alan P.

1959   "An Evaluation of the Phase Concept in Southwestern Archaeology as Applied to the Eleventh and Twelfth Century Occupations at Point of Pines, East-Central Arizona." Ph.D. dissertation, Department of Anthropology, University of Arizona, Tucson.

1962a   A History of the Phase Concept in the Southwest. *American Antiquity* 27:457–72.

1962b   Review of *Jeddito 264*, by Hiroshi Daifuku. *American Antiquity* 27: 604–5.

Parker, Marion L.

1967   "Dendrochronology of Point of Pines." Master's thesis, Department of Anthropology, University of Arizona, Tucson.

Pfeiffer, John E.
1972   *The Emergence of Man*. 2nd edition. New York: Harper and Row.

Pizza, Andrea C.
1999   "Correlate Construction and Craft Specialization: An Evaluation of the Ceramic Standardization Hypothesis." Master's thesis, Department of Anthropology, University of Arizona, Tucson.

Platt, John
1964   Strong Inference. *Science* 146:347–53.

Plog, Fred
1985   Status and Death at Grasshopper: The Homogenization of Reality. In *Status, Structure, and Stratification: Current Archaeological Reconstructions*, edited by M. Thompson, M. T. Garcia, and F. J. Kense, 161–65. Calgary: University of Calgary.

Price, T. Douglas, Clark M. Johnson, Joseph A. Ezzo, Jonathan Ericson, and James H. Burton
1994   Residential Mobility in the Prehistoric Southwest United States: A Preliminary Study Using Strontium Isotope Analysis. *Journal of Archaeological Science* 21:315–30.

Quimby, George I.
1993   A Thing of Sherds and Patches. *American Antiquity* 58:7–21.

Raab, L. Mark, and Albert C. Goodyear
1984   Middle-Range Theory in Archaeology: A Critical Review of Origins and Applications. *American Antiquity* 49:255–68.

Reed, Erik K.
1948   The Western Pueblo Archaeological Complex. *El Palacio* 55:9–15.
1950   Eastern-Central Arizona Archaeology in Relation of the Western Pueblos. *Southwestern Journal of Anthropology* 6:120–38.

Reid, J. Jefferson
1973   "Growth and Response to Stress at Grasshopper Pueblo, Arizona." Ph.D. dissertation, Department of Anthropology, University of Arizona, Tucson.
1974   Behavioral Archaeology at the Grasshopper Ruin. *The Kiva* 40:1–2.
1978   Response to Stress at Grasshopper Pueblo, Arizona. In *Discovering Past Behavior: Experiments in the Archaeology of the American Southwest*, edited by P. F. Grebinger, 195–213. London: Gordon and Breach.
1982   (editor) *Cholla Project Archaeology*. 5 vols. Archaeological Series 161. Tucson: Arizona State Museum.
1984a   Implications of Mogollon Settlement Variability in Grasshopper and Adjacent Regions. In *Recent Research in Mogollon Archaeology*, edited by S. Upham, F. Plog, D. Batcho, and B. Kauffman, 59–67. Occasional Papers 10. Las Cruces: New Mexico State University.
1984b   What Is Black-on-White and Vague All Over? In *Regional Analysis of Prehistoric Ceramic Variation: Contemporary Studies of the Cibola*

Whitewares, edited by A. P. Sullivan and J. L. Hantman, 135–52. Anthropological Research Papers 31. Tempe: Arizona State University.

1985a Formation Processes for the Practical Prehistorian: An Example from the Southeast. In *Structure and Process in Southeastern Archaeology*, edited by R. S. Dickens Jr. and H. T. Ward, 11–33. Tuscaloosa: University of Alabama Press.

1985b Measuring Social Complexity in the American Southwest. In *Status, Structure, and Stratification: Current Archaeological Reconstructions*, edited by M. Thompson, M. T. Garcia, and F. J. Kense, 167–73. Calgary: University of Calgary.

1986 Historical Perspective on the Concept of Mogollon. In *Mogollon Variability*, edited by C. Benson and S. Upham, 1–8. Occasional Papers 15. Las Cruces: New Mexico State University.

1989 A Grasshopper Perspective on the Mogollon of the Arizona Mountains. In *Dynamics of Southwest Prehistory*, edited by L. S. Cordell and G. Gumerman, 65–97. Washington, D.C.: Smithsonian Institution Press.

1991 Editor's Corner. On the History of Archaeology and Archaeologists. *American Antiquity* 56:195–96.

1993 Emil Walter Haury 1904–1992. *Kiva* 59:243–59.

1995 Four Strategies after Twenty Years: A Return to Basics. In *Expanding Archaeology*, edited by J. M. Skibo, W. H. Walker, and A. E. Nielsen, 15–21. Salt Lake City: University of Utah Press.

1998a Return to Migration, Population Movement, and Ethnic Identity in the American Southwest: A Peer Reviewer's Thoughts on Archaeological Inference. In *Vanishing River: Landscapes and Lives of the Lower Verde Valley; The Lower Verde Archaeological Project*, edited by S. M. Whittlesey, R. S. Ciolek-Torrello, and J. H. Altschul, 629–38. Tucson: SRI Press.

1998b Wickiup 2 at the Grasshopper Spring Site and the Dating of Western Apache Occupation. In *Vanishing River: Landscapes and Lives of the Lower Verde Valley; The Lower Verde Archaeological Project*, edited by S. M. Whittlesey, R. S. Ciolek-Torrello, and J. H. Altschul, 197–99. Tucson: SRI Press.

1999 The Grasshopper–Chavez Pass Debate: Existential Dilemmas and Archaeological Discourse. In *Sixty Years of Mogollon Archaeology: Papers from the Ninth Mogollon Conference, Silver City, New Mexico, 1996*, edited by S. M. Whittlesey, 13–22. Tucson: SRI Press.

Reid, J. Jefferson and David E. Doyel (editors)
1986 *Emil W. Haury's Prehistory of the American Southwest*. Tucson: University of Arizona Press.

Reid, J. Jefferson, and Donald A. Graybill
1982 Cholla Project Chipped Stone Identification Procedures. In *Cholla*

Project Archaeology, vol. 1: *Introduction and Special Studies*, edited by J. J. Reid, 27–34. Archaeological Series 161. Tucson: Arizona State Museum.

Reid, J. Jefferson, and Barbara K. Montgomery
1997 The Brown and the Gray: Pots and Population Movement in East-Central Arizona. *Journal of Anthropological Research* 54:447–59.
1999 Ritual Space in the Grasshopper Region, East-Central Arizona. In *Sixty Years of Mogollon Archaeology: Papers from the Ninth Mogollon Conference, Silver City, New Mexico, 1996*, edited by S. M. Whittlesey, 23–29. Tucson: SRI Press.

Reid, J. Jefferson, Barbara K. Montgomery, and M. Nieves Zedeño
1995 Refinements in Dating Late Cibola White Ware. *Kiva* 61:31–44.

Reid, J. Jefferson, Barbara K. Montgomery, M. Nieves Zedeño, and Mark A. Neupert
1992 The Origin of Roosevelt Redware. In *Proceedings of the Second Salado Conference, Globe, AZ, 1992*, edited by R. C. Lange and S. Germick, 212–15. Phoenix: Arizona Archaeological Society.

Reid, J. Jefferson, Michael B. Schiffer, and Jeffrey Neff
1975 Archaeological Considerations of Intrasite Sampling. In *Sampling in Archaeology*, edited by J. W. Muller, 209–24. Tucson: University of Arizona Press.

Reid, J. Jefferson, Michael B. Schiffer, and William L. Rathje
1975 Behavioral Archaeology: Four Strategies. *American Anthropologist* 77: 864–69.

Reid, J. Jefferson, Michael B. Schiffer, Stephanie M. Whittlesey, Madeleine J. Hinkes, Alan P. Sullivan, Christian E. Downum, William A. Longacre, and H. David Tuggle
1989 Perception and Interpretation in Contemporary Southwestern Archaeology: Comments on Cordell, Upham, and Brock. *American Antiquity* 54:802–14.

Reid, J. Jefferson, and Izumi Shimada
1982 Pueblo Growth at Grasshopper: Methods and Models. In *Multidisciplinary Research at Grasshopper Pueblo, Arizona*, edited by W. A. Longacre, S. J. Holbrook, and M. W. Graves, 12–18. Anthropological Papers 40. Tucson: University of Arizona Press.

Reid, J. Jefferson, John R. Welch, Barbara K. Montgomery, and M. Nieves Zedeño
1996 A Demographic Overview of the Late Pueblo III Period in the Mountains of East-Central Arizona. In *The Prehistoric Pueblo World, A.D. 1150–1350*, edited by M. A. Adler, 73–85. Tucson: University of Arizona Press.

Reid, J. Jefferson, and Stephanie M. Whittlesey
1982 Households at Grasshopper Pueblo. *American Behavioral Scientist* 25: 687–703.

1990   The Complicated and the Complex: Observations on the Archaeo-
        logical Record of Large Pueblos. In *Perspectives on Southwestern
        Prehistory*, edited by P. Minnis and C. Redman, 184–95. Boulder:
        Westview Press.

1997   *The Archaeology of Ancient Arizona*. Tucson: University of Arizona
        Press.

1998   A Search for the Philosophical Julian: American Pragmatism and
        Southwestern Archaeology. *Kiva* 64:275–86.

1999   *Grasshopper Pueblo: A Story of Archaeology and Ancient Life*. Tucson:
        University of Arizona Press.

Renfrew, Colin

1994   Towards a Cognitive Archaeology. In *The Ancient Mind: Elements of
        Cognitive Archaeology*, edited by C. Renfrew and E. B. W. Zubrow,
        3–12. Cambridge: Cambridge University Press.

Reynolds, William E.

1981   "The Ethnoarchaeology of Pueblo Architecture." Ph.D. dissertation,
        Department of Anthropology, Arizona State University, Tempe.

Rice, Glen E.

1998   *A Synthesis of Tonto Basin Prehistory: The Roosevelt Archaeology
        Studies, 1989 to 1998*. Archaeological Field Studies 41. Tempe: Ari-
        zona State University.

Riggs, Charles R., Jr.

1994   "Dating Construction Events at Grasshopper Pueblo: New Tech-
        niques for Architectural Analysis." Master's thesis, Department of
        Anthropology, University of Arizona, Tucson.

1999a   "The Architecture of Grasshopper Pueblo: Dynamics of Form, Func-
        tion, and Use of Space in a Prehistoric Community." Ph.D. disserta-
        tion, Department of Anthropology, University of Arizona, Tucson.

1999b   Spatial Variability in Room Function at Grasshopper Pueblo. In *Sixty
        Years of Mogollon Archaeology: Papers from the Ninth Mogollon Con-
        ference, Silver City, New Mexico, 1996*, edited by S. M. Whittlesey,
        3–11. Tucson: SRI Press.

2001   *The Architecture of Grasshopper Pueblo*. Salt Lake City: University of
        Utah Press.

Robinson, William J.

1958   A New Type of Ceremonial Pottery Killing at Point of Pines. *The Kiva*
        23:12–14.

1959   "Burial Customs at the Point of Pines Ruin." Master's thesis, Depart-
        ment of Anthropology, University of Arizona, Tucson.

Robinson, William J., and Roderick Sprague

1965   Disposal of the Dead at Point of Pines, Arizona. *American Antiquity*
        30:442–53.

Rock, James T.

1974   The Use of Social Models in Archaeological Interpretation. *The Kiva* 40:81–91.

Scarborough, Robert, and Izumi Shimada

1974   Geological Analysis of Wall Composition at Grasshopper with Behavioral Implications. *The Kiva* 40:49–66.

Scheper-Hughes, Nancy

1992   Hungry Bodies, Medicine, and the State: Toward a Critical Psychological Anthropology. In *New Directions in Psychological Anthropology*, edited by T. Schwartz, G. White, and C. Lutz, 221–47. Cambridge: Cambridge University Press.

Schiffer, Michael B.

1972   Archaeological Context and Systemic Context. *American Antiquity* 37:156–65.

1976   *Behavioral Archeology.* Academic Press, New York.

1983   Toward the Identification of Formation Processes. *American Antiquity* 48:675–706.

1985   Is There a "Pompeii Premise" in Archaeology? *Journal of Anthropological Research* 41:18–41.

1987   *Formation Processes of the Archaeological Record.* Albuquerque: University of New Mexico Press.

1988   The Structure of Archaeological Theory. *American Antiquity* 53:461–85.

1989   Formation Processes of Broken K Pueblo: Some Hypotheses. In *Quantifying Diversity in Archaeology*, edited by R. D. Leonard and G. T. Jones, 37–58. Cambridge: Cambridge University Press.

1995a   *Behavioral Archaeology: First Principles.* Salt Lake City: University of Utah Press.

1995b   Social Theory and History in Behavioral Archaeology. In *Expanding Archaeology*, edited by J. M. Skibo, W. H. Walker, and A. E. Nielsen, 22–35. Salt Lake City: University of Utah Press.

1999   *The Material Life of Human Beings: Artifacts, Behavior, and Communication.* London: Routledge.

2000a   Social Theory in Archaeology: Building Bridges. In *Social Theory in Archaeology*, edited by M. B. Schiffer, 1–13. Salt Lake City: University of Utah Press.

2000b   (editor) *Social Theory in Archaeology.* Salt Lake City: University of Utah Press.

Schoenwetter, James

1986   "A Palynological Approach to a Chronometry Problem on the Colorado Plateau." Manuscript on file, Department of Anthropology, Arizona State University, Tempe.

Schoenwetter, James, and Alfred E. Dittert Jr.

1968   An Ecological Interpretation of Anasazi Settlement Patterns. In

Anthropological Archeology in the Americas, edited by B. J. Meggers, 41–66. Washington, D.C.: Anthropological Society of Washington.

Shipman, Jeffrey H.

1982   "Biological Relationships among Prehistoric Western Pueblo Indian Groups Based on Metric and Disease Traits of the Skeleton." Ph.D. dissertation, Department of Anthropology, University of Arizona, Tucson.

Skibo, James M.

1999   *Ants for Breakfast: Archaeological Adventures among the Kalinga.* Salt Lake City: University of Utah Press.

Smiley, Terah L.

1949   Tree-Ring Dates from Point of Pines. *Tree-Ring Bulletin* 15:20–21.

1952   *Four Late Prehistoric Kivas at Point of Pines, Arizona.* University of Arizona Bulletin 23(3), Social Science Bulletin 21. Tucson: University of Arizona.

Smith, Watson

1962   Schools, Pots, and Potters. *American Anthropologist* 64:1165–78.

1992   One Man's Archaeology. *Kiva* 57:2.

Snead, James E.

2001   *Ruins and Rivals: The Making of Southwest Archaeology.* Tucson: University of Arizona Press.

South, Stanley

1972   Evolution and Horizon as Revealed in the Ceramic Analysis in Historical Archaeology. In *The Conference on Historic Site Archaeology Papers* 6(I):71–106. Columbia: University of South Carolina Institute of Archaeology and Anthropology.

Spielmann, Katherine A.

1998   *Migration and Reorganization: The Pueblo IV Period in the American Southwest.* Anthropological Research Papers 51. Tempe: Arizona State University.

Stein, Mercedes C.

1962   "An Analysis of the Human Skeletal Remains from Turkey Creek Ruin, Point of Pines, Arizona." Master's thesis, Department of Anthropology, University of Arizona, Tucson.

Stein, Walter T.

1962   "Mammals from Archaeological Sites, Point of Pines, Arizona." Master's thesis, Department of Anthropology, University of Arizona, Tucson.

1963   Mammal Remains from Archaeological Sites in the Point of Pines Region, Arizona. *American Antiquity* 29:213–20.

Stillman, Calvin W.

1995   Learning from Landscape and Nature. In *Landscape in America*, edited by G. F. Thompson, 51–60. Austin: University of Texas Press.

Sullivan, Alan P., III

1974   Problems in the Estimation of Original Room Function: A Tentative Solution from the Grasshopper Ruin. *The Kiva* 40:93–100.

1978   Inference and Evidence in Archaeology: A Discussion of the Conceptual Problems. In *Advances in Archaeological Method and Theory 1*, edited by M. B. Schiffer, 183–222. New York: Academic Press.

1980   "Prehistoric Settlement Variability in the Grasshopper Area, East-Central Arizona." Ph.D. dissertation, Department of Anthropology, University of Arizona, Tucson.

1982   Mogollon Agriculture: An Appraisal and a New Model. *The Kiva* 48:1–15.

1984   Design Styles and Cibola White Wares: Examples from the Grasshopper Area East-Central Arizona. In *Regional Analysis of Prehistoric Ceramic Variation: Contemporary Studies of the Cibola White Wares*, edited by A. Sullivan and J. Hantman, 74–93. Anthropological Papers 31. Tempe: Arizona State University.

1988   Prehistoric Southwestern Ceramic Manufacture: The Limitations of Current Evidence. *American Antiquity* 53:23–35.

1995   Behavioral Archaeology and the Interpretation of Archaeological Variability. In *Expanding Archaeology*, edited by J. M. Skibo, W. H. Walker, and A. E. Nielsen, 178–86. Salt Lake City: University of Utah Press.

Sullivan, Alan P., III, Matthew E. Becher, and Christian E. Downum

1995   Tusayan White Ware Chronology: New Archaeological and Dendrochronological Evidence. *Kiva* 61:175–88.

Sullivan, Alan P., III, and Jeffrey L. Hantman (editors)

1984   *Regional Analysis of Prehistoric Ceramic Variation: Contemporary Studies of the Cibola White Wares*. Anthropological Papers 31. Tempe: Arizona State University.

Sumner, Dale R.

1984   "Size, Shape, and Bone Mineral Content in the Human Femur in Growth and Aging." Ph.D. dissertation, Department of Anthropology, University of Arizona, Tucson.

Tanner, Clara Lee

1954   Byron Cummings, 1860–1954. *The Kiva* 20:1–20.

Taylor, Walter W.

1954   Southwestern Archaeology: Its History and Theory. *American Anthropologist* 56:561–70.

Thompson, Marc, Maria T. Garcia, and F. J. Kense (editors)

1985   *Status, Structure, and Organization: Current Archaeological Approaches*. Calgary: University of Calgary.

Thompson, Raymond H. (editor)

1956   The Subjective Element in Archaeological Inference. *Southwestern Journal of Anthropology* 12:327–32.

1958a   (editor) *Migrations in New World Culture History*. Social Science Bulletin 27. Tucson: University of Arizona Press.

1958b   Preface. In *Migrations in New World Culture History*, edited by R. H. Thompson, v–vii. Social Science Bulletin 27. Tucson: University of Arizona Press.

1958c   *Modern Yucatecan Maya Pottery Making*. Memoir 15. Society for American Archaeology.

1963   Archaeological Excavations by University of Arizona Archaeological Field School, Fort Apache Indian Reservation, June, July, and August, 1963. Report to the Bureau of Indian Affairs, Washington, D.C.

1972   Interpretive Trends and Linear Models in American Archaeology. In *Contemporary Archaeology*, edited by M. P. Leone, 34–38. Carbondale: Southern Illinois University Press.

1995   Emil W. Haury and the Definition of Southwestern Archaeology. *American Antiquity* 60:640–60.

Thompson, Raymond H., and William A. Longacre

1966   The University of Arizona Archaeological Field School at Grasshopper, East-Central Arizona. *The Kiva* 31:255–75.

Triadan, Daniela

1989   "Defining Local Ceramic Production at Grasshopper Pueblo, Arizona." Master's thesis, Lateinamerikainstitut, Freie Universität, Berlin, Germany.

1994   "White Mountain Redware: Expensive Trade Goods or Local Commodity? A Study of the Production, Distribution, and Function of White Mountain Redware during the 14th Century in the Grasshopper Region, East-Central Arizona." Ph.D. dissertation, Lateinamerikainstitut, Freie Universität, Berlin, Germany.

1997   *Ceramic Commodities and Common Containers: Production and Distribution of White Mountain Red Ware in the Grasshopper Region, Arizona*. Anthropological Papers 61. Tucson: University of Arizona Press.

Trigger, Bruce G.

1995   Expanding Middle-Range Theory. *American Antiquity* 69:449–58.

Tuggle, H. David

1970   "Prehistoric Community Relationships in East-Central Arizona." Ph.D. dissertation, Department of Anthropology, University of Arizona, Tucson.

Tuggle, H. David, Keith W. Kintigh, and J. Jefferson Reid

1982   Trace Element Analysis of White Wares. In *Cholla Project Archaeology*, vol. 5: *Ceramic Studies*, edited by J. J. Reid, 22–38. Archaeological Series 161. Tucson: Arizona State Museum.

Tuggle, H. David, and J. Jefferson Reid

2001   Conflict and Defense in the Grasshopper Region of East-Central Arizona. In *Deadly Landscapes: Case Studies in Prehistoric Southwestern*

Warfare, edited by G. E. Rice and S. A. LaBlanc, 85–107. Salt Lake City: University of Utah Press.

Tuggle, H. David, J. Jefferson Reid, and Robert C. Cole Jr.

1984   Fourteenth Century Mogollon Agriculture in the Grasshopper Region of Arizona. In *Prehistoric Agriculture Strategies in the Southwest*, edited by S. F. Fish and P. R. Fish, 101–10. Anthropological Research Papers 33. Tempe: Arizona State University.

Upham, Steadman

1978   "Final Report on Archaeological Investigations at Chavez Pass Ruin: The 1978 Season." Manuscript on file at the Coconino National Forest, Flagstaff, Arizona.

1982   *Polities and Power: An Economic and Political History of the Western Pueblo*. New York: Academic Press.

1989   East Meets West: Hierarchy and Elites in Pueblo Society. In *The Sociopolitical Structure of Prehistoric Southwestern Societies*, edited by S. Upham, K. G. Lightfoot, and R. A. Jewett, 77–102. Boulder: Westview Press.

Upham, Steadman, and Gail M. Bockley

1989   The Chronologies of Nuvakwewtaqa: Implications for Social Processes. In *The Sociopolitical Structure of Prehistoric Southwestern Societies*, edited by S. Upham, K. G. Lightfoot, and R. A. Jewett, 447–90. Boulder: Westview Press.

Upham, Steadman, Kent G. Lightfoot, and Gary Feinman

1981   Explaining Socially Determined Ceramic Distributions in the Prehistoric Plateau Southwest. *American Antiquity* 46:822–33.

Upham, Steadman, Kent G. Lightfoot, and Roberta A. Jewett (editors)

1989   *The Sociopolitical Structure of Prehistoric Southwestern Societies*. Boulder: Westview Press.

Upham, Steadman, and Fred Plog

1986   The Interpretation of Prehistoric Political Complexity in the Central and Northern Southwest: Toward a Mending of Models. *Journal of Field Archaeology* 13:223–38.

Van Keuren, Scott

1994   "Design Structure Variation in Cibola White Ware Vessels from Grasshopper and Chodistaas Pueblos, Arizona." Master's thesis, Department of Anthropology, University of Arizona, Tucson.

1999   *Ceramic Design Structure and the Organization of Cibola White Ware Production in the Grasshopper Region, Arizona*. Archaeological Series 191. Tucson: Arizona State Museum.

2001   "Ceramic Style and the Reorganization of Fourteenth Century Pueblo Communities in East-Central Arizona." Ph.D. dissertation, Department of Anthropology, University of Arizona, Tucson.

Varien, Mark D.

1999   *Sedentism and Mobility in a Social Landscape*. Tucson: University of
        Arizona Press.

Watson, Richard A.

1991   What the New Archaeology Has Accomplished. *Current Anthropology*
        32:275–91.

Welch, John R.

1991   From Horticulture to Agriculture in the Late Prehistory of the Grass-
        hopper Region, Arizona. In *Mogollon V*, edited by P. H. Beckett,
        75–92. Las Cruces, New Mexico: COAS Publishing Co.

1996   "The Archaeological Measures and Social Implications of Agricul-
        tural Commitment." Ph.D. dissertation, Department of Anthro-
        pology, University of Arizona, Tucson.

Welch, John R., and Daniela Triadan

1991   The Canyon Creek Turquoise Mine, Arizona. *Kiva* 56:145–64.

Wheat, Joe Ben

1952   Prehistoric Water Sources of the Point of Pines Area. *American An-
        tiquity* 17:185–96.

1954a   *Crooked Ridge Village (Arizona W:10:15)*. University of Arizona Bul-
        letin 21(3), Social Science Bulletin 24. Tucson: University of Arizona.

1954b   Southwestern Cultural Interrelationships and the Question of Area
        Co-tradition. *American Anthropologist* 56:576–86.

1955   *Mogollon Culture Prior to A.D. 1000*. Memoir 82, American Anthro-
        pological Association. Memoir 10, Society for American Archae-
        ology.

Wheat, Joe Ben, James C. Gifford, and William W. Wasley

1958   Ceramic Variety, Type Cluster, and Ceramic System in Southwestern
        Pottery Analysis. *American Antiquity* 24:34–47.

White, Hayden

1987   *The Content of the Form: Narrative Discourse and Historical Represen-
        tation*. Baltimore: Johns Hopkins University Press.

Whittaker, John C.

1984   "Arrowheads and Artisans: Stone Tool Manufacture and Individual
        Variation at Grasshopper Pueblo." Ph.D. dissertation, Department of
        Anthropology, University of Arizona, Tucson.

1986   Projectile Points and the Question of Specialization at Grasshopper
        Pueblo, Arizona. In *Mogollon Variability*, edited by C. Benson and
        S. Upham, 121–40. Occasional Papers 15. Las Cruces: New Mexico
        State University.

1987a   Individual Variations as an Approach to Economic Organization:
        Projectile Points at Grasshopper Pueblo, Arizona. *Journal of Field
        Archaeology* 14:465–79.

1987b   Making Arrowpoints in a Prehistoric Pueblo. *Lithic Technology* 16:
        1–12.

Whittlesey, Stephanie M.

1974   Identification of Imported Ceramics through Functional Analysis of Attributes. *The Kiva* 40:101–12.

1978   "Status and Death at Grasshopper Pueblo: Experiments Toward an Archaeological Theory of Correlates." Ph.D. dissertation, Department of Anthropology, University of Arizona, Tucson.

1982   Summary of Cholla Project Chipped Stone Studies. In *Cholla Project Archaeology*, vol. 1: *Introduction and Special Studies*, edited by J. J. Reid, 51–61. Archaeological Series 161, vol. 1. Tucson: Arizona State Museum.

1984   Uses and Abuses of Mogollon Mortuary Data. In *Recent Research in Mogollon Archaeology*, edited by S. Upham, F. Plog, D. Batcho, and B. Kauffman, 276–84. Occasional Papers 10. Las Cruces: New Mexico State University.

1989   The Individual, the Community, and Social Organization: Issues of Evidence and Inference Justification. In *Households and Communities*, edited by S. MacEachern, D. Archer, and R. Garvin, 227–34. Calgary: University of Calgary.

1998a   Archaeological Landscapes: A Methodological and Theoretical Discussion. In *Vanishing River: Landscapes and Lives of the Lower Verde Valley; The Lower Verde Archaeological Project*, edited by S. M. Whittlesey, R. S. Ciolek-Torrello, and J. H. Altschul, 17–28. Tucson: SRI Press.

1998b   Landscapes and Lives along the Lower Verde River. In *Vanishing River: Landscapes and Lives of the Lower Verde Valley; The Lower Verde Archaeological Project*, edited by S. M. Whittlesey, R. S. Ciolek-Torrello, and J. H. Altschul, 703–21. Tucson: SRI Press.

1999a   Engendering the Mogollon Past. In *Sixty Years of Mogollon Archaeology: Papers from the Ninth Mogollon Conference, Silver City, New Mexico, 1996*, edited by S. M. Whittlesey, 39–48. Tucson: SRI Press.

1999b   Preface. In *Sixty Years of Mogollon Archaeology: Papers from the Ninth Mogollon Conference, Silver City, New Mexico, 1996*, edited by S. M. Whittlesey, vii–xiv. Tucson: SRI Press.

1999c   (editor) *Sixty Years of Mogollon Archaeology: Papers from the Ninth Mogollon Conference, Silver City, New Mexico, 1996*. Tucson: SRI Press.

2003   *Rivers of Rock: Stories from a Stone-Dry Land; Central Arizona Project Archaeology*. Tucson: SRI Press.

Whittlesey, Stephanie M., Eric J. Arnould, and William E. Reynolds

1982   Archaeological Sediments: Discourse, Experiment, and Application. In *Multidisciplinary Research at Grasshopper Pueblo*, edited by W. A. Longacre, S. J. Holbrook, and M. W. Graves, 28–35. Anthropological Papers 40. Tucson: University of Arizona Press.

Whittlesey, Stephanie M., Richard S. Ciolek-Torrello, and Jeffrey H. Altschul (editors)

1998   *Vanishing River: Landscapes and Lives of the Lower Verde Valley; The Lower Verde Archaeological Project.* Tucson: SRI Press.

Whittlesey, Stephanie M., and J. Jefferson Reid

1982a   Cholla Project Perspectives on Salado. In *Cholla Project Archaeology*, vol. 1: *Introduction and Special Studies*, edited by J. J. Reid, 63–80. Archaeological Series 161, vol. 1. Tucson: Arizona State Museum.

1982b   Cholla Project Settlement Summary. In *Cholla Project Archaeology*, vol. 1: *Introduction and Special Studies*, edited by J. J. Reid, 206–16. Archaeological Series 161, vol. 1. Tucson: Arizona State Museum.

Wilcox, David R.

1975   A Strategy for Perceiving Social Groups in Puebloan Sites. In *Chapters in the Prehistory of Eastern Arizona IV. Fieldiana: Anthropology* 65:120–59.

1982   A Set-Theory Approach to Sampling Pueblos: The Implications of Room-Set Additions at Grasshopper. In *Multidisciplinary Research at Grasshopper Pueblo, Arizona*, edited by W. A. Longacre, S. J. Holbrook, and M. W. Graves, 19–27. Anthropological Papers 40. Tucson: University of Arizona Press.

1991   Changing Contexts of Pueblo Adaptations, A.D. 1250–1600. In *Farmers, Hunters, and Colonists*, edited by K. A. Spielmann, 128–54. Tucson: University of Arizona Press.

Willey, Gordon R.

1988   *Portraits in American Archaeology.* Albuquerque: University of New Mexico Press.

Willey, Gordon R., and Philip Phillips

1958   *Method and Theory in American Archaeology.* Chicago: University of Chicago Press.

Willey, Gordon R., and Jeremy A. Sabloff

1993   *A History of American Archaeology*, 3rd edition. New York: W. H. Freeman.

Wood, W. Raymond, and Donald L. Johnson

1978   A Survey of Disturbance Processes in Archaeological Site Formation. In *Advances in Archaeological Method and Theory 1*, edited by M. B. Schiffer, 315–81. New York: Academic Press.

Woodbury, Richard B.

1961   *Prehistoric Agriculture at Point of Pines, Arizona.* Memoir 17. Society for American Archaeology.

1993   *Sixty Years of Southwestern Archaeology: A History of the Pecos Conference.* Albuquerque: University of New Mexico Press.

Zedeño, María Nieves

1991   "Refining Inferences of Ceramic Circulation: A Stylistic, Technological, and Compositional Analysis of Whole Vessels from Chodistaas,

Arizona." Ph.D. dissertation, Department of Anthropology, Southern Methodist University, Dallas.

1992　Roosevelt Black-on-White Revisited: The Grasshopper Perspective. In *Proceedings of the Second Salado Conference, Globe, AZ, 1992*, edited by R. C. Lange and S. Germick, 206–11. Phoenix: Arizona Archaeological Society.

1994　*Sourcing Prehistoric Ceramics at Chodistaas Pueblo, Arizona: The Circulation of People and Pots in the Grasshopper Region.* Anthropological Papers 58. Tucson: University of Arizona Press.

1995　The Role of Population Movement and Technology Transfer in the Manufacture of Prehistoric Southwestern Ceramics. In *Ceramic Production in the American Southwest*, edited by B. J. Mills and P. L. Crown, 113–41. Tucson: University of Arizona Press.

Figure Credits

Grasshopper Pueblo and the Field School camp. Photograph by Jefferson Reid; originally published in Reid and Whittlesey 1999, 25.

Grasshopper Trading Post and cowboy camp. Photograph by Jefferson Reid.

Bion Griffin excavating a room floor at Grasshopper Pueblo. Photograph by R. Gwinn Vivian.

Byron Cummings at Rainbow Bridge. Photograph by E. Tad Nichols; courtesy of the Arizona State Museum; neg. no. 18821.

Alfred V. Kidder and Emil W. Haury. Photograph by E. B. Sayles; courtesy of the Arizona State Museum; neg. no. 3208.

Field School staff and students in 1964. Photograph by Raymond H. Thompson; courtesy of the Arizona State Museum; neg. no. 10479.

Field School staff and students in 1971. Photograph by Susan E. Luebbermann; courtesy of the Arizona State Museum; neg. no. 31131.

Field School staff and students in 1979. Photograph by Jefferson Reid; courtesy of the Arizona State Museum; neg. no. 52110.

Field School staff and students in 1989. Photograph by Jefferson Reid; courtesy of the Arizona State Museum; neg. no. 16-8.

Stephanie Whittlesey and Tim O'Meara. Photograph by Jefferson Reid.

Painted pottery from Grasshopper Pueblo. Photograph by Jefferson Reid; originally published in Reid and Whittlesey 1999, 3.

Map Credits

The Grasshopper region. Drawing by Charles R. Riggs; originally published in Reid and Whittlesey 1999, 72.

Grasshopper Pueblo. Drawing by Charles R. Riggs; originally published in Reid and Whittlesey 1999, 64–65.

Chodistaas Pueblo. Drawing by Charles R. Riggs. Originally published in Reid and Whittlesey 1999, 39.

Grasshopper Spring Pueblo. Drawing by Charles R. Riggs; originally published in Reid and Whittlesey 1999, 42.

Grasshopper Pueblo as of 1965. Drawing by Charles R. Riggs; adapted from Thompson and Longacre 1965:260, Fig. 2.

Grasshopper Pueblo as of 1968. Drawing by Charles R. Riggs.

Grasshopper Pueblo as of 1973. Drawing by Charles R. Riggs.

East and West Villages of Grasshopper Pueblo. Drawing by Charles R. Riggs; originally published in Reid and Whittlesey 1999, 113.

Room 216 at Grasshopper Pueblo. Drawing by E. Wesley Jernigan.

Room 359 at Grasshopper Pueblo. Drawing by E. Wesley Jernigan.

Index

Note: The letter *f* after a page number indicates a figure. *Passim* is used for a cluster of references in close sequence.

Names

Zedeño, Nieves, 135, 164–65, 167f, 171, 172

Zubrow, Ezra, 121

Subject

aggregation, 67, 83, 103, 198

American Anthropological Association memoirs, 56

American Antiquity, 166, 168, 169

Anasazi, 4, 38

Apaches, 68; archaeology and, 7, 61–62, 96, 162, 166; Cibecue, 25, 35, 133, 134, 187, 192–93, 214–15, 216; as field crews, 52, 53, 95–109 *passim*, 117—27; *passim*; 143–72 *passim*; Western, 4, 11, 25, 187; White Mountain, 25, 47, 105, 144, 159, 161

Archaeological Resources Protection Act, 138, 144

archaeologist-as-explorer image, 19, 20–21, 22

Arizona Archaeological Council, 168

Arizona State Historic Preservation Office, 39, 126, 136, 141, 148

Arizona State Museum, 11, 34–35, 42, 46, 49, 76, 128–29, 136, 161

Arizona State University, 39, 128, 152, 165, 168–69, 197–200, 209

behavioral archaeology, 4, 9–10, 111–12, 113, 114–15, 131, 175; and processual archaeology, 181, 196–212; research in, 190–96, 213–14

Black Mountain Pueblo, 159, 160

Blue House Pueblo, 160

Broken K Pueblo, 32, 87, 88

Bureau of Indian Affairs, 121, 137

Bureau of Reclamation, 165

burials: human, 34–35, 60, 80–81, 86, 88, 117–18, 120, 127, 128, 139, 141, 143–44, 163–64, 189, 199, 202

camps, 216; cowboy camp, 27, 28f; Grasshopper, 27–30, 68–73, 133; maintenance of, 134, 137–38, 141; Point of Pines, 53–54

Canyon Creek project, 106

Canyon Creek Pueblo, 39, 122, 123, 176

Central Arizona Project (CAP), 128, 165, 209

ceramics, 20, 52, 84, 94, 164–65, 168, 170, 172; Chavez Pass, 161–62, 200; Chodistaas, 139, 151; cross-dating with, 61–62, 177

Chacmool Conference, 154–55, 159, 166, 169, 203, 204

Chavez Pass Ruin, 32, 148, 152, 161, 168, 197, 199–204, 207–8

Chediski Farms, 96

Chevelon region, 39–40, 129

Chodistaas Pueblo, 32, 34, 35–37, 139, 143, 151, 157, 158, 162, 164, 166; excavation of, 122–23, 124, 127, 152, 153, 155–56, 163, 168, 170, 183, 216; settlement system around, 160–61

Cholla Project, 24f, 38, 39, 115, 116, 125, 133, 139, 150, 160, 186; and Grasshopper research, 128–32, 141, 153, 188

chronology, 56, 57, 176, 177, 196, 200. *See also* dendrochronology

Cibecue, 25, 26, 150

cliff dwellings, 39, 122, 124, 176, 195

climate, 20, 21, 24–25, 83

Coconino National Forest, 197, 198, 208

Colorado Plateau, 32, 44–45

construction unit project, 96, 99–100, 101, 104, 107

contract archaeology, 12–13, 15, 209–10; Cholla Project, 128–32

convergence principle, 195–96

cornering project, 86–87, 88–89, 93, 96, 100, 101, 104, 108, 109

Crooked Ridge Village, 55, 56

culture history: as research approach, 4, 7–8, 59–60, 64–65, 68, 84, 174, 175–81, 212–13

Dames & Moore, 165, 209

dendrochronology, 49, 60, 61–62, 122, 194–95, 200–201

dissertations, 93, 101, 108, 114, 116, 151, 171, 204, 218, 221, 223; in processual archaeology, 189–90; research for,

About the Authors

Jefferson Reid and Stephanie Whittlesey are professional archaeologists who specialize in writing about archaeology and ancient history for the general reader. This is their third book about archaeology and ancient life in prehistoric Arizona. The first book, *The Archaeology of Ancient Arizona*, published by the University of Arizona Press, introduces the history of Arizona archaeology and the prehistoric cultures of vanished Arizona. It sets the stage for a closer look at the Mogollon people of Grasshopper Pueblo, offered in their second book, *Grasshopper Pueblo: A Story of Archaeology and Ancient Life*, also published by the University of Arizona Press. The story presented here is about archaeology and the archaeologists who unearthed the data Reid and Whittlesey used to reconstruct life at Grasshopper Pueblo. The book discusses the University of Arizona Archaeological Field School tradition as exemplified by thirty years of fieldwork at Grasshopper.

Jefferson Reid is a professor in the Department of Anthropology at the University of Arizona, from which he received his Ph.D. in 1973. He was director (1979–1992) of the University of Arizona Field School at Grasshopper and editor of *American Antiquity*, the scholarly journal of the Society for American Archaeology. His forty years of fieldwork ranged from large prehistoric pueblo ruins of the American Southwest to temple mounds in the Southeast and Mayan pyramids in the Mexican jungle. His research interests include the method, theory, and philosophy of reconstructing past human behavior and culture; the Mogollon culture of the Arizona mountains; the historical period of southern Arizona; and especially the fascinating history of southwestern archaeology.

Stephanie Whittlesey holds a Ph.D. in anthropology from the University of Arizona (1978). She was associated for many years with the Field School at Grasshopper. In the 1970s, she became immersed in the field of cultural resource management and has dedicated her career to meshing the goals of reconstructing the past and preserving it for future generations. Along the way, she discovered the vital importance of involving the public in archaeology. Since 1989, she has worked for Statistical Research, Inc., a private cultural resource management consulting firm based in Tucson, where she now serves as senior principal investigator. She pioneered the application of cultural landscape studies in Hohokam archaeology, as reflected in the SRI Press books *Vanishing River: Landscapes and Lives of the Lower Verde Valley; The Lower Verde Archaeological Project*, coedited with Richard Ciolek-Torrello and Jeffrey Altschul, and *Rivers of Rock: Stories from a Stone-Dry Land; Central Arizona Project Archaeology*, which was written for a general audience and is distributed by the University of Arizona Press. Her research interests include Native American ceramics, social organization, and the Mogollon and Hohokam cultures of Arizona's mountains and deserts.

Mogollon Village, 51, 52
multidisciplinary research, 50–51, 60, 102
Museum of Northern Arizona, 23, 101, 104

National Science Foundation, 197, 209; Advanced Science Seminar Program, 13–14, 74, 76, 77–78, 84, 86, 88, 97; other proposals and grants, 90–92, 94, 101, 102–8, 116–25 *passim*, 129–30, 133, 153, 159, 171, 217–18, 220, 222
Native American Graves Protection and Repatriation Act, 143–44
Native Americans, 19–20, 141. *See also* Apaches
Nuvakwewtaqa. *See* Chavez Pass Ruin

paleoenvironmental research, 60, 96–97, 100, 106, 121, 156
Papaguería Project, 11, 50–51
Pecos Conference, 55, 111
phase concept, 176–78
Pinnacle Flats, 120–21, 122
pit-house sites, 122, 127
Point of Pines, 8, 11, 50f, 51, 58, 59, 60–63, 174, 176, 180, 181; field school at, 53–57, 72
postprocessualism, 192–93
pragmatism: American, 192, 215
processual archaeology, 4, 8–9, 32, 66, 74, 113; at Chavez Pass, 196–211; and culture history, 84, 175, 178–87; dissertations in, 93–94, 189–90; flaws in, 110, 204–5, 212; at Grasshopper, 82–83, 97, 100–101, 103–4, 105–8, 175, 181–90, 213; NSF and, 90–92; and social theory, 187–89
publications, 208, 209–10, 218, 219–22

Q Ranch region, 38–39, 129, 131, 152, 160

Red Rock House, 39, 77, 122, 123
research papers, 89–90
research questions, 83–84, 91, 103, 176, 198

Ringo site field school, 7, 66–67
room reports, 84–85, 184–85
Roosevelt Archaeology Project, 165, 209

Salado, 67, 172, 209
Salado Conference, 172
Salt River Canyon, 25, 26
Salt River Draw, 28, 73–74, 96, 100, 125, 149
sampling, 185–86, 209, 213
San Carlos Apache Reservation, 53
School of American Research Seminars, 139–40, 153–54
SELGEM, 106, 107, 110, 114, 119
settlement systems, 148–49, 158–61, 162, 186, 201–2
social organization, 83, 93, 124, 189, 193, 198, 204–5, 206–7
social status, 87–88, 189
social theory, 187–89, 199, 203
Society for American Archaeology, 56, 62, 97, 100, 101–2, 148, 156, 171
Southwest Center conference, 165–66
Southwestern Anthropological Association, 171
Southwestern Anthropological Research Group, 38, 99, 103
Spotted Mountain Ruin, 127
Spring Ridge Pueblo, 149–50
staff, 194; Grasshopper, 72–73, 74–127 *passim*, 131–32, 137–38, 142–72 *passim*
students, 12–13, 14; graduate, 15, 16, 54, 60, 111, 134–35, 221; Grasshopper, 74–127 *passim*, 141–172 *passim*; skills of, 183–85, 194
subflooring, 96, 99, 104, 120
surface collections, 122, 126, 158, 160
survey, 21–22, 128; catchment, 122, 125–26; Grasshopper region, 35, 38–40, 94, 106, 119, 120–21, 141, 144, 152, 159–61, 180, 189; macroregional, 131–32; nonsite, 158–59

teaching, 16, 124–25, 217–18
Tonto-Roosevelt region, 40, 129
topography: Mogollon Rim, 24–25